S. A. Moran.

JOHN RUSKIN

The Portrait of a Prophet

By the Same Author

BAUDELAIRE AND THE SYMBOLISTS

A SUPERFICIAL JOURNEY (*Travel*)

THE PRIVATE LETTERS OF PRINCESS LIEVEN (*Edited with Introduction*)

CAROLINE OF ENGLAND

BYRON: THE YEARS OF FAME

BYRON IN ITALY

FOUR PORTRAITS: *Studies of the Eighteenth Century*

John Ruskin

JOHN RUSKIN

THE
PORTRAIT OF A PROPHET

By

PETER QUENNELL

COLLINS
ST JAMES'S PLACE LONDON
1949

PRINTED IN GREAT BRITAIN
COLLINS CLEAR-TYPE PRESS : LONDON AND GLASGOW
1949

To

Elizabeth von Hofmannsthal

ILLUSTRATIONS

FOREWORD

THE object of this book is to portray John Ruskin both as a writer and as a personality: to show the close connection between his personal growth and his literary development: and to suggest how the frustration of his private hopes finally brought to an end his career of public usefulness. The theme is vast. Ruskin was an extraordinarily copious writer and an industrious correspondent; and his Collected Works in the massive Library Edition, including his Letters, run to thirty-nine volumes. The present study does not pretend to give a detailed account of Ruskin in all his numerous phases. His opinions as an art-critic themselves demand a separate essay: his efforts and influence as a social reformer deserve far more intensive examination than I have sought to give them. The student who wishes a closer view must fall back on the admirably thorough-going biographies produced by Cook and Collingwood. But, since the appearance of those pious and affectionate tributes, certain new material has been put before the general reader. In *The Order of Release* Admiral Sir William James published a series of deeply interesting letters, written by Ruskin to the young woman who became his wife, which throw fresh and somewhat disconcerting light upon the problems of his personal temperament. The light they shed is necessarily partial; and, while making full use of the information they provided, I have attempted to incorporate it in a balanced and (as I hope even Ruskin's most fervent admirers may be prepared to agree) though admittedly imperfect and incomplete, neither intellectually prejudiced nor unsympathetic portrait.

First I wish to express my gratitude to Mrs. Detmar

Blow, who with great generosity has allowed me to examine forty unpublished letters from Ruskin to her aunt Mrs. Cowper Temple, afterwards Lady Mount Temple, which supplied the basis of many passages in Chapters VII, VIII and IX. For permission to quote from these letters, and from other copyright material, including letters printed in the Library Edition, I am indebted to Sir Stanley Unwin, acting on behalf of the Ruskin Trustees, and Messrs. Allen & Unwin; for permission to make use of material printed in *The Order of Release*, to Admiral Sir William James, the author, and Sir John Murray, the publisher. I am also indebted to Sir John Murray and to Sir Ralph Millais, Bart., for permitting me to reproduce the portrait of Effie Gray by G. F. Watts. The portrait of Ruskin by J. E. Millais I reproduce by kind permission of Sir William Acland, Bart.; Ruskin's drawings of "The Castelbarco Tomb, Verona," and "A Coast Scene near Dunbar," I owe to the kindness of J. Howard Whitehouse, Esq., and of The City of Birmingham Museum and Art Gallery respectively. The frontispiece and the three photographs opposite pages 113, 208 and 288 appear by permission of the Picture Post Library. In conclusion I wish to thank Sir Sydney Cockerell, who has given me the benefit of his deep knowledge of all Ruskinian questions, and my friend Sir Edward Marsh, who, not for the first time, has been good enough to act as my stylistic conscience.

"I seem born to conceive what I cannot execute, recommend what I cannot obtain, and mourn over what I cannot save."

John Ruskin to his father, 1848

. . . . No wreck is so frequent, no waste so wild, as the wreck and waste of the minds of men devoted to the arts . . ."

John Ruskin to Mrs. Hugh Miller, 1857

I

IN the daily career of the virtuous businessman, there comes a hushed and solemn moment when, free at length from his office but still irradiated by the glow of satisfied commercial zeal, he sits down to unfold to his wife a detailed, unsparing chronicle of his efforts and endeavours during the previous six hours. This was the invariable practice of James Ruskin. Having returned, never unpunctually, from his City counting-house, he dined in his front parlour at exactly half-past four; and while he dined, watched over by his wife Margaret, who always sat beside him, he would talk, complacently or despondently, of his progress in the wine trade. " My father " (wrote John Ruskin) " was apt to be vexed if orders for sherry fell the least short of their due standard, even for a day or two." John, an only child, was not admitted to these conferences. At such times it would have been a grave misdemeanour—and life was hedged in by possible offences: he had been whipped on numerous occasions for tumbling downstairs—so much as to approach the parlour door or in any other way disturb his parents' discourse. But afterwards the family was reunited. On summer evenings they drank tea in their suburban garden beneath a white-heart cherry or, if the weather was cold, at six o'clock in the drawing-room. John Ruskin had his cup of milk and his slice of bread and butter, which he consumed in a little recess, fenced off by a table. There he remained as in a niche—the alcove was considered his peculiar territory—his mother knitting and his father reading aloud, usually from the Waverly novels; till James Ruskin threw down the last volume with an " intense expression of sorrow mixed with scorn," recognising in *Count Robert of Paris* that the career of Scott had ended.

For the Ruskins were cultivated, as well as affluent and virtuous. James Ruskin's leisure was limited: he had spent many years rescuing his fortunes from ruin, and owed his later success to a long miserable period of struggle and self-sacrifice. But he loved beauty, venerated antiquity, and prided himself on keeping an open mind in all questions of the intellect. Moreover he enjoyed travel; and his career as a sherry merchant provided many excuses for rambling round the country. Neither of his two partners—Monsieur Domecq, the wine-grower, who seldom came to England, and Mr. Telford, an amiable old gentleman who rarely left his country house—played a particularly active part in the business at Billiter Street. During the summer months, nevertheless, Mr. Telford consented to ride up to London daily; and the Ruskins borrowed his travelling-chariot and set off, the three of them, on expeditions that took their carriage across the length and breadth of England. In the chariot, as in the drawing-room, John had his appointed place. He sat well forward, between his father and mother, on a box which contained his clothes, perched up high enough in the high-hung carriage to command a wide view, over dykes and hedgerows, of the whole surrounding landscape. Thus England, at least in the South not yet much scarred and disfigured by the industrial revolution, flowed away beneath his infant eyes—the prosperous market towns with their coaching inns, from which postilions clattered instantly at the cry of " Horses out! ": the cathedral cities, their vast decaying churches still largely unrestored: and the noblemen's seats for which Mr. Ruskin, who, in an unambitious way, was a considerable snob, had a romantic predilection. John Ruskin possessed a receptive brain: he was also a composed and obedient child, who followed his elders' direction and shared their tastes and interests. For he had been brought up on regular and inflexible lines by a mother who, having given birth to her only child at the age of thirty-eight, had " dedicated him to God " and still intended him to be a bishop. From the grim mythology of

Genesis to the obscure horrors of *Revelation*, there was no part of the Bible, including, of course, the most tortuous genealogical passages, with which John Ruskin, since early childhood, had not been thoroughly familiar. The greater part of his schooling he owed to Mrs. Ruskin, who, besides controlling his Biblical studies, was at pains to provide a solid groundwork in other less abstruse and more elementary subjects. Meanwhile the process of self-education was proceeding somewhat rapidly. With few toys and few playmates, he became, like many lonely children, precociously self-sufficient and by the time he was seven years old had begun to " lead a very small, perky, contented, conceited, Cock-Robinson-Crusoe sort of life," the central point of a circular universe created and maintained for his especial benefit.

Behind its frontiers he contrived to amuse himself with unusual success and skill. Writing and drawing both absorbed him; and when he was six, in a little red-covered note-book with narrow blue ruled pages, he embarked on a composition entitled *Harry and Lucy Concluded*, which owed a good deal to Maria Edgeworth but borrowed some of its material from Byron's *Manfred* and Joyce's *Scientific Dialogues*. The mixture was significant, as he afterwards observed, of the " interwoven temper of my mind, at the beginning of days, just as much as at their end . . ." In the same note-book, employing a careful script that imitated printed letters, he copied out a poem in rhymed couplets on the subject of the steam-engine, and another, in blank verse, inspired by the contemplation of a rainbow. Highly imaginative, he was yet extremely practical. Among the few toys in his bare and secluded nursery, he was most devoted to a box of building-bricks, which could be assembled to form the scale model of a dignified two-arched bridge, perfect with " voussoir and keystone " and a course of inlaid steps. He loved its solid mathematical elegance, and was never tired of assembling, dismantling and patiently rebuilding it. Yet his instinctive appreciation of the solid and definite was accompanied by imaginative stirrings of a very different tendency. Streams and rivers had always fascinated him; and, on occasional visits to Perth, the home of a family of lively Scottish cousins—the children of his Aunt Jessie, his father's only sister—he was captivated by the waters of the Tay, "which eddied, three or four feet deep of sombre crystal," beyond the garden boundary, and higher up, "where Tay gathered herself like Medusa," broke into "swirls of smooth blackness", filling him, as he passed, with sensations of delight and dread. Such was the background of his imaginative development: on the side of the emotions, the life that he led was strangely bleak and empty. Demonstrative displays of feeling were not encouraged or countenanced in the sober Ruskin household. Father and mother were omnipotent and omnipresent. His sense of obligation to these mighty entities was passive and unreflecting.

Both his parents had suffered deeply; and on each the effect of suffering had been to increase the weight and harden the edge of an already serious character. James Ruskin's father, having brought his affairs to the verge of ruin, had at length committed suicide. The whole of his son's youth passed in an unremitting struggle to restore the family credit; but, before he left his Scottish home, at the age of twenty-two or twenty-three, on his way to the City of London to set up his own business, he had proposed marriage to, and had been accepted by his cousin, Margaret Cox, who since she was twenty had lived with the Ruskins in the capacity of housekeeper. Four years older than himself, the daughter of a widow who kept an inn at Croydon, educated, nevertheless, in all the ladylike accomplishments, Margaret was a "tall, handsome, and very finely made girl," an exceedingly capable manager and a "natural, essential, unassailable, yet inoffensive, prude." She waited for James until she was thirty-seven. "My father" (wrote John Ruskin) "chose his wife much with the same kind of serenity and decision with which afterwards he chose his clerks." Margaret was perhaps the more deeply in love; but James, through continued observation, had acquired a habit of complete reliance upon her sympathy and friendship. The long period of probation was followed by an harmonious and uneventful marriage. "Neither of them" (we are told) "ever permitted their feelings to degenerate into fretful or impatient passion"; and the mood of sobriety in which they had embarked on life they afterwards transferred to the little universe they had created. Their rule was strict but equable. "Nothing" (remembered their only child) "was ever promised me that was not given; nothing ever threatened me that was not inflicted, and nothing ever told me that was not true." He learned "peace, obedience, faith"—faith in his parents and blind obedience to their dictates, coupled with a peaceful acceptance of the well-ordered world around him.

Certainly, he was not unhappy. Punishments that seem outrageously severe by any modern standard, he accepted as a part of the scheme of things and, since he was a quick and submissive pupil, soon no longer merited. Not till much later did it occur to John Ruskin that the influence of his early education had perhaps been somewhat negative. Besides the cousins who lived at Perth, he had another family of cousins, offspring of his mother's sister, domiciled at Croydon, whose existence was as high-spirited and independent as his own was quiet and circumscribed. His aunt had married a local baker, but appeared cheerfully unconscious that she had thereby lost caste; and of one of her sons it was recorded that he had taught a younger brother to swim by tossing him head over heels into the waters of a deep canal. Suppose such treatment had been applied to *him*, John Ruskin sometimes speculated, would not the effect have been salutary? Might he not, by the experience of danger and the exercise of free will, have grown up a happier, more exuberant being? As it was, "my judgment of right and wrong, and powers of independent action" (as distinct from independent thought) "were left entirely undeveloped; because the bridle and blinkers were never taken off me." Outwardly at least he remained the creation of his parents' wishes, poised observant on his seat in the travelling-chariot, alone in the drawing-room alcove, like an idol in its niche, listening, drawing, reading. Meanwhile, by mysterious processes that no parent, even the most devoted, could survey or supervise, there developed within him the complex pattern of an individual character.

* * *

John Ruskin was born in London, in Hunter Street off Brunswick Square, on February 8th, 1819. When he was thirteen years old, in 1832, after a period of violent social unrest that seemed to threaten revolution, the passing of the first Reform Bill crowned the hopes of English Liberals and ensured (though this was a result that Whig aristocrats would neither have understood nor welcomed) the future political predominance of the English middle classes. If every age has a representative building, and if the gentleman's house was the most characteristic architectural product of eigthteenth-century civilisation, with its sense of space and its regard for human dignity—for the dignity, at least, of a privileged and happy few—the merchant's suburban residence, degenerating at a later stage into the clerk's Victorian villa, was the architectural expression of the age that followed. Now that the affluent tradesman no longer lived above his counting-house, the hills around London were tamed by the enterprise of a hundred speculative builders. With his top hat beneath the carriage seat, waiting to be donned as soon as he had entered the City, the British merchant drove in from the suburbs every morning and every evening drove back again to his trim domestic Eden. It had some of the pretensions, without the amplitude, of a genuine country house; the park had shrunk to "ornamental grounds"; but there was a stable-yard attached to the main building, and conservatories flamed in the sun; aproned gardeners weeded the gravel paths, and tended gaudy circular flower-beds and picturesque umbrageous shrubberies. John Ruskin was already four when his father, who during the last few years had been making steady progress, moved his household from urban Bloomsbury to suburban Herne Hill, where he occupied a semi-detached house, with a front garden full of laburnum and lilac, and a back garden, measuring seventy yards long by twenty wide, which was "renowned all over the hill for its pears and apples" and enclosed by an unbroken hedge of gooseberry and currant bushes. Though they had many neighbours, neither of the Ruskins was of a sociable, expansive turn. James Ruskin was far too busy: his health, moreover, had been much damaged by early overwork: while Margaret, conscious always of her own undistinguished origins, was too proud or too shy to cultivate acquaintances of whom she did not feel herself the perfect social equal. Besides, their plutocratic shopkeeping neighbours maintained a style of living, with "great cortège of footmen . . . glitter of plate . . . costly hothouses, and carriages driven by coachmen in wigs," that the prudent and modest Ruskins, who kept no menservants and burned only tallow candles, did not seek to emulate. Mrs. Ruskin could not boast a barouche: Mr. Ruskin travelled to London daily by the omnibus.

Yet, as his affairs improved, the need for strict economy became, even to Mr. Ruskin's eyes, no longer quite so evident. When John was fourteen, a momentous change occurred. A year earlier, Mr. Telford, that kind old country gentleman, had given him Samuel Rogers' *Italy*, with vignette illustrations engraved after Stothard and Turner. To-day as we skim the pages of this supremely pedestrian poem, and examine the accompanying vignettes—grim crags, contorted pine-trees and feathery cascades, marble-smooth moonlit seas and deeply-shadowed mountain slopes, all hatched-in with exquisite precision by the engraver's laborious needle—it is difficult to understand the impression they made on Ruskin's youthful fantasy. But the effect they produced was immediate: Turner's illustrations opened before him a series of wide and brilliant pathways, down which his imagination raced from London to Lake Leman, and thence across the Alpine passes to Verona, Venice, Naples. Early in the spring of the following year, fresh excitement was provided by the publication of Prout's *Sketches in Flanders and Germany*. A copy was procured for Herne Hill; and, when Mrs. Ruskin observed the delight which Prout's drawings aroused both in her son and in her husband, she suggested that this year—it was 1833—there was no reason why their annual holiday should not be extended to the Continent. Thus was formed a habit, that soon became almost a rite, in the existence of the Ruskin household, consecrated by their community of tastes and interests, and by the strong, if unexpressed, devotion that held the family together. Accompanying them was John's cousin Mary, now the only surviving daughter of his Scottish Aunt Jessie, who, after the death of her mother and sisters and the break-up of her own home (which brought to an end John's visits to Perth and his expeditions along Tayside) had joined the Ruskins at Herne Hill and ranked as an adopted child. "A rather pretty, blue-eyed, clumsily-made girl, very amiable and affectionate in a quiet way," Mary added "a serene . . . neutral tint" to the existing household harmony. "When we travelled" (Ruskin wrote) "she took somewhat of a governess position towards me," John being four years younger and by his anxious middle-aged parents considered very delicate. Together with Anne, the Ruskins' cross-grained nurse, and a courier named Salvador, in a comfortable travelling-carriage specially equipped for the occasion, the party left England in mid-May 1833 as soon as they had celebrated Mr. Ruskin's birthday. They journeyed from Calais to Cologne, up the Rhine and through the Black Forest, explored northern Switzerland and crossed the Splügen into Italy, where they visited Como, Milan, Genoa; but at Genoa the weather was so torrid it was decided they should turn back. They re-crossed into Switzerland, and travelled north through France by the cities of Dijon and Lyons.

Their expedition was to be the first of many, each bringing with it some new, precious increase of knowledge and enjoyment. For pleasure and knowledge were now inseparable. Only in the life of the mind and imagination did John Ruskin breathe easily or exist completely. Though he delighted in the spectacle of the outer world and was training himself to record what he saw with a minuteness of observation that would have done credit to the patient engraver of one of Turner's vignettes, he loved and admired it always at a certain distance. He was still the solitary of Herne Hill ; about his temperament there was still something of the lonely and pensive child who had spent hours gazing with rapt abstraction from his nursery window. Again, he was not unhappy. It is doubtful if, at any later period of life, he recaptured the exhilaration of those early journeys. Every stage possessed some separate charm—the departure, in a newly-chosen, newly-fitted travelling-carriage ; the early trot through the London suburbs, enlivened by a " sense of pity for all the inhabitants of Peckham who weren't going, like the pity of lovers on their wedding day for everybody who is not being married ; the change of horses at Dartford, feeling that the last link with Camberwell was broken, that we were already in a new and miraculous world " ; to the entrancing moment when, one fine summer afternoon, the travellers entered a well-remembered town, for instance half-medieval Abbeville, and he could jump out into the courtyard of the Hôtel de l'Europe and rush down the narrow street " to see St. Wulfran again before the sun was off the towers. . . ."

Yet delight in foreign voyaging did not breed in John Ruskin any disgust for domestic life at Herne Hill. He returned always with satisfaction, and even abroad, among the Alps or in a French cathedral city, was faithful to the " beloved sameness " of the life he led there. Thus, on his return to England in 1833, he plunged immediately and without regret into the atmosphere of " self-engrossed quiet " that his parents spread around them. The family trio, as John grew up, and James and Margaret grew older and richer, far from expanding its interests, was becoming more and more exclusive. The Ruskins had their *égoïsme à trois*, as a later critic called it. They had, moreover, a pleasing sense of their own intrinsic superiority, " the sense " (Ruskin afterwards confessed) " that we were, in some way or other, always above our friends and relations —more or less patronising everybody, favouring them by our advice, instructing them by our example, and called upon, by what was due both to ourselves, and the constitution of society," to refrain from approaching them in any closer contact. John neither envisaged any possible change nor felt the smallest stirring of dissatisfaction with the existent scheme of things. Both as a precocious child and as a gifted boy, he "already disliked growing older —never expected to be wiser, and formed no more plans for the future than a little black silkworm does in the middle of its first mulberry leaf."

The leaf was unquestionably large and verdant. Just as John acknowledged and bowed to his parents' adult wisdom, so they had come to acknowledge in their son a degree of intellectual capability verging upon genius; and they were happy to supply the nourishment that genius needed. During their original tour, he had had his introductory glimpse of the Alps, "clear as crystal, sharp on the pure horizon sky. . . . Infinitely beyond all that we have ever thought or dreamed—the seen walls of lost Eden could not have been more beautiful . . . not more awful, round heaven, the walls of sacred Death"; and to this glimpse, from a garden-terrace at Schaffhausen, he dated back all that in his destiny was to be most "sacred and useful." During their second tour, which took place in 1835 and was somewhat delayed because, in the spring of that year, John was laid low by a brief but dangerous attack of pleurisy, he enjoyed his first sight of Rouen (to which dear Abbeville was the "preface and interpretation"), one of the three cities, Rouen, Geneva and Pisa, that "have been, in sum, the three centres of my life's thought. . . ." Venice was also studied; and John, who had set out equipped with a "cyanometer," to measure the blue of the sky, "a ruled note-book for geological observations, and a large quarto for architectural sketches, with square rule and foot-rule ingeniously fastened outside," returned home, intending to compose a poetic journal of the tour "in the style of Don Juan, artfully combined with that of Childe Harold." This particular project was never completed; but others took its place. Industry was Ruskin's natural element; and, though it may already have been becoming obvious, even to his mother and father, that their hopes of seeing John a prince of the Church were unlikely to be realised, in all else he was a model son, with just enough vivacity and independent thought to make perfection palatable. Margaret Ruskin had begun to concentrate upon him the full force of her grave and pious nature. For James Ruskin he was the crown of a life's work, the symbol of credit redeemed and of triumphant commercial virtue. John would enter the world as a scholar and a gentleman : the disgrace of his grandfather's ruin would finally be wiped away.

John himself acquiesced : he had none of that resentful restlessness which is the torment of many youths between fifteen and twenty-five : he understood the meaning of gratitude and felt the charm of loyalty. Given parents so well-intentioned and a son so talented, high-minded and admirably brought up, what opening could be found for the entry of those perverse spirits which combine to keep men miserable ? Yet, looking back to his childhood across the gulf of nearly fifty years, Ruskin thought that he detected one main flaw running through his education : ". . . I had nothing to love." The veneration he originally felt for his parents had developed into an unquestioning devotion, now that he no longer regarded them as mere " visible powers of nature " whose existence was inevitable and necessary like the existence of sun and moon ; but there was more of piety in his affection than of genuine emotional zest. Thus the vicissitudes of love were still unknown to him, unknown the agony of loving in vain and the bewildering happiness of love returned and satisfied. He had had no friends whom he adored ; he had never been spoiled or favoured ; completely unversed in the management of his feelings—there had been few feelings in his experience of life that needed to be managed—he had yet a capacity for emotion which, though still undiscovered and unsuspected, was already growing dangerous. But the first hint of calamity did not materialise till Ruskin was seventeen, and then it was so slight and conventional as to seem relatively unimportant. A vague warning—a hint of the hint—had been sounded three years earlier. On their way home through Paris from their Swiss and Italian journeyings in 1833, the Ruskins had paid a formal visit to the family of Monsieur Domecq, and had dined at his house, and met his five delightful daughters. They had impressed the English boy, but he had naturally not impressed them ; and the only comfort had been provided by the youngest of the quintet, Elise, who, " seeing that her elder sisters did not choose to trouble themselves with me, and being herself of an entirely benevolent and pitiful temper," had advanced across the drawing-room and, leaning her elbow on his knee, had chattered to him for an hour and a half, mellifluously and incessantly, neither demanding nor receiving any sort of answer. Now, in 1836, the Domecqs came to London, the wine-grower and his wife, accompanied by Adèle Clotilde, " a graceful oval-faced blonde of fifteen," Cécile, who was thirteen and dark and finely browed, Elise, " round-faced like an English girl," and still a treasure of kindliness and native good sense, and Caroline, " a delicately quaint little thing of eleven." With some difficulty they were all fitted into the modest house on Herne Hill; and their visit, so far as the parents were concerned, passed off smoothly and agreeably. But for John its results were startling. This " curious galaxy, or southern cross, of unconceived stars, floating on a sudden into my obscure firmament of London suburb," were the first luminaries of their kind that he had ever met with. They were, indeed, literally the " first well-bred and well-dressed girls I had ever seen—or at least spoken to," beautifully but simply attired, devout Catholics, of course, but worldly and intelligent, speaking fluent French and Spanish, and English " with broken precision." At their side—especially at Adèle's side: for, though all the sisters stirred his imagination, the eldest had conquered his heart—his shortcomings sprang into cruel relief, and he both felt and appeared cold and shy and awkward. His jealous silences were long and miserable; and as often as he attempted to shine or endeavoured to please his mistress, his " patriotic and Protestant conceit " induced him to embark on just those subjects most likely to offend her, to talk of the triumph of Protestant arms or the defects of Catholic doctrine. He was equally unsuccessful when he did his best to win her over by a display of literary talent, and wrote a story called *The Bandit Leoni* for which he managed to find a place in the pages of *Friendship's Offering*. His only reward was to watch the " rippling ecstasies of derision " that overcame her while she read it.

Then the nymphs departed—such a frieze of young girls in flower as Marcel Proust (whose genius had many striking affinities with that of John Ruskin) was to describe for a later generation with no less poignant emphasis—unconscious of the change they had caused, still laughing, no doubt, at the recollection of Adèle's naïve admirer, his conceit and his sentimentalism, his manifold Protestant absurdities and Anglo-Saxon crudities. If Ruskin's world had not been revolutionised, the possibility of a revolution was at least becoming obvious. It is arguable that our early experiences of violent love determine all the others: that they fix an emotional pattern from which any subsequent escape is often strangely difficult: and from the pattern that Adèle imposed—which was strengthened, of course, by the idiosyncrasies of his temperament—Ruskin (one may hazard) would never escape completely. Love for him was always nympholeptic. He wrote of women—or rather of girls: youth, frequently extreme youth, was part of the provocation—as witches or fairies or delusive mocking spirits. There was pain in the immediate rapture, and, mixed with the pleasure of loving, a sense of impending loss. . . . To these experiences, and their implications, John Ruskin's devoted parents remained luckily impervious. His father was not displeased when he saw John paying attention to his partner's charming daughter, and hoped that, if he wrote her verses, they might turn out to be as good as Byron's *Hours of Idleness*, while his mother, " who looked upon the idea of my marrying a Roman Catholic as too monstrous to be possible in the decrees of Heaven, and too preposterous to be even guarded against on earth, was rather annoyed at the whole business, as she would have been if one of her chimneys had begun smoking. . . ." But she did not suspect that the house had caught fire, and that henceforward a faint odour of combustion, portent of a series of disastrous conflagrations, would continue to hover through the building.

More serious projects were afoot: John must go to Oxford. He should have the best education there that was purchasable by money; but James Ruskin, with characteristic caution, first consulted the Dean of Christ Church on the propriety of a mere City merchant entering his son as a gentleman-commoner (which entitled him to the use of a separate table in Hall, and to a velvet cap and a silk gown) rather than as a studious, plebeian commoner. The Dean replied that in nineteenth-century England, if one could pay for those flattering distinctions, one might certainly enjoy them; and, since the expense was no obstacle, Ruskin went up to Oxford as gentleman-commoner on January 14th, 1837. There he acquitted himself with prudence and, on the whole, not without distinction. Unworldly he might be; but he had sufficient knowledge of the world to hold his own among the knowing and aristocratic young men by whom he was surrounded. They received him with off-hand kindliness, which afterwards developed into appreciation when they heard one of his questions, innocently but unexpectedly put, completely floor their tutor, and when they saw that he understood wine and had a head for it as solid as most of his contemporaries. If he was a puritan, he was not a prig. He made no attempt to reform his acquaintances; and they, in their good-humoured fashion, refrained from comment on Ruskin's curious habit of spending the evenings with his mother. For Mrs. Ruskin had come to Oxford. She lodged at an old house in the High Street; and regularly at seven o'clock, after dinner in Hall and wine given or accepted, John would hurry round to meet her at tea and linger in her company till the bell summoned him from Tom Tower. On Sundays they were joined by James Ruskin, and all three, according to family custom, attended morning service at St. Peter's. But this was their only joint appearance. Otherwise father and mother remained considerately unobtrusive.

They were repaid by the spectacle of John's steady upward progress. He read diligently if not excessively, entertained his fellow gentlemen-commoners in a handsome but moderate style, and made friends of the right sort, without acquiring as he did so any complementary vices. There was Henry Acland, who delighted him "as a leopard or a falcon would," and Francis Charteris, "on the whole the grandest type of European Circassian race hitherto visible to me," an engaging young man, possessed of delicate good looks, much sense and a fund of "subtle, effortless, inevitable, unmalicious sarcasm," who "never troubled himself about anything" yet succeeded in all he did. Ruskin admired ; but he was not influenced. Always slightly a stranger at Oxford, upheld, moreover, by that sense of intrinsic moral worth he had acquired at Herne Hill, he drifted smoothly through his years of residence, emerging unspotted and unscathed, none the worse (as his parents gratefully noticed) but also none the wiser. He was still in love, or clung to the idea with strange and touching obstinacy. Adèle herself had done nothing to encourage him. Indeed, when, during the latter part of 1838, Monsieur Domecq announced that he was bringing over his four unmarried daughters to conclude their education at a Convent near Chelmsford, and Adèle and her sisters returned at Mrs. Ruskin's invitation to spend their holidays at Herne Hill, he found her, if possible, even less responsive; never "in the least amiable," though "firm, and fiery, and high-principled," her character had grown no more ingratiating, her attitude towards John Ruskin no more sentimental. Physically, too, she had changed. Beautiful at fifteen, Adèle Domecq at eighteen was not prettier or more beguiling than the average French girl. Ruskin saw and felt the change; but his passion had now established itself in depths of his nature from which the critical faculty alone was powerless to dislodge it, and from which it proceeded to lay a maleficent spell upon his whole existence. Months slipped by in miserable confusion, in a welter of "complex absurdity, pain, error, wasted affection and rewardless semi-virtue. . . ."

The life of the mind, however, in spite of the confusion that possessed his heart, continued almost without interruption. In 1839 he won the Newdigate Prize, and two years earlier had begun a series of architectural essays, published in the *Architectural Magazine* under the pen-name "Kataphusin," which were well received by the public and remained "curiously right up to the points they reach" according to the essayist's considered later judgement. Already he had a vision distinctly his own, already the gift of translating that vision into eloquent, harmonious imagery. His prose-style was clear and sensible, formed on the Johnsonian pattern. But, although unusually precocious in everything that touched the intellect, in other important respects he was astonishingly immature. Had John Ruskin been one of those human beings from whose composition the instinct to love, and the desire to possess what we love, unaccountably have been omitted, he might have developed without regret or misgiving into a self-sufficient celibate, happy among his books and drawings and costly mineral specimens, spending his income and canalising his emotions in the pursuit of art and science. But the passion that was to make of him an artist also destined him to be an amorist. Adèle might have changed and deteriorated; but nothing could shake his conviction that he deeply, passionately loved her. His love existed with a life of its own. James Ruskin, now becoming vaguely alarmed, endeavoured to distract his attention and even introduced him to a Miss Wardell, a "softly moulded slender brunette" of ample fortune and charming disposition, whose parents lived at Hampstead; but John merely announced that she was "not his sort of girl"—he liked long uncurling fair hair, oval clear-skinned faces; his visits were suspended, and Miss Wardell died soon afterwards. It must be Adèle, or it should be no one. The impossibility of possessing Adèle enriched her like a halo.

The moment arrived when he heard she was to be

married or, rather, when he learned that negotiations with a view to marriage were taking place between the Domecqs and the family of an eligible French sportsman whose name was Baron Duquesne. During the autumn of 1839 he wrote her a poetic Farewell; and in the following March, when Ruskin had already celebrated his twenty-first birthday, Adèle Domecq achieved the fate for which by upbringing and disposition she had obviously been intended, and emerged from the chrysalis of the *jeune fille bien élevée* as a dashing young married woman. It was the right, appropriate, inevitable step. But not all his recognition of her social unsuitability, emotional poverty and intellectual nullity could shake Ruskin's attachment to the image that he had built up. In his *Farewell* he had given it a Byronic colouring:

Yet come—and let thy glance be dim,
And let thy words be low;
Then turn—for ever turn—from him
Whose love thou canst not know;—
And reck not of the faithful breast
Whose thoughts have now no home—no rest—
That wreathed, with unregarded light,
Thy steps by day, and sleep by night.
And when the wildest word is past,
And when mine eyes have looked their last,
By every barrier earth can twine
Cast in between my soul and thine—
The wave, the wild, the steel, the flame
And all that word or will can frame:
When God shall call or man shall claim,
Depart from me . . .

Yet, unlike the average youthful passion, having assumed a literary form, it did not thereupon begin to lose its potency. The crisis deepened: the hurt enlarged itself: a sense of frustration, which combined a touch of wounded idealism with something of the wayward child, gradually extended through the background of his daily life, till the troubles of the spirit found concrete expression in disorders of the body. Against the advice of his excellent holiday-tutor, Osborne Gordon, who had warned him: "When you have got too much to do, don't do it," Ruskin had changed his plan of work, and, no doubt by way of emotional relief, often dragged out his Oxford working-day from six o'clock in the morning to close on midnight. Suddenly the climax materialised. One evening—it was, as he remembered, a Saturday or a Sunday—a "short tickling cough . . . preceded by a curious sensation in the throat, and followed by a curious taste in the mouth," surprised him while he sat at his desk, and sent him round to seek comfort and counsel at his parents' High Street lodgings. The taste had been that of blood. Mrs. Ruskin was an expert in cases of pulmonary consumption; at her direction John left Oxford and returned obediently to Herne Hill. His first adventure as an adult human being, which coincided with his first experience of the pleasures and pains of love, thus terminated in a strategic withdrawal, behind the frontiers of the eclectic private universe he had been constructing since his childhood.

James and Margaret Ruskin at the same time—Margaret more particularly—gained over their son's obedience an additional hold which, though it was greatly weakened by the passage of years, they never quite relinquished. He seldom fretted at the restraints they imposed, notwithstanding grieved speculations several decades later as to the harm they might have done him; for with much that was masculine and wilful, his character preserved always a certain strain of self-indulgent femininity. Wishing for protection, appreciating devotion, gifted, moreover, with the art of slipping away as often as he pleased into a closed garden of the intellect, where his parents could not pursue but admired him from afar across the boundary-hedge raised by his superior knowledge, he was well-suited to the career of the invalid only child, for whom nothing was too good and every sacrifice was justified. The household, of which he had once formed an inconspicuous fraction, now revolved around its son and heir, being gradually remodelled to meet his tastes and interests. Mr. Ruskin was induced to purchase Turner's, and, though often alarmed to notice that his son was an extremely bad business man, abetted him in founding a collection of water-colour sketches. On John's twenty-first birthday his father had given him Turner's sketch of Winchelsea, a little drawing which, with its "thundrous sky and broken white light of storm round the distant gate and scarcely visible church," seemed to contain a prophetic reflection of troubles still impending. Amid the confusion and distress of feeling which had accelerated, if it did not produce, the breakdown of his health at Oxford, and in which he remained plunged months after he had left Oxford and fallen back on Herne Hill, his intense love of natural beauty provided a solitary guiding beam. The doctors had ordered him abroad, and it was with "some renewal of spirit," some relief from the "sickly fermentation of temper" under which he had been labouring, that he looked forward to revisiting Italy and viewing the classical prospects that Turner's genius had illuminated. His expectations were far too sanguine. The disease of the body might slowly yield; the adversary lodged in the mind proved subtler and more obstinate.

He did not enjoy his Italian tour; for although the idea of beauty continued to draw him, and he had by no means lost his early delight in the pleasures of the intellect, a shadow perpetually intruded itself, disfiguring and discolouring every landscape that he passed through. He was sick and weary and fretful. To spare John unnecessary pain, the family cortège did not on this occasion travel south by way of Paris. From Rouen they made for the Loire, and thence, across Auvergne, to the cities of the sea-coast. The South of France proved eminently displeasing; and in Italy, during the first few weeks, John found little enough to interest or distract him. The Arno at Pisa appeared a dull and muddy stream. Florence he explored with feelings of "grievous disappointment," hating the "Newgate-like palaces," considering "the inside of the Duomo a horror, the outside a Chinese puzzle," and the whole city, country round about included, " a provocation and weariness, except for one master, M. Angelo." At Siena, where he had a bad headache, " the cathedral seemed to me every way absurd—over-cut, over-striped, over-crocketed, over-gabled, a piece of costly confectionery and faithless vanity "; while " the first sight of St. Peter's dome, twenty miles away, was little more to any of us than the apparition of a grey milestone, announcing twenty miles yet of stony road before rest." As for the sluggish flood of the Tiber, what a " vile and saddening sight "! A nearer view of St. Peter's, and a brief inspection of the " clumsy dulness of the façade, and the entirely vile taste and vapid design of the interior," confirmed him in the dislike he felt for most Renaissance monuments. The ceremonies of the Catholic Church were equally confusing and exasperating; and if he ever consented to attend them, it was in the hope that he might catch a momentary glimpse, over the heads of the Italian crowd, of the fair regular features of an exquisite English girl, a certain Miss Tollemache, whom he did not approach or speak to, but whose beauty—" statuesque severity with womanly sweetness joined "—was among the rare consolations of a dismal overclouded winter.

As yet the clouds showed no signs of lifting; and his state of mind continued to puzzle himself as much as it perplexed and mortified his parents. Flashes of happiness suddenly visited him—for instance at Sestri di Levante, described in a memorable passage of his early journals. But such enlightenment was seldom long-enduring; and on December 30th, after a touch of local fever, he describes in his diary how he has been walking to and fro upon the Pincian, with the loveliest of prospects before him——

> ". . . A light Decemberish mist, mixed with the slightest vestige of woodsmoke, hovering between the distances, and giving beautiful grey outlines of every form between the eye and the sun. . . . It was not like moonlight, nor like sunlight, but as soft as the one, and as powerful as the other. . . ."

——unable to decide why it was that "every imaginable delight palls so very rapidly. . . ." Gardens, obelisks, palaces, the vision of far-away Apennines, "with one principal pyramid of pure snow, like a piece of sudden comet-light fallen on the earth," could not disguise from him the fact that he felt, above all else, tired and sullen and despondent. But still he saw, though he could not enjoy; and his record, kept at the time, of the Ruskins' expedition from Rome to Naples during the early days of January is full of felicitous images and brilliantly descriptive strokes, which reveal both his precocious command of language and the quickness and hyper-sensitiveness of his perceptions when he confronted natural beauty. He reached Naples, nevertheless, as usual disappointed, almost weeping with exhaustion, and, on the return journey at Albano, experienced a further haemorrhage, which, although no more serious than the first, caused James Ruskin to look extremely troubled and hurry ahead to Rome to fetch the English doctor. But the doctor's verdict was reassuring; and meanwhile there were other hopeful symptoms—intimations, dim at first, it is true, of an improvement in his mental health. Rome revisited during Easter week seemed far less void and desolate than his impressions of the winter months; even the church services had begun to touch and interest him; and as the family travelled northwards, John's spirits gradually rose, achieving a pitch of real rapture, when they arrived at the lagoons of Venice and he saw "the black knot of gondolas on the canal of Mestre." "Thank God I am here," he wrote in his diary on May 6th, 1841; "it is the Paradise of cities." At last he had found a spiritual home, a refuge which could be compared only to his beloved Alpine solitudes. "This and Chamouni," he concluded, "are my two bournes of Earth."

During the same summer, among the mountains themselves, he received as it were a confirmation that he had made his peace with destiny. Ruskin's intelligence had a highly symbolic turn. His original glimpse of the Alps "had been to me as a direct revelation of the benevolent will in creation," while, later, the volcanic landscape around Naples, where the primeval fires beneath the earth are still manifest in lava-streams, burning ash and clouds of poisonous vapour, had represented its malevolent counterpart—" if not the personality of an Evil Spirit, at all events the permitted symbol of evil, unredeemed; wholly distinct from the conditions of storm, or heat, or frost, on which the healthy courses of organic life depended." Typical both of primitive man and of the poet in the civilised world, an addiction to such symbolism is also characteristic of certain nervous maladies. Ruskin's cast of mind was strongly poetic; that his mental equilibrium was somewhat precarious might already have been inferred from the state of prostration to which he had been reduced by the disappointment of his first love. Now the mountains brought him symbolic succour, and completed the beneficent effect of those enchanted weeks in Venice. At six o'clock of a summer morning, he woke from sound sleep in a one-windowed, wood-walled bedroom, dressed quickly, ran along the village street, crossed a brook and climbed a grass slope opposite. Beneath the pine-boughs he had a moment of illumination. Hope, a sense of purpose, belief in the future, were suddenly rekindled. "I had found my life again; all the best of it. . . . I went down thankfully to my father and mother, and told them I was sure I should get well."

Thus the crisis passed. Returning to England, John Ruskin was permitted for the first time to make an independent journey—to North Wales, where he wished to visit and sketch the mountains of Snowdonia—though subsequently enjoined to break it off, when his mother and father learned that Dr. Jephson of Leamington Spa had decided that their young invalid was in need of further treatment. Dr. Jephson's treatment proved efficacious, and by May he was well enough to take his degree, a double-fourth, at Oxford. During the autumn months of 1842, the Ruskin family, after anxious and prolonged discussion, moved from their semi-detached house on Herne Hill to a considerably larger house on nearby Denmark Hill which, besides the genteel quality of detachment, possessed many other attributes of a decorous and distinguished kind, such as a big garden, hothouses and stables, even a miniature home-farm which gave them milk and butter. The central building, a merchant's residence of the late-Georgian period, was square and plain and dignified; and within its shelter the life of the Ruskin family was soon re-established on the customary agreeable pattern, self-sufficient, unassuming yet modestly luxurious. Here, among his pictures and books, waited on by a devoted valet, secure in the enjoyment of the adequate personal allowance his father now contributed, John was free to pursue studies and to cultivate inclinations which, as he himself felt and as his parents agreed, were alike completely admirable. From 1842 to 1847, between the critical ages of twenty-three and twenty-eight, there was little outward change in the life he led; while suggestions of inward strain, at least on the scale of the previous crisis, were very rarely evident. Richmond painted him in 1843, a pensive yet engaging youth, who turns away from a mahogany writing-desk, a portfolio at his feet, a pen poised between his fingers. Diligence and good breeding are implied by every detail—the apparatus of his work around him, varnished boots, slim trouser-legs, the fine velvet-collared frock-coat. This was the young man who, when some congenial and cultivated visitor gained admittance to the house on Denmark Hill, having survived the preliminary inspection that must be gone through at the porter's lodge, would come running downstairs, the blue of his neckcloth a match for the blue of his eyes, both hands outstretched in welcome, to show his Turners and the Tintoretto, the Joshua Reynolds or the alleged Titian that James Ruskin had collected. He was exceedingly busy, yet naturally hospitable. But, once the visitor had gone, he would dart back to his work-room, remaining there till Margaret Ruskin, who still watched over his health with the same assiduous attention she devoted to her house and servants, packed him off for his afternoon walk, which usually took him to the Dulwich Gallery or to the house of a fellow-enthusiast who could show him Turner drawings. After dinner, it was his custom to work another hour or two. But he went early to bed—Mrs. Ruskin had not forgotten the disastrous result of those protracted Oxford vigils—and at breakfast he would read aloud some eloquent addition to the book his family knew him to be writing, a celebration of the genius of the modern landscape painters. Occasionally, neglectful of Turner, mineralogy, and the beauties of Venetian art, he would devote his attention to some less important project. Thus, when, in 1841, a little girl named Euphemia Gray, the daughter of friends who lived near Perth at Bowerswell, visited Denmark Hill and spent some days among the Ruskins, he amused her by writing a fairy story, afterwards published as *The King of the Golden River*.

II

OVER the modest signature, " A Graduate of Oxford," the opening volume of *Modern Painters* was published by Smith, Elder, of Cornhill, in April, 1843. It had been written during the previous twelve months; but its genesis can be traced back to a far remoter period of Ruskin's education—to his earliest glimpse of Rogers' *Italy*, to the memorable occasion when he first acquired a Turner water-colour, or to his original meeting with the great man, which had brightened the disturbed and dreary days between the time he left Oxford and his departure for the Continent. Though warned that he might think the old Academician " coarse, boorish, unintellectual, vulgar," when they came face to face Ruskin found him " a somewhat eccentric, keen-mannered, matter-of-fact, English-minded gentleman: good-natured evidently . . . shrewd, perhaps a little selfish, highly intellectual, the powers of the mind . . . flashing out occasionally in a word or a look." Admirer and master made a curiously-assorted pair: the one youthful, innocent, enthusiastic, the handsome and fastidious product of a well-to-do, adoring family; the other a short, seventy-year-old " Jewish-nosed man in an ill-cut brown tail-coat, striped waistcoat, and enormous frilled shirt," whose habits were both miserly and crapulous, and whose bare, dirty London rooms, haunted by a troop of skeleton-thin Angora cats and an elderly and squalid concubine, were further encumbered by a vast decaying accumulation of partly-finished pictures. But Ruskin's enthusiasm was uncritical; the study of human nature, after all, would never be his *forte*; and, on noticing some newspaper abuse of Turner's recent " Juliet " he had already, at the age of seventeen, dashed off a spirited defence of his favourite painter's life-work, which James Ruskin, with his usual caution, decided the artist himself must see before it reached the public. Turner's response had been politely discouraging; and Ruskin continued to hold his peace, until a renewed attack, published by the art critic of the *Athenaeum*, reawoke his ardour. At once he embarked on a vindication of Turner's latest mannerisms, which gradually developed into an essay on the whole method and tendency of modern landscape art.

The book was immediately successful. True, its hero, who had had the somewhat overwhelming experience of seeing himself compared to the great angel of the Apocalypse "glorious in conception—unfathomable in knowledge—solitary in power . . . sent as a prophet of God to reveal to men the mysteries of His universe," prudently refrained from uttering any comment; and fifteen months had passed before he could bring himself to refer to those outrageous eulogies. But then, after a dinner-party, Turner abruptly thanked his champion, drove home with him in the same carriage, and, when they arrived at his door, "vowed he'd be damned if we shouldn't come in and have some sherry. We were compelled to obey" (wrote Ruskin) "and so drank healths again . . . by the light of a single tallow candle in the under room. . . ." Turner's fellow-painters were equally reserved. Literary judges, on the other hand, were very much less backward; and Sydney Smith, an urbane and delightful link between the Georgian and Victorian ages, was reported to James Ruskin as having spoken "in the highest terms of your son's work, on a public occasion, and in the presence of several distinguished literary characters," declaring that it was "a work of transcendent talent, presented the most original views, and the most elegant and powerful language, and would work a complete revolution in the world of taste." Apart from its literary charm, which was compulsive, *Modern Painters* had many obvious claims to general popularity. In a period enamoured of its own achievements, convinced that the nineteenth century represented a critical, perhaps a concluding, stage in the history of human progress, the book, which set out to prove with a dignified parade of learning that modern artists—what was more, modern *English* artists—were immensely superior to the Old Masters, French or Dutch, whose pictures filled our galleries, was bound to receive the suffrage of many progressive and patriotic readers. Besides, its moral tone was reassuring. The intention of the book might not be plainly pietistic; yet repeatedly the author expressed his conviction that the true object of the artist's life was to celebrate the supreme beauty, diversity and ingenuity of the god-made world around him. He was less a creator than an interpreter. The æsthetic side of the artist's functions, if not summarily discounted, was nowhere over-emphasised; for the artist's business (so the reader gathered) was to appeal to beholders in clear and simple language; and this language, with all its complexities, though "invaluable as the vehicle of thought," was "by itself nothing. . . . All those excellences which are peculiar to the painter as such, are merely what rhythm, melody, precision and force are in the words of the orator and poet, necessary to their greatness, but not the test of their greatness. It is not" (decided Ruskin) "by the mode of representing and saying, but by what is represented and said, that the respective greatness either of the painter or the writer is to be finally determined."

As an example of the magnificent uses to which the language of painting might be applied by a really accomplished and rightly conscientious artist, Ruskin proceeded to describe a canvas by Edwin Landseer, entitled "The Old Shepherd's Chief Mourner":

"Here" (he wrote) "the exquisite execution of the glossy and crisp hair of the dog, the bright sharp touching of the green bough beside it, the clear painting of the wood of the coffin and the folds of the blanket, are language—language clear and expressive in the highest degree. But the close pressure of the dog's breast against the wood, the convulsive clinging of the paws, which has dragged the blanket off the trestle, the total powerlessness of the head . . . the fixed and tearful fall of the eye . . . the quietness and gloom of the chamber, the spectacles marking the place where the Bible was last closed, indicating how lonely has been the life—how unwatched the departure of him who is now laid solitary in his sleep—these are all thoughts—thoughts by which the picture is separated at once from hundreds of equal merit, as far as mere painting goes, by which it ranks as a work of the highest art, and stamps its author, not as the neat imitator of the texture of a skin, or the fold of a drapery, but as the Man of Mind."

Having thus affirmed his æsthetic beliefs and borne witness to the super-eminent virtues of what he called "sincerity"—a mixture of right feeling and accurate observation, through which the artist becomes a devout and truthful interpreter of the divine message implicit in the beauty of the sensuous world—Ruskin got to grips with the Old Masters, with such of them as he knew, particularly with Claude and Poussin, whose observation he considered usually weak, and whose interpretation of nature was coarse, conventional and earth-bound. In contrast to the brilliance of his prose style, the critical methods he employed were very often naïve to the point of downright crudity. Turner was judged superior to Claude because, unlike the Old Master, he understood as a scientist how clouds were formed, how trees branched and how the rocks were stratified. Clouds were especially important; for to Ruskin, with his love of subtle, interwoven, swiftly-changing movement, the mysterious architecture of the sky was an intense preoccupation, almost an obsession. He loved clouds as he loved rivers; and when he wrote of a rushing, rebounding stream, of some "colossal mountain of grey cumulus, through whose shadowed sides the sunbeams penetrate in dim, sloping, rain-like shafts," of the "quiet multitudes of the white, soft, silent cirrus," or of the "veily transparency" of the rain-cloud "with its ragged and spray-like edge," the austere Graduate of Oxford forgot to be a moralist, forgot that it was his duty to enlighten and instruct the commercial age he lived in; while his style expanded into long elaborate discursive paragraphs of a bewildering eloquence and fluency.

Modern Painters, in fact—or, to give it its full title, *Modern Painters: Their Superiority in the Art of Landscape Painting to all the Ancient Masters proved by Examples of the True, the Beautiful, and the Intellectual from the Works of Modern Artists, especially from those of J. M. W. Turner, Esq., R.A.*—is one of the most presumptuous, most poetic, most brilliant yet most wrong-headed volumes ever published by a very young man. Ruskin was twenty-four, and at a single stroke now established himself in the forefront of modern English art critics. He was not ill-pleased with the result of his labours. Though always prone to moods of self-critical depression verging on abjection, he rarely questioned his own æsthetic judgment; for he was deeply imbued with that sense of natural superiority, both moral and intellectual, which he had first absorbed at Herne Hill. It had begun to dawn on him, nevertheless, that his examination of the Old Masters had not been quite exhaustive. For example, there were the Italian painters of whom he knew little or nothing, but whose works, he now surmised, might have an important bearing upon his central thesis. A continental tour with his parents in the winter of 1844 led to long sessions at the Louvre, which helped to whet his appetite. He announced that he must go abroad again before he wrote another volume, and, since James Ruskin was detained by his business affairs, John took the bold step of suggesting that he should cross the Channel unaccompanied. His parents were doubtful; but they consented to humour his whim; and, during the spring of 1845, the celebrated author of *Modern Painters* set forth from Denmark Hill to enjoy, at the age of twenty-six, his first independent foreign journey.

The independence, of course, was relative. For, besides being squired by George, his English valet, who, though once caught smoking on the Piazza San Marco, proved in every other respect a virtuous and staunchly loyal body-servant, he was escorted by Couttet, the Swiss courier, whom his parents knew and trusted, who had learned to nurse him should he fall sick, and could be relied on to hold an umbrella over his head lest he expose himself when sketching. The three formed an harmonious trio. Only occasionally did George lament himself in the accents of Byron's Fletcher, amid the summer heats of an Italian city regretting the fresh strawberries and the cool acacia-walk at Denmark Hill; while Couttet now and then grew impatient with the moods of deep despondency from which his young employer suffered, dropping behind him on a walk and murmuring to George, with a shrug of the shoulders: " *Le pauvre enfant, il ne sait pas vivre.*" Ruskin would perhaps have concurred. On the other hand, since the disappointment of his hopeless love for Adèle, he had shown few signs of wishing for any life wider or more adventurous than that which his own talents and his father's wealth and devotion so liberally provided. New impressions came in a tumultuous flood; uplifted by the splendours of Florentine painting, he was no less astonished and delighted by the achievement of the great Venetian artists, and wrote home that he had been " crushed to the earth " by the concentration of intellect revealed in Tintoretto's pictures. But Venice, he promised, should not persuade him to prolong his stay unnecessarily: in the meantime he would take good care of his health and be constantly attentive not to fall off ladders. When he got back, he added, " I hope I shall write a very nice book, and one that I need not be ashamed of. . . ." Yet, in spite of his promises and Couttet's precautions, on the way home, at Padua, he became seriously unwell. His complaint was described as a " nervous fever "; and during his convalescence he learned of the death of one of the robust Croydon cousins, whose noisy companionship had relieved the monotony of his quiet and lonely childhood. Feeling depressed and weak and feverish, he began to despair of existence and to speculate " what my own selfish life was to come to. . . ." Would he reach England alive? Reflecting on the intense grief his death would cause his parents, the invalid took refuge in prayer, continuing his spiritual exercises as he travelled slowly homewards; till, as he approached Paris, he was suddenly visited by an experience that " people who are in the habit of praying know as the consciousness of answer," a " sense of direct relation with Heaven," which did not desert him till he had crossed his parents' threshold, when (as he remembered in later years) he almost at once sank back " into the faintness and darkness of the Under-World." How are we to explain that last perplexing phrase? In what underworld did the high-minded, innocent, dutiful young man already feel that he existed? For the moment we must dismiss the problem, observing merely that a conviction of sin—a conviction at least of profound personal unworthiness, oddly at variance with his sense of inherited superiority—was one of the disabilities under which he sometimes laboured, and which reappeared to torment him according to the vicissitudes of his general health and spirits. But his nerves were steady enough, in the winter months of 1845 and the spring of 1846, to permit him to take up work again as soon as he returned to Denmark Hill. Five months saw the completion of his second volume—a book that his father and mother found exceedingly impressive: " they used both to cry a little, at least my father generally did, over the pretty passages, when I read them after breakfast. . . ."

That summer it had been agreed that the whole family should revisit Italy, to view, under the young man's guidance, " all the things and pictures " he had written of. Though tired, he was " in excellent health and proud hope; they also at their best and gladdest." He landed at Calais in a calm and happy mood. Yet by one of those rapid and sweeping revolutions to which the student of John Ruskin's life soon becomes accustomed, in Italy, almost for the first time, a hint of conflict developed between father and son, John growing impatiently—even angrily—conscious of the inevitable limitations of the old man's aims and outlook: James Ruskin, though he continued to love and admire, recognising regretfully that since the publication of John's second volume it was more and more difficult to share in his pursuits and studies. Sad that his son would never wear lawn-sleeves: sad that his poetic ambitions had now been definitely abandoned! And then, his methods as a draughtsman were changing. No longer did he produce the kind of large carefully-finished water-colour sketch that looked so well at Denmark Hill—" such as in former days " (wrote James Ruskin to a friend) " you or I might compliment in the usual way by saying it deserved a frame " —but brief disconnected notes which he stuffed into his waistcoat-pockets, " fragments of everything from a cupola to a cartwheel . . . all true, Truth itself, but Truth in mosaic." Glancing back at this period across the gulf of many years, Ruskin was to accuse himself both of " arrogance " and of " vicious stubbornness." Yet his arrogance, he remarks, was not founded on vanity so much as upon sorrow—on the sorrow occasioned in him by other people's shortcomings, the obliquities of their vision, the failures of their sensitiveness. It was his mission to reopen the eyes of England. Alas, the belief that one's life is dedicated is hard to support without a certain touch of vanity, without a tinge of that spiritual pride which has more often a more unpleasing, more subtly disfiguring influence, on any human character than most of the vices and follies that Ruskin despised and shunned. The first conflict with his devoted but tactless father revealed in John's temperament an underlying vein of obstinacy, manifested now and then in small but significant explosions of petulance and harshness.

Thus, one sunny afternoon in Pisa, at the gates of the Spina chapel, there was a distressing little scene about the payment of a cabman's fare. How much ought he to give the man, inquired the thrifty merchant; and John, disturbed in contemplation—for the chapel was at that moment among the chiefest objects of his reverence—retaliated with some caustic observations on his father's commercial instincts and want of true æsthetic nicety. Long afterwards this incident remained " one of the worst, wasp-barbed, most tingling pangs " in Ruskin's recollection; just as he could never forget the look of deep anguish that had crossed his father's face when, five years earlier, he had suffered a relapse on the road between Rome and

Naples. But the harm done was not yet beyond repair. Each attempted, honestly and anxiously, to understand the other; and if they failed, as they were bound to fail, it was not for any lack of love or thought or patience. The weeks that they spent in Switzerland, at the conclusion of their tour, proved as usual mollifying; and John lost himself in the delights of observation pure and simple—simple as happiness could make it, pure of the trace of spiritual conceit, which emerged as often as he attempted to translate observation into doctrine, and sacrificed the joy of pleasing himself to the interest of enlightening others. He noted, near the source of the Arveron, the " intense scarletty purple of the shattered larch stems . . .; the alder stems looking much like birch, covered with the white branchy moss that looks like a coral," or watched the formation of the rain-clouds—" long, continuous and delicate "—as they wreathed and undulated beneath the mountain crests.

Had those two adversaries, the Moralist and the Æsthete, battled alone for supremacy in the depths of Ruskin's nature, the difficulties that confronted him would have been acute but not perhaps insoluble. The existence of the Lover, clamorous for his rights but not by any means certain of his own objectives, made the development of the conflict immeasurably more confused, since he could neither be suppressed nor quite accommodated to any æsthetic, moral or intellectual system. Adèle's image had gradually lost its power. Now, when Ruskin returned from Italy, a second image, as vivid if slightly less disturbing, arose to take its place, and he decided that he was again in love—again with a very young girl, who dawned on his mind like a vision and eluded him, when he attempted to grasp her, with visionary swiftness. Her name was Charlotte Lockhart, the daughter of the critic and biographer, the granddaughter of Walter Scott. Once again the passion was nympholeptic. " Little high-foreheaded Charlotte " became in Ruskin's fervid imagination " a Scottish fairy, White Lady, and witch of the fatallest sort, looking as if she had just risen out of the stream in Rhymer's Glen, and could only be seen by favouring glance of moonlight over the Eildon." In fact, he often saw, and was even able to speak to her, though never happily or satisfactorily, " by the dim lamplight of this world"—in Park Street, for example, in Lady Davy's drawing-room, where the old bluestocking gathered around her many of Sir Walter's friends. But Charlotte was in love with a Mr. Hope; and then, Ruskin's methods of courtship had neither improved nor changed since he attempted to win Adèle. Other approaches having come to nothing, he hit on the plan of attacking through her father, who, as editor of the *Quarterly Review*, had proposed that the author of *Modern Painters* should write a critical notice of Lord Lindsay's *History of Christian Art*. Ruskin at first hesitated, but presently decided, " with " (he commented wryly) " my usual wisdom in such matters," that a triumphant *Quarterly* review might help him to gain Charlotte, and set out for the English Lakes, determined to complete his essay. There, whether it was love or Lord Lindsay, " the grilled salmon for breakfast, or too prolonged reflections on the Celestial Hierarchies," he fell into a state of gloom and lassitude more intense and unrelieved than any he had yet experienced, spending his forenoons laboriously balancing phrases and his afternoons afloat on Windermere, observing that the waters were leaden and the hills were low and dull. Nor did the completion of his task bring the expected rewards: Lockhart, a conservative editor, insisted on cutting out the " best bits ": Charlotte, cool, virginal, remote, looked inflexibly the other way.

Their last encounter was unfortunate and characteristic. At a party in Lady Davy's house, Ruskin was given Charlotte Lockhart to take down to dinner; but he found it impossible to begin a conversation; and, in the spirit of desperate contrariety peculiar to unhappy lovers, he squandered his opportunities by talking across her at considerable length to her other neighbour, Mr. Gladstone, with whom he disputed about the condition of the Neapolitan gaols; for Gladstone, that pillar of common sense, " couldn't see, as I did, that the real prisoners were the people outside." Whatever Gladstone thought or Charlotte suffered during the course of this protracted and inappropriate dialogue, the paradoxical opinion which Ruskin expressed seems indicative of the phase through which his mind was passing. Though there was no upheaval which could be compared with the crisis that had overtaken him when he heard of Adèle's marriage, temporarily at least the effects of Charlotte's unkindness were even more demoralising, darkened the colours of his imagination, gave the workings of his fancy a curious and morbid twist. He was a prisoner of adult life, already a forlorn exile from the beloved world of childhood. And in a letter to his father, written on a visit to a Scottish friend during the summer months of 1847, appears a passage of nostalgic lamentation as confused and mysterious as it is musically worded. He was at Dunkeld, where he had intended remaining.

". . . But I must go on" (he wrote). "I feel so utterly down-hearted to-night that I must get away to-morrow without going out again, for I am afraid of something seizing me in the state of depression. I never had a more beautiful, nor half so unhappy a walk as this afternoon; it is so very different from Switzerland and Cumberland that it revives all sorts of old feelings at their very source—and yet in a dead form, like ghosts—and I feel myself so changed, and everything else so ancient, and so the same in its ancientness, that, together with the name and fear, and neighbourhood of the place, I can't bear it. The flow of the Tay before the window under the bridge, with its banks of shingle and clear, soft, sliding, ringing water, is so unlike the Arve, and every other stream, and so like itself—old Tay—the very Tay that I remembered in the Bridge-end house at the bottom of the garden—the very Tay for the association with which, however impartial or imperfect, I believe it is that I have so loved all other running streams—that it is enough to break one's heart to look at it."

Though the ripple of the Tay had delighted his childhood, why (his reader is bound to inquire) should its associations for Ruskin, as a free and celebrated and well-loved young man, have been so oddly moving? The recollection of his vanished Scottish cousins, however deep his attachment or profound his regret, would not in itself have affected him thus strongly. His regret, indeed, would seem to be focused, not on any person, living or dead, but upon childhood for its own sake, as if, between present and past times—the past warm and luminous, the present cold and overclouded—there had occurred some loss of candour, some fatal fall from innocence, an introduction to the knowledge of good and evil, for which no subsequent success could ever console or compensate him. James Ruskin was naturally alarmed—distressed, too, when, in letters similarly despondent, John reverted to the subject of former woes and grievances. He replied at length, patiently, elaborately: "You say we could not by a whole summer give you a tenth of the pleasure that to have left you a month in the Highlands in 1838 would have done, nor by buying Turner and Windus's gallery the pleasure that two Turners would have done in 1842, you having passed two or three years with a sick longing for Turner. I take blame to myself for not sending you to the Highlands in 1838 and not buying you a few more Turners; but the first I was not at all aware of, and the second I freely confess I have been restrained in from my very constitutional prudence. . . ." As he saw it, he added somewhat pathetically, his life-work had two purposes—"to indulge you and to leave you and Mamma comfortably provided for"—and wound up with a plea that, should John have "any longings like 1842," he would at once disclose them. James Ruskin's professions were whole-hearted. When John next confessed to a desperate longing, he found in the older man an anxiously sympathetic, if injudicious, ally.

At this point, some relief is needed. Though it is true that a dark strain of spiritual hypochondria ran through Ruskin's temperament, his constitution had other attributes at least as noteworthy and, from the point of view of the world at large, very much more reassuring. New friends found him a delightful companion. There was something

Effie Gray by G. F. Watts

about the gifted young critic, not dashing perhaps—for his character at the first glance revealed itself as naturally and deeply serious—but debonair and, as regards his outward appearance, even somewhat dandified. Thus he made an immediate conquest of his parents' old friend, the elderly but still vivacious woman of letters, Mary Russell Mitford, who announced that John Ruskin was " certainly the most charming person I have ever known . . . Just what, if one had a son, one should have dreamt of his turning out—in mind, manner, conversation, everything . . . He is by far the most eloquent and interesting young man that I have ever seen, grace itself and sweetness." After this promising introduction, Ruskin paid several visits to Miss Mitford's cottage. They exchanged numerous and friendly letters; but when his friend, with a courage and discrimination unusual in literary women of that period, recommended him to read Balzac's *Illusions Perdues*, he confessed that he could not finish it—" there was too much of what was exquisitely painful to be endured sympathetically."

In John Ruskin, the history of Lucien de Rubempré was not likely to gain an appreciative or understanding audience: it is more difficult to decide why the impact of the book on his imagination should have been so violent and unexpected that he could not reach the last page. Was he disturbed by the demonic aspect of Balzac's amoral heroes and darkly heroic villains? Did they point the way towards fields of experience he still preferred to disregard? His beliefs and ambitions were orthodox, his feelings and inclinations complex. His own demon was always uneasily stirring, only half held down by an inherited religious creed and by the habit of moral conformity he had learned in early childhood. The obvious symptoms of its struggles were restlessness and ill-health; and, when James Ruskin implored his son to make a frank disclosure of any secret longings that they might at once be satisfied, he showed his appreciation of the extent of the danger, though its causes, emotional and intellectual, were far beyond his mental scope. He made a promise, and he would keep his word. But the test did not come till the autumn months of 1847.

The longing that John then voiced was not for tours or Turners, but for a living acquisition, a delectable human toy, another materialisation of the image he had already failed to grasp in Adèle and in Charlotte.

Euphemia Gray had returned to Denmark Hill—and returned not as the little girl for whom he had written *The King of the Golden River* in 1841, but as a marriageable young person, just now becoming pleasantly conscious of the power her beauty exercised. Fate seemed already to have linked the Grays and Ruskins; for not only were they distantly connected, but the house which the Grays inhabited had belonged to John's ill-omened grandfather, and, by a curious and alarming coincidence, the room in which their daughter was born—on May 7th, 1828—was that in which John Ruskin the elder had committed suicide. George Gray, Euphemia's father, was a Writer to the Signet. Moderately well to do, he had made unfortunate speculations in the future of English railways; and, during 1847 and 1848, his financial position was clearly somewhat difficult. But both Euphemia and her brother George had been educated at English schools; and, on their way to and from school, the more affluent and always hospitable Ruskins often entertained them. Euphemia's last visit as a schoolgirl was paid during the autumn of 1846; but on that occasion, when she was accompanied by her father, her reception by Mr. and Mrs. Ruskin had not been very cordial. Recognising their son's susceptibility and knowing the damage his unlucky passions did him, his parents would appear to have observed with dismay John's attraction towards their old friends' evidently seductive and now almost grown-up daughter. But no sooner had the Grays departed than John had begun to plead that Euphemia should be lured back. Mrs. Ruskin suggested that he should wait till next year; and John, who believed her to be twelve months younger than, in fact, she was, tells us that he had consented, although reluctantly and sulkily. When spring came, her visit was repeated. This time she arrived alone; John saw and made much of her; and it was presently plain that his original interest had by no means died down. There followed consultations between anxious mother and father. James Ruskin was extremely disquieted by what he had heard of Mr. Gray's investments and by the " speculative propensities he believed to prevail in Perth." He dreaded the effect on John's constitution of another unsuccessful love-affair. Besides, John was supposed, among their acquaintances, to be a serious suitor for the hand of Charlotte Lockhart. The whole situation was immensely troublesome. Since his commercial experience had led him to imagine that any danger could be averted, and any problem solved, by a becoming display of firmness, probity and candour, James Ruskin decided on bold and straightforward methods. With appropriate gravity he took up his pen, and proceeded to lay his doubts at considerable length before Mr. Gray at Bowerswell.

Neither as a diplomatist nor as a correspondent was Mr. Ruskin gifted. His epistolary style was equally tortuous and sententious; and in his anxiety to do himself justice, to be firm yet completely fair, sincere yet always dignified, he contrived at times to produce more mischief than many haphazard, and even some dishonest, letter-writers. Avenues were explored to no purpose; not a stone was allowed to remain unturned—though the process of turning over merely revealed a host of lurking platitudes—as he crept back and forth across his subject with laborious ant-like industry. Thus, when opening his heart to Euphemia's father, he began by giving a diffuse account of John's early sentimental mishap, and explained that his son had recently encountered " a young lady who has engaged his affections and has made proposals the result of which is not yet known." After this reference, perhaps slightly disingenuous, to John's love for Charlotte Lockhart—it is difficult to believe that he had made an explicit proposal: but then, James Ruskin was not the man to emit a casual untruth—he went on to announce that Mrs. Ruskin, remembering her own unhappy years in Scotland, had conceived an insuperable dislike to that country as a whole and to the neighbourhood of Perth particularly, and regarded the idea of a Scottish alliance with almost superstitious horror. True, " our young people " were not yet in love: and " I would not presume to say that Miss Gray cannot be daily with my son without the smallest danger to herself but I deem it more than possible from what I already see that both may fall into some danger and that very great embarrassment might arise to all of us should the favourable impression which each may be already making on the other proceed to take a more definite form." In short, he would be greatly obliged if Mr. Gray would arrange for the immediate removal of his much too charming daughter. Mr. Gray at once assented, promising that Euphemia should be removed but adding, a little tartly, that it struck him Mrs. Ruskin might have saved them all much trouble had she quietly hinted to Euphemia that John was an engaged man. His daugher, he knew, had " always expressed herself favourably of John as a person for whom she had a high respect as a man of talent and refined manners "; but he knew also that she had a " great deal of good sense and maidenly pride," and would be " the very last person in the world " either to give her affections to John if he were previously committed or, were he free, to accept him at the expense of his mother's feelings. Thus the relationship might have reached an abrupt conclusion, had Mr. Ruskin, in his next letter, not seen fit to reveal an unexpected change of attitude. No doubt John, when he learned that Euphemia was soon to leave Denmark Hill, protested vehemently and passionately. His father, at least, composed a hurried reply, withdrawing his earlier objections, affirming that " we had no grounds whatever to think that Miss Gray was . . . interested about my son beyond the interest of one young person for another on a renewed acquaintance " and begging that her visit might be allowed to run its course. That he was apprehensive, he frankly admitted; " . . . his Mother and myself see every day that he is too sensibly affected by Miss Gray's presence for his own peace—still no sudden steps can be taken without too much wounding his feelings and showing a distrust in his strength of mind which not knowing his own danger, he would ill brook from any one . . ." Till the end of June, when she returned to Scotland, Euphemia remained the Ruskins' guest, driving out daily with John, listening to her hostess' good advice or lending a patient ear to Mr. Ruskin's table-talk. By the time she left, she had established just such a hold on John's affections as both his parents dreaded.

To what extent was Euphemia Gray's subjugation of her promising, eligible admirer either conscious or deliberate? Effie or Phemy—to give her the names usually current among her friends and family—though in her composition there was nothing of the blue-stocking, possessed, besides unusual physical grace, a certain native shrewdness. Her face had a rounded feline charm; but whereas the line of the cheeks was full, the nose straight and delicate, the mouth small and sensuous with its slightly swelling underlip, the large eyes were serious and intent, and looked out from beneath level brows with a steady glance that seemed equally blended of candour and sophistication. Her tastes were worldly, if not frivolous; and during her stay at Denmark Hill, whether she drove in the Park, visited exhibitions, or watched the aged Duke of Wellington riding up St. James's Street, she had derived endless amusement from the spectacle of London life. She loved clothes: she delighted in parties: the observation of her fellow human beings very seldom failed to interest her. Thus her comments on the Ruskin household were sharp, though not uncharitable. Mr. Ruskin (she informed her parents) was "as kind as ever and as droll"; Mrs. Ruskin appeared to be feeling her age and was inclined to drowse off when they sat together in the lamplight. As for John—well, she herself inclined to think that this affair of the heart, of which his parents made so much and talked so deliberately, had been somewhat over-emphasised; he seemed reluctant to leave the house but, "queer being" that he was, preferred to sit at home painting, while the two devoted old people planned his future marriage: "Mr. and Mrs. R. are always talking about marrying from reason, rather odd, isn't it." Should John marry at all, she concluded, she could only suppose that he would do so in obedience to a mistaken sense of duty. "He adores them and will sacrifice himself for them . . ." Mrs. Ruskin had now imparted the secret of John's alleged attachment "in case as she says that John and I should *love each other*. Wasn't it good, I could not help laughing."

If she was indeed unconscious of John's attraction, his behaviour during the months that followed did little to enlighten her. Though he visited Perth, he made no halt at Bowerswell, explaining in a letter to Mrs. Gray that the emotions aroused by revisiting the neighbourhood after an interval of twenty years were too painfully disturbing, and that the city and its surroundings "have been to *me* so peculiarly and constantly unfortunate that I would not willingly associate any of my present pleasures with its hitherto ill-boding scenes." This was the period of nameless gloom already described in a letter to his father. Then, it is permissible to suppose, the image of Charlotte Lockhart had not been wholly expunged, though a second image had begun to emerge like the writing of a palimpsest. But by mid-September he had so far conquered his fears and elucidated his private feelings as to summon up resolution to pay his friends a visit, and wrote at length to Mrs. Gray suggesting he should call upon them. Meanwhile, under the pressure of John's appeals, reinforced by the belief that, if he were thwarted or disappointed, his health was bound to suffer, the opposition of his parents had gradually been worn down. They assured him that they were anxious to see him married; waiving their previous objections to Perth and the speculative tastes that businessmen imbibed there, they expressed their complete confidence in Mr. Gray's stability; on the subject of Effie herself, and her qualities and gifts and virtues, Mrs. Ruskin poured out a flood of maternal approbation. It was improbable, she said, that John would find another girl so well-suited to the needs of his exacting mind and character. With his parents' license to be happy, John Ruskin arrived at Bowerswell during October 1847.

He proposed, and he was presently accepted—in what circumstances we do not know nor after how hard a siege; and, when he returned to London at the beginning of November, Effie had promised to marry him, her mother and father had consented, and the wedding had been fixed for the spring, so that a honeymoon in the English Lake District could be followed by a family tour among the mountains and monuments that the bridegroom knew and loved best. Ruskin's state of mind was feverishly exalted. The old depression did not completely vanish; and there were moments at which he believed that he was losing his delight in nature: that, robbed of its beauty and innocent freshness, the world had become "a mere board-and-lodging house." Did a friend object that by forfeiting some of his youthful inspiration, he was perhaps "coming down more to fellowship with others," Ruskin retorted that the company in which he joined them was "a fellowship of blindness. I may be able to get hold of people's hands better in the dark, but of what use is that, when I have nowhere to lead them, but into the ditch?" He was writing beside the sea, which "was once to me a friend, companion, master, teacher; now it is *salt water*, and salt water only." But on the same expedition, which had taken the whole family for a week to Folkestone, in a letter to his betrothed at Bowerswell he wrote of sea and sky and a large moon rising over the chalk cliffs, "nearly as large as the great cliff itself," while the twilight sea below "sobbed out its subjection," with visionary enthusiasm and undiminished eloquence. No suggestion of gloom was allowed to spoil his love-letters. Stinted of love when he was a child, long thwarted in his pursuit of the beloved image during early manhood, he threw himself recklessly into the rôle of adorer, and lavished upon Effie—or upon the idea of Effie—all the accumulated emotion of the previous ten years. Later, he was to sum up his predicament sadly, briefly and concisely. As a child he had had nothing to love: ". . . when affection did come, it came with violence utterly rampant and unmanageable . . ." Though its objective might be open to question, the violence of his feeling for Effie is underlined by almost every paragraph of the lengthy and frequent letters that flew from London to Bowerswell during the winter months of 1847 and the spring of 1848. Yet as love-letters they make incongruous reading. Passion is there in full force; and, though the tone is modest and the expressions used are guarded, they produce an air of erotic intensity hard to reconcile with the other glimpses we have had of Ruskin's private character. His excitement is uncontrollable; his premonitions of happiness are so acute and vivid that he can hardly bear to contemplate them. He is dazzled, breathless and bewildered. True to his habit of regarding any young woman whom he found attractive as a nymph, witch or fairy destined to delude or madden, he rhapsodises over the poetic and supernatural associations of Effie's human beauty. Like Charlotte's, hers is a fatal face. Unconscious though she may be of the dreadful power she exercises, she can intoxicate with a syllable and destroy with a passing look. "Ah, Effie" (he was writing on December 15th, 1847), "you have such sad, wicked ways without knowing it—such sweet silver undertones of innocent voice—that when one hears, one is lost—such slight—short—inevitable—arrowy glances from under the bent eyelashes—such gentle changes of sunny and shadowy expression about the lovely lips—such *desperate* ways of doing the most innocent things—Mercy on us—to hear you ask anybody 'whether they take sugar with their peaches'?—don't you recollect my being 'temporarily insane' for all the day afterwards?..." Elsewhere he had given the fancy a wider, more dramatic setting. An earlier suitor had died or disappeared, victim of those arrowy glances, of those desperate delusive smiles:

"Now are you not a terrible creature, Effie . . . I don't know anything dreadful enough to liken you to . . . You are like a sweet forest of pleasant glades and whispering branches—where people wander on and on in its playing shadows they know not how far—and when they come near the centre of it, it is all cold and impenetrable . . . You are like a wrecker on a rocky coast luring vessels to their fate. Every flower that you set in your hair—

every smile that you bestow—nay—every gentle frown even—is a false light lighted on the misty coast of a merciless gulph . . . You are like a fair mirage in the desert—which people follow with weary feet and longing eyes—until they faint on the burning sands—or come to some dark salt lake of tears. You are like the bright—soft—swelling—lovely fields of a high glacier covered with fresh morning snow—which is heavenly to the eye—and soft and winning on the foot—but beneath, there are winding clefts and dark places in its cold—cold ice—where men fall and rise not again. And then you say you ' don't know how it is . . .' "

When due allowance has been made for an element of hyperbole, and for the delight in the use of language natural to any writer æsthetically so gifted, one need not be a psychologist to find the symbolism of this remarkable letter both surprising and illuminating. Lured into the depths of an impenetrable forest, where the adventurer sees at last that he is caught among thorns and briers—beckoned towards a " merciless gulph " in which travellers are dashed to pieces—tempted out on to virginal snow-fields that give way beneath his tread to discover dark and tortuous ice-caves—Ruskin regarded his emotional plight with a mingling of joy and terror. But his descent towards the fascinating abyss included many cautious pauses, when he sufficiently recovered his balance to recollect that he was the son and heir of Denmark Hill. Mrs. Ruskin had some useful advice to give, and the lover obediently passes it on, though he feels quite sure " you will know this without her telling you . . ." Still, a reminder may not come amiss. Effie's dresses, bought to be worn next year, should be of the plainest and neatest kind—" of stuffs that will not crush—nor spoil, nor be bulky in a carriage—for you know we shall be *four*—and very simply made . . ." There was " no *dressing* at Chamouni—the higher the rank commonly the plainer the dress—and it would be no use to leave handsome dresses behind you, merely to find them out of fashion when you come back." He trusted—but, conscious as he was of her own perfect good taste, it seemed hardly worth while saying so—that in her wardrobe she would avoid any suggestion of the ostentatious or expensive; "your beauty is conspicuous without the slightest adornment"; and, far from attracting attention, "it should be your study to dress if possible—so as to *escape unobserved*." Never, never should Effie be in the very least conspicuous; indeed, "I have a great fancy that I shall ask you sometimes to put on your finest dresses when we are alone—and always your simplest when we are going into public."

When they were *alone*!—but it was inconceivable that he would ever reach such happiness. He had been trying to imagine how, at Keswick, they would sit together after dinner. "I couldn't do it—it seemed so impossible I should ever get you all to myself . . ." But his fantasies about their future life were sometimes much less nebulous, and he fell to conjuring up visions of Effie as a keen ecclesiologist, picturing to himself how, while he drew and measured, scrambling over leads and tiles, or "creeping into crypts on my hands and knees, and into rood-lofts and turrets by inexplicable stairs," Effie in the dusky nave of the church would be quietly looking over the building's early written history or, pencil in hand, making her "own unpretending little memoranda of a capital here—an ornament there"; till a time came when he could command her services in the capacity of unpaid draughtsman, and set her to record a frieze while he ascended to examine the vault. For Effie understood, of course, that "I must go on with my *profession*," and that, although during a part of the day he would be completely hers, during another part, usually the longer, "you will have to be *mine*—or to sit at home." Nevertheless, he experienced no apprehensions. On one score alone did he suffer anxious misery, tormented by the thought of the time he had lost and regretting (just as he regretted the semi-starvation of his early appetite for Turners) that their engagement had been so long delayed, and that he had missed "the sight of you—in your *girlish* beauty—which I might have had three years back." Oppressed by reflections of this sort, "I *could* feel very bitter." The harm was evidently irreparable

—" I hardly know *how* great a misfortune it may yet turn out to be." He had injured his health; he had squandered precious happiness. Would not Effie persuade her mother to agree to their marriage at the very earliest opportunity? During Easter week would be most convenient; " for you know my father's birthday is the 10th of May, and we must—God willing—be at Denmark Hill for that."

Effie's replies were affectionate and sensible. Besides hoping that he would not be jealous and reminding him that in the other each of them had much to find out, she promised to mend his gloves and prevent him wearing white hats: for her part she would never wear " an *excessively* Pink Bonnet . . . Pink is a very favourite colour of mine "; but she would subdue the shade in deference to his superior judgement. From Bowerswell, during October, Ruskin had written to a friend, admitting that he knew little enough of the girl he hoped to marry. " I love Miss Gray very much and therefore cannot tell what to think of her. Only this I know, that in many respects she is unfit to be my wife, unless she also loved me exceedingly." She was surrounded by attentive admirers; and, " though I believe most of them inferior in some points to myself," these admirers were " far more calculated to catch a girl's fancy. Still " (he concluded) " Miss Gray and I are old friends." Of such doubts little would seem to have survived the ardours of his courtship. His only dread was that the vision floating before him might somehow not materialise: that he would die of joy or that Effie would vanish from his arms " like the white lady of Avenel." Hence his determination to hurry on the marriage. He left London during the month of April, unaccompanied by his parents. John Ruskin and Euphemia Chalmers Gray were married in the Bowerswell drawing-room on April 10th, 1848.

Around the whole subject of his marriage, Ruskin himself, his friends and his official biographer, agreed in later years to draw heavy curtains of silence and obscurity. What information they provided was deliberately designed to mislead; and a report was put about, to be sedulously propagated by the Ruskinian faithful, that Ruskin had married " to please his parents," who " saw in a marriage with Euphemia the means by which they might gain a daughter and not lose a son." It was they, according to this version of the story (which Holman Hunt adopted), who assured John that he was attached to Effie and implored him to " make them all happy " by admitting that he loved her; he had resisted, but a sense of filial duty and feelings of misplaced chivalry, in spite of earnest struggles, slowly and disastrously had weakened his resistance . . . The publication of the Millais papers has at length destroyed this legend: for the picture of a chivalrous but reluctant bridegroom we must substitute that of an impetuous and excited lover: while John's parents are shown to have agreed to the match only under the pressure that their son himself exerted. The wedding at Bowerswell was an event to which for the last six months he had been feverishly looking forward. Finally his hopes were realised. The married couple left for Aberfeldy, then turned south to pass the remainder of their honeymoon among the mountains of the Lake District. In the meantime, every day's newspapers were making their plans for a foreign tour—either with or without John's parents—seem more and more impracticable. Not since the Napoleonic Wars had the fabric of European civilisation appeared to rock so perilously; —revolution broke out in Paris, in Vienna, in many of the German States; monarchs were dethroned and fled; statesmen vanished overnight; Louis Philippe, abandoning the Tuileries to the mob and his powers to a provisional government, hurriedly left Paris and caught the English packet-boat; Metternich, " Grand Inquisitor of Europe," re-emerged as a private citizen beside the sea at Brighton. In England, though the Chartists organised a monster petition, they failed to build a barricade. But from an English point of view the implication of changes abroad was none the less alarming; and, when Ruskin learned that the smoke and stench of war had drifted across Italy, he trembled for the cities he loved, struck once again by the chilling conviction that on nothing he loved and valued could he hope to keep a firm hold.

"I should be very, very happy just now," he wrote to tell Miss Mitford, "but for these wild storm-clouds bursting on my dear Italy and my fair France, my occupation gone, and all my earthly treasures (except the one I have just acquired and the everlasting Alps) perilled amidst 'the tumult of the people,' 'the imagining of vain things.'" Disappointment over the tremendous drama being enacted outside England had produced "a depression and fever of spirit which, joined with some other circumstances nearer home, have, until now that I am resting with my kind wife among these quiet hills, denied me the heart to write cheerfully . . . ." The quiet hills from which Ruskin addressed his old friend were the pastoral mountains of the Lake District; and there his honeymoon passed, unobtrusively and, so far as the world could judge, conventionally and smoothly. An affectionate and well-brought-up young woman, Effie sent home to Bowerswell long enthusiastic descriptions of local food and landscapes. Scenic prospects were duly impressive, the inn rooms warm and comfortable. They had dined off "Ham and eggs and fine Potatoes with small trout": John had been "quite amused" to see how much she loved the Highlanders. At Penrith the pea soup was bad: but then, the fish was excellent. After Scottish sublimities, the mountain slopes round Keswick were somewhat uninspiring—they were "merely good hills without crag or colour": "still everything looks very sweet," and they had made several enchanting tours and had enjoyed a good picnic luncheon of sandwiches and rhubarb tart . . .

No contrast could be more distinct, no association more pregnant with hints of future conflict. On the one hand, Effie, healthily young, innocently sensuous, munches her sandwiches and admires the April view, content in John's society, delighted with the new importance that marriage seems to give her: on the other, her self-questioning, self-tormenting husband, even now, as he listens to the rumour of faraway disturbances, begins to feel that "all the work I have been doing, and all the loves I have been cherishing, are vain and frivolous—that these are not times for watching clouds or dreaming over quiet waters, that more serious work is to be done, and that the time for endurance has come rather than for meditation, and for hope rather than for happiness." The happiness of the moment, such as Effie enjoyed, warm, physical, uncomplicated, if not beyond his comprehension, was certainly beyond his grasp; and, although there is no doubt that the political events of 1848 affected him profoundly, it seems probable that his rejection of happiness had a more personal and deeper origin, and that he welcomed the opportunity of attributing his discontent to obvious external causes, in which his real motives for unhappiness were temporarily swallowed up. He had discovered—he was still discovering—that his own temperament as a passionate human being concealed a fatal cleavage. There could be no compromise, in the last resort, between the real and the ideal. Between imagination and passion, between spiritual and sensual love, there existed a disastrous dichotomy which, although it did not kill desire, reduced his faculties to impotence. His marriage was never consummated. In spite of the fervour of his approach, he could not, or would not, when the time came, translate imaginative adoration into terms of adult love-making. He had worshipped the shadow, only to reject the substance. Of his love for the virginal, remote, child-like, unreal Effie, the letters written during their engagement provide abundant and convincing proof; he had pursued her as Pan pursued Syrinx, as Apollo followed Daphne. His fate was the reverse of theirs. He exchanged a cool and unearthly illusion for the disturbing reality of human flesh and blood.

It would be convenient—at times, comforting—could we dissociate the facts of a writer's existence from the work he left behind him, the adventures of the spirit from the experiences of the body: were his voice disembodied like the utterances of Dodonan Zeus. But, since works of art are never complete and perfect, we are bound, as we examine them, to observe their individual colouring, and to note the psychological flaws and fissures that give the achievements of the artist their special shape and quality.

Ruskin's was, throughout his career, an extremely individual genius; and the conflict that frustrated his marriage was the reflection of a larger conflict, perceptible, in varying degrees and under various guises, through almost everything he said and wrote. It may be traced back to his relations with his parents, and to the effect on his emotional development of their jealous and possessive love; but other factors, to which we have as yet no clue, probably determined it; and we must beware of the facile analysis that leaves out of account the complex stratification of any human ego. The soul leans on the body, as the body leans on the soul: both are exposed to the influence of the age, to the mysterious currents that flow through society, determining the destiny of entire races, epitomised or parodied in the behaviour of the individual. Ruskin's dilemma, as I shall attempt to show, was one highly characteristic of the period he lived in, his attitude to the problem of personal happiness—a problem that Ruskin could neither solve nor set aside—one that occurs again and again in nineteeth-century literature . . . But for the moment we must return to Effie, personification of ordinary human desires, the desires that had drawn Ruskin on, only to repel him. With prophetic insight he had spoken of her as the wrecker who attracts the ship, as the siren who remains innocently unconscious of the deadly spell she exercises. She was still innocent; perhaps she was a little puzzled; but the advantages and amusements of the position she occupied as yet outweighed the difficulties.

Neither husband nor wife seemed anxious to prolong the honeymoon. Proofs of a second edition of *Modern Painters* awaited John in London; and, towards the end of April, they travelled south by railway. At Euston they were met by Mr. Ruskin. The days were long past when the Ruskins did not own a carriage; and the vehicle that took them to Denmark Hill struck Effie, always appreciative of material comforts, as "very nice and handsome"; for it had been newly painted and lined, and in honour of their homecoming the coachman had donned a new coat, with multiple impressive capes, and was seated above his horses on a new imposing hammercloth. Arrived at Denmark Hill, they found that the whole household had been drawn up to receive them. Beside the gate stood the gardener, tendering a "most splendid bouquet of Geraniums, Orange Blossom, Heath of the most delicate kinds, Myrtles, Cineraria, etc., all tied in ornamental paper and with White Satin Ribbon"; while at the front door, they were welcomed by Mrs. Ruskin arrayed in the spreading splendour of prosperous middle-class gentility. With a quick eye over the flowers and ribbons of her bouquet Effie noted every detail—Mrs. Ruskin's dress, a "splendid rich drab or pale brown satin with rich fringe on the front," and how nice the maidservants looked, in their aprons and white caps and "green and stone-coloured mousselines." During dinner, a German band played beneath the windows: "we spent the evening very happily," the old people complimenting their daughter-in-law on their son's improved appearance and expressing the delight that it gave them to behold him so contented. Plans for the future were equally exhilarating: "Mr. Ruskin, John and I go to-morrow to the private view of the Academy where we shall see all the *nobs*."

For the time being at least, Effie's desire to consort with nobs received the complete approval of John's admiring family. If he had a fault, it was that he was inclined to despise the world and look down on its advantages; and Mr. Ruskin wrote to Mr. Gray that he was "glad to see Effie gets John to go out a little . . . He is very indifferent to general society and reluctantly acknowledges great attentions shown him . . . Seven years ago he refused to spend a month at the Duke of Leinster's . . ." There could be no question, on the other hand, of Effie's social gifts and instincts. With the excitement of a young girl and the gusto of a newcomer, she made her way on John's arm through the elaborate ceremonial of a mid-Victorian season, which revolutions abroad and riots at home had neither discouraged nor dimmed. Clothes enchanted her, and she described them at length, in an epistolary style at

John Ruskin by Sir J. E. Millais, P.R.A.,
1853-54

once ingenuous and vivid: as we read, we can hear the crunch of silks, see the bloom of the velvets, the aqueous gleam of satins. Thus for a private view—" you know" (she reminded her provincial audience) " it is a great compliment getting these tickets and you only meet there the artists themselves and the nobility "—she wore her " pale glacée silk, white lace bonnet, black Mantilla, pale gloves, etc.," while John for his part was " also very well dressed." The spectacle was entrancing; and now her attention was caught by three Dukes in a row with their complement of Duchesses; now it wandered to a youthful dandy, one of Lord Ravensworth's sons (all of them, it turned out, John's great admirers) conspicuous for a talkativeness most unusual " in this age of Nonchalance " and for the " exquisite gloves which he kept drawing off and on with the same energy he displayed in conversation."

John's distinguished friends—those friends of whom old Mr. Ruskin was so proud—paid her gratifying homage. Samuel Rogers, ivory-headed, octogenarian poetaster, invited them to breakfast—a meal that Effie pronounced the most perfect that she ever saw—showed her his *bibelots* and *objets de vertu*, and, when she commented on one of his chiefest treasures, patted her cheek and said she had a fine taste. That same morning they visited Turner, and, after knocking for some time, were admitted by the painter himself, who entertained them with wine and biscuits in his " bare and miserly " room, then " took us up to his gallery where we saw *such* pictures," among others an incandescent canvas called " The Fighting Téméraire." Dinner with Lady Davy proved extremely sumptuous. It was followed by a dinner-party of a more elderly and instructive kind, at which John and the Bishop of Norwich " got into a long and learned discussion upon the migratory habits of seagulls." Grisi and Lind sang for her delectation. Lansdowne House flung open its doors; and, moving through the crowded ballroom, Effie remarked the Duke of Cambridge looking like " the public Auctioneer," the aged Lady Morgan, " painted up to the eyes," and an enviable creation in "pale primrose satin with black lace flounces and velvet bows all about it with diamonds inside." No shadow had yet appeared: none, that is to say, was reflected in her letters home. "I am happier every day with John" (she informed her mother and father) "for he really is the kindest creature in the world and he is so pleased with me . . ."

On both sides, the contentment was superficial. While the small bright figure of the young woman goes sailing confidently forward, afloat on the stream of ordinary life, dipping in rapturous acknowledgement of the salutations that acclaimed her, we watch her husband, gradually at first, then more and more determinedly, withdrawing into a private universe where, as nowhere else, he felt free and strong and guiltless. His mission reclaimed him, and once more there was a book to write. This time it was a book on architecture; and, after an enjoyable visit to Oxford, enlivened by "fine music and scientific pleasures such as looking at the circulation through a living Frog in a microscope," John and Effie set out on a tour of the English cathedral cities. Both the elder Ruskins had decided to accompany them. Effie did not demur; but, away from London and its distracting gaieties, some indefinable change in the atmosphere made their joint expedition, even at the outset, slightly inharmonious. John was eager to get to work again: "my son" (complained old Mr. Ruskin, writing to a friend from Salisbury) "occupies himself with the architecture of the cathedral, a lovely edifice, but I find it very slow." Then John caught cold, and Effie was amused, puzzled, and at length exasperated by the tremulous solicitude with which Mr. and Mrs. Ruskin hung about his sick-bed. Their alarm seemed to infect the patient. If his mother and father "would only let him alone," Effie felt sure that he would very soon get better; but to release their hold upon their ewe-lamb, their delicate and brilliant child, a man who had entered his thirtieth year but whom they still treated as an ailing youth to be guided and protected, was something that his parents neither would nor could do. The rôle assigned to her in their existence, Effie had begun to see, was very largely decorative. That it was decorative and nothing more—that no physical relationship underlay her marriage—old Mr. and Mrs. Ruskin had not yet suspected; and when during John's illness he was put into a separate room, he told Effie that his father supposed that conjugal passion must have overtaxed his energies, adding with a laugh that his father's view of the situation was curiously misinformed. Years later, that laugh, and the odd coldness that it implied, stuck in Effie's memory. It afforded a dim premonition of discoveries she had still to make.

Some lights, confused and confusing, she had already obtained on the problem of John's character. In the privacy of their room, he had spoken to her at length and strangely; and though the account of what he said is necessarily one-sided (for Ruskin's apologia still remains unpublished), there seems no reason to doubt that, given the limitations of her understanding, the tale that Effie told was truthful. Unhappiness is often loquacious; and, exposed to the disillusionment of marriage, Ruskin would appear to have taken refuge in elaborate and tormented sophistries. "For days" he talked of the married relation, explaining why he shunned it, alleging that he disliked children and did not wish to have them round him, pleading that he wished to preserve her beauty, and implying vague "religious motives." Effie (she tells us) "argued with him and took the Bible but he soon silenced me"; and he concluded by promising that in six years' time, when she was twenty-five, their marriage should be consummated. Such was the background of the Ruskins' married life: Effie is bemused but patient, while on John's side, through the fog of mystery and perversity, we see an unhappy attempt to excuse or sublimate his failure. That failure, it must be emphasised, according to all the evidence, was primarily psychological: the passion that flowered at a distance withered in proximity: like Lohengrin in the story by Jules Laforgue, from the beloved's too-physical presence he longed to escape into the free world of the intellect . . . Luckily, by the summer months of 1848, the revolutionary clouds that covered Europe were rising and dissolving. It was again safe to cross the English Channel; and during August, John and Effie, accompanied by old Mr. Ruskin as far as Boulogne, embarked on a tour of the Norman churches and cathedrals. With him Ruskin carried the plan of his *Seven Lamps of Architecture*.

III

IF RUSKIN had always tended to distrust the purely sensuous approach to beauty—the tremor of instinctive delight with which he himself, for example, observed the wreathing of clouds on a mountainside, the rush of an Alpine torrent, or the " intense scarletty purple " of the trunk of a shattered larch—his distrust was certainly strengthened by the disillusionment of marriage. Since happiness had eluded him, and the promise of pleasure proved abortive, it became more than ever necessary to discover some principle in beautiful objects less dangerous and more praiseworthy than the exquisite enjoyment their contemplation gave him. Æsthetic qualities must, with all the ingenuity at his command, be linked to moral virtues, and one set of standards shown as directly dependent upon the existence of the other. His lamps of architecture were to be beacons of truth; and in pursuit of this lofty ideal, Ruskin now flung himself into just such an assiduous round of measuring, sketching, climbing as he had already outlined for Effie's benefit during the period of their courtship. Writing home, she described her diligent husband as " quite in his element here and very happy "; but hard work soon overtired him; and in a letter of birthday congratulations, written from Rouen to Effie's brother, George Gray, he hinted at, though he did not describe, a burden of inexplicable sorrows and irremediable grievances. He trusted, he said, that, " by the time that you are my age," his brother-in-law would be a better man and have been more useful in his generation. His last ten years had " passed like a fable ", and, though many of their days had been happy, he had begun to feel " the pain of looking back upon happiness which has been profitless." Effie had read aloud to him their mother's account of a long walk from Blair Atholl. It had reminded him of many happy wanderings of his own, of which all that he could remember now was that they had indeed been happy—" their only effect has been that of deadening my powers of present enjoyment "; and he wound up by recommending the advantages of a life of strenuous labour as, in retrospect, probably " far more gladdening " than the life of leisure and independence in which he himself had dissipated his best years. . . .

George's existence was laborious enough; and, it so happened, a somewhat acid exchange on the question of the young man's future was, at this moment taking place, between the Gray and Ruskin families. The suggestion that, by marrying their daughter to John Ruskin, the improvident Grays had hoped to benefit financially, has now been revealed as baseless by the publication of the Millais papers: Mr. Gray was undoubtedly hard pressed, but his financial affairs eventually recovered without assistance from the Ruskins. Yet not unnaturally he assumed that, as a rich man and an old friend, Mr. Ruskin might be willing to do him a small service, and he had asked the merchant to help George, then a struggling provincial clerk, to find employment in the City. Mr. Ruskin, however, declined, alleging with conspicuous want of tact that George, as a clerk in London, would be a source of social embarrassment both to his famous brother-in-law and his fashionable sister. His reasoning he set forth in a tone of proud Podsnappery that Dickens himself could scarcely have improved upon; for, besides mentioning the superior education that John had received as a " Gentleman Commoner at Christ Church, Oxford," his introduction to the " highest men " by two young grandees he had encountered on his travels, and his refusal (with which the Grays were already acquainted) to accept a flattering invitation from the Duke of Leinster, he glanced complacently over John's subsequent progress and the company he kept at the " Tables of Ministers, Ambassadors and Bishops," adding with a touch of mock modesty that he was "aware this arose from his having shown some knowledge in the fine Arts, a subject chiefly interesting to the higher Classes . . ." Be that as it might, John and, by extension, Effie had now outsoared the shadows of the workaday commercial universe. In fact, from the sphere to which they had now risen, not only George Gray but Mrs. Ruskin and himself were definitely excluded; "John has brought Lords to our table but we are very marked in regarding them as John's visitors . . ." Meanwhile he was preparing for John and his wife a house at 31 Park Street, off Grosvenor Square, "to be among their own set—when they like to put up with Wine Merchants or Colonial Brokers they may dine here now and then—but I hope there is no undue pride in my desiring the young couple to retain some hold of good Society."

Mr. Gray had retired discomfited; and the younger Ruskins, having concluded their tour, returned to England and proceeded to live up to old Mr. Ruskin's highest expectations. They entertained, and they were entertained. "As John says" (wrote Effie) "we are getting into the thick of it," mixing with company both serious and frivolous, art-collectors and scholars, divines and *dilettanti*, and observing at close quarters all the lions of the social season. For example, at dinner with Sir Robert Inglis (who is "very agreeable" and "appears very religious and clever") Effie found herself sitting opposite Mr. T. B. Macaulay, whose new history was being eagerly read and who dazzled her by the exuberance of his dinner-table conversation. She had "never heard such a man . . . He goes from St. Chrysostom's sermon at Antioch . . . to M. Thiers's speeches twenty years ago . . . then back again to Greek Mausoleums 4 Centuries B.C. . . . then to Seringapatam streets and mud houses and going at such a pace. . . ." So long as she remained in Park Street, if not completely tranquil, Effie's mood, so far as we can judge, was moderately contented; but over Christmas she was claimed by Denmark Hill, and by a round of solemn family festivities which left her very little respite, and from which she emerged, at the beginning of the New Year, feeling ill and gloomy. Though she would have preferred to keep her room, while she was their guest the benevolent tyranny of the Ruskin parents made this quite impossible. They were determined that Effie must play her part, and persisted in their determination until, at last recognising that she was genuinely indisposed, they were obliged to send for doctors. The doctors disagreed. One thing, however, seemed clear—Effie would not be well enough to accompany the Ruskins on the Swiss tour they were planning for the spring months of 1849, now that John had written finis to the *Seven Lamps of Architecture*. Effie withdrew to Bowerswell, in search of health and peace of mind, and the Ruskin trio, restored to its original integrity, departed for the Continent.

John Ruskin did not forget his wife: some prickings of the passion she had inspired, though it was already in decline, were still felt intermittently. To love at a distance was perhaps easier than to cherish and protect the Effie whom he had gradually come to know in twelve months' daily intercourse, the Effie who loved pink bonnets and liked attending dinner-parties, whose interests were material and whose deepest needs were physical. Again he could credit her with a remote ethereal beauty, and dream of their re-union, now that a distance of many hundred miles luckily divided them. His letters home addressed her in the familiar adoring strain, telling her how much he looked forward to "your next bridal night" and to the moment when he would once more "draw your dress from your snowy shoulders" and would lean his cheek upon them, "as if you were still my betrothed only; and I had never held you in my arms." Later he was to complain that his frivolous and self-willed wife had refused to share his interests; but this allegation is scarcely borne out by a request that she would make notes for his benefit upon Venetian history, or by his reference, a week afterwards, to her attempts at drawing, in which she is counselled not to be discouraged and directed to copy from the Old Masters "a feature here and there—a hand, foot—head—arm—bit of drapery—or of foliage—taking the easiest—that is to say that which has fewest lines, the first. . . ." But his parents, meanwhile, were bent on improving the occasion which this separation offered. Alone with their adored son, it would appear that they made overt criticisms of Effie's character and conduct, and insinuated to John that she was both secretive and intractable. They wished to help her, but she would not be helped. "I often" (wrote John to Effie) "hear my mother or father saying poor child—if she *could* but have thrown herself openly upon us, and trusted in us, and felt that we desired only her happiness . . . how happy she might have been; and how happy she might have made us all." Stimulated by the air of crisis, Mr. Ruskin's remarkable epistolary gifts overflowed in a long and officious communication to Mr. Gray at Bowerswell. He sincerely regretted, he said, that his daughter-in-law's "bad state of health" showed no signs of improvement, and begged to inform her father of "the trouble we are all in from not knowing what should be done—if anything can be done on our part," to speed her convalescence. It was natural enough that she should not be able to enter into John's extensive range of interests: cathedral cities were sometimes dull, and "ninety women out of a hundred . . . would prefer what I have heard Effie say she would, the flying over a desert on horseback"; but he expected from her "great good sense and talent" that her ambition, "of which she has too much mind not to have good share, would be little gratified by her husband abandoning the haunt, where his genius finds food and occupation, to seek for stirring adventures, which might end in more mishap than profit." He closed with a fragment of good advice. If, he wrote, he might take the liberty of offering a prescription "for her own comfort and amendment," he would suggest that Effie made an effort "to sacrifice everything to duty, to become interested and delighted in what her husband may be accomplishing by a short absence and to find a satisfaction in causing him no unnecessary anxiety. . . ."

Effie herself had no part in this courteous, but envenomed wrangling. From the dead calm of an English close or a French cathedral square, she may occasionally have longed to escape on a romantic Arab steed and go "flying over a desert" in quest of vague adventures; yet she would have been well satisfied with the rewards of a humdrum domestic life. To John in France she wrote reminding him again how much she wished for children; but the reply that she received, though tender, was evasive. He had been thinking of her, he remarked, "as of course I always do when I am not busy." While he was measuring churches or drawing mountains, he forgot himself and Effie alike—if he did not do so (he explained) he could hardly bear their separation—and began to wonder whether he had ever been married, "and to think of all my happy hours, and soft slumber in my dearest lady's arms, as a dream." He, too, hoped for "a little Effie . . . only I wish they weren't so small at first that one hardly knows what one has got hold of." Yet, even while he wrote of "little Effies" and continued to retain her interest yet keep her at bay with all the dexterity and delicacy of which his style was capable, his intelligence, which was both subtle and indirect, was attacking the problem of their relationship from an entirely different point of view; and, ten days after his letter to Effie, he wrote to her father, propounding his personal theory that her reason was disordered. Ruskin's approach was curiously casuistical; for Mr. Gray was given the choice of believing that his daughter was either mad or bad, and warned that John *might* have considered her conduct and attitude in the highest degree blameworthy, were he not convinced that they were due to bodily weakness, "that is to say—and this is a serious and distressing admission—to a nervous disease affecting the brain." As to the exact symptoms of this disease, he was not at all explicit, merely alleging that it had originally manifested itself, as it did now, "in tears and depression." He had his own opinion, he wrote, of the principal cause; but it did not "bear on matter in hand." Meanwhile, he must admit that, before coming to the conclusion that Effie was no longer entirely responsible for everything she said and did, he had thought it right to administer a private scolding—when for the first time she "showed causeless petulance towards my mother." The incident in itself had been trivial, and merely provoked by Mrs. Ruskin's suggestion that John should take a blue pill. But Effie had resented her interposition, and resented still more her husband's kindly criticism, with the result that she had grown increasingly jealous and suspicious of Mrs. Ruskin's influence. Still, there had been no further " unpleasantness " and they had got abroad at last. But, whether he had overtired her by visits to cathedrals or allowed her to drink too much coffee in the evening, her indisposition had gradually increased and she had returned home none the happier. At Denmark Hill, finding her daughter-in-law in tears when she should have been dressing for dinner, Mrs. Ruskin had given her " a scold " which, had she not been indisposed, she would certainly have merited. Well, poor Effie had dressed as she was told and come down " looking very miserable. I had seen her look so too often to take particular notice of it." But she had appeared ready to faint at the dinner-table and a doctor, who happened to be present, had recommended remedies which, " good girl," she swallowed to please her husband, but which had weakened her system till she contracted influenza. The question, in short, was a " purely medical one." Yet, thus far carefully restrained, Ruskin wound up his communication with something like a menace. Had Effie, while " in *sound mind* ", been annoyed by the " contemptible trifles " which had caused her so much misery, had she rejected his parents' " affection in any other circumstances but those of an illness bordering in many of its features on incipient insanity," he would not now be writing. He hoped " (he concluded) " that together with her girl's frocks, he would see her outgrow her " contemptible dread of interference and petulant resistance of authority . . . . Restiveness I am accustomed to regard as an unpromising character even in horses and asses."

Between the tone of this extraordinary letter and the benignity and gentleness stated by most biographers to have been Ruskin's ruling traits, it may seem difficult—perhaps impossible—to establish any correspondence. A profoundly self-centred man, he must be assumed to have had an almost unequalled gift of sweeping aside facts that his pride or his self-love encouraged him to disregard; while his was the type of sensitiveness that, if sufficiently exasperated, often flashes out in cruelty. Rather than confess that he had failed his wife—and that the ambiguous attentions to which, judging by the evidence of his letters, he still occasionally exposed her, must at length have a disastrous effect upon her health and spirits—he decided to believe that Effie had failed him, but (as if to soften a deception) transferred the main burden of responsibility from Effie to her state of health. In such crises on the terrestial plane, thank heavens for the refuge of scholarship and literature! He had published *Seven Lamps*, and had seen his equation of beauty with truth, and of architectual merits with social and moral virtues, receive the approval, loudly expressed, of an enthusiastic audience. But the book was brief—an outline of convictions, illustrated by detailed architectural references, rather than the systematic examination of any style or period; and in his next book, though its central thesis would be the same, the subject was to be more specialised and the general treatment more elaborate. During the aftermath of a previous crisis, Venice, from the moment he arrived at Mestre, had comforted and inspired him. The drawings and notes made in 1845 had not yet been fully used; and Venice, he determined, should be the focus of the book he was now planning—Venice in her decline and Venice in her glory, with the background of Venetian history to furnish a supreme example of the decadence that overcame any race of European artists as soon as the community to which they belonged had ceased to think devoutly and govern itself wisely.

Thus, a fortnight after his return to London, where Effie rejoined him, looking calmer and more cheerful, he again boarded the Channel packet, accompanied this time by his wife, who took with her, to keep her company while John worked, a childhood friend named Charlotte Ker. Travelling through Switzerland and Northern Italy, they reached Venice in November. There they remained till the following March. For Effie, those few months were an agreeable holiday from Denmark Hill and its associations: for her husband, a period of furious intellectual effort. Already fortified by a course of historical reading, he set himself to revisit the whole city and digest its entire fabric, down to the very smallest detail, first committing his sketches and measurements to a series of little square notebooks, then transferring his memoranda to a growing pile of larger volumes, each of them presently equipped with an index and cross references. He worked all day, in all weathers; and Venice (he reminded a correspondent) though balmy and beautiful on luminous summer days, "when pomegranate blossoms hang over every garden wall, and green sunlight shoots through every wave," was an exceedingly inclement place during the long and bitter winter months. "Fighting with frosty winds at every turn of the canals takes away all the old feelings of peace and stillness; the protracted cold makes the dash of the water on the walls a sound of simple discomfort, and some wild and dark day in February one starts to find oneself actually balancing in one's mind the relative advantages of land and water carriage, comparing the Canal with Piccadilly, and even hesitating whether for the rest of one's life one would rather have a gondola within call or a hansom."

There were other distractions—from frost-bitten fingers, idle gondoliers, and a fisherman who pounded up live crabs for bait every morning underneath his window, to the tiresome behaviour of "my little sea-horses, who wouldn't coil their tails about sticks when I asked them." His work itself had a deadening effect; analysis (he decided) was an "abominable business"; and after a while he felt that he had lost sight of the city he loved in the information he was collecting, and Venice "presented itself to me merely as so many 'mouldings,' and I had few associations with any building but those of more or less pain and puzzle and provocation. . . ." Yet he persisted, and the opening volume of *The Stones of Venice* began gradually to take shape.

Ruskin's third and closing volume was not to be completed till October, 1853: the book contains, in fact, the records of two successive visits which, since the ideas and emotions they provoked fall into a characteristic and uninterrupted pattern, must be treated as one for the purpose of the present survey. In spite of fatigue and temporary losses of faith, between the winter of 1849 and the autumn of 1853 Venice dominated Ruskin's imagination, far more definitely though less insidiously than, some thirty years earlier, it had dominated Byron's. For, whereas Byron had surrendered to its sleepy spell, enjoying the oddity of the Venetian *patois*, admiring the Amazonian carriage and painted eyelids of the bold Venetian courtesans, appreciating the " gloomy gaiety " of the bird-necked gondolas, neglecting or ignoring the city's monuments but engrossed in vague dreams of the magnificent Venetian past, Ruskin kept his faculties in a state of constant wide-awakeness, and though he was as alive to beauty as the romantic poet and had a considerably richer gift of rendering it in detail, subordinated his sensuous impressions to his intellectual prejudices. Yes, Venice taught a spiritual lesson, as stern and as distinct as that of the cathedrals of Normandy: he had had (he declared afterwards in *A Crown of Wild Olive*) " from beginning to end, no other aim than to show that the Gothic architecture of Venice had arisen out of, and indicated in all its features, a state of pure national faith, and of domestic virtue; and that its Renaissance architecture had arisen out of, and in all its features indicated, a state of concealed national infidelity, and of domestic corruption." Such, at least, was the writer's avowed aim; but so curiously intermixed were the various strands of feeling which joined in Ruskin's character, that a modern reader may be excused if the moral intention of *The Stones of Venice* frequently escapes him. The moralist is always in pursuit of, but seldom quite pins down, the artist. He loved his subject for its own sake, and was shrewd enough to suspect, and admit, that the desire to teach and to do good was not his sole incentive. " I don't think myself a great genius " (he was to confess to his father in 1852)

" but I believe I have genius; something different from mere cleverness, for I am *not* clever in the sense that millions of people are. . . . But there is a strong instinct in me, which I cannot analyse, to draw and describe the things I love—not for reputation, nor for the good of others . . . but a sort of instinct like that for eating or drinking. I should like to draw all St. Mark's . . . stone by stone, to eat it all up into my mind, touch by touch."

If *The Stones of Venice* represents the pleasures of assimilation, as he gazed at the façade of St. Mark's, or, having tied his boat to a water-worn post, " half-way between the end of the Giudecca and St. George of the Seaweed," saw " the Euganeans . . . and all the Alps and Venice " hover behind him in the rosy evening sunlight, it also represents the arduous process of digestion—of rationalisation, too; since it was essential that what one enjoyed must somehow be related to a purifying moral concept. Beauty must have a reason, delight a justification. The " interwoven temper " of his mind (as he called it in *Praeterita*) is nowhere more fully or more dramatically illustrated than in *The Stones of Venice*. The little boy who had adored his building-blocks—rudiments of a miniature bridge, complete with " voussoir and keystone "—has developed into an authoritative art-historian who devotes page after laborious page to a precise examination of arches, friezes, capitals. In these passages he is the exacting schoolmaster—the reader is being given his opportunity: should he fail to profit by it, well, so much the worse for him! But elsewhere the *tempo* changes; and we think of that early impressionable self who had wandered, rapt and lonely, along a Scottish river-bank, watching the Medusa-like coilings of the Tay, " swirls of smooth blackness, broken by no fleck of foam." Then his style becomes more intricate, more intense and highly coloured: he launches out into one of those " pretty passages," of which secretly he was always a trifle ashamed —as of some unseemly indulgence in uncensored, unsanctified feeling—but which correspond to an important aspect of the writer's divided nature. He yearned after the things he loved, as he had once yearned after the image of Effie's earthly beauty. Yet his passionate affection for things and places was now balanced by the dislike or distrust that, beyond the bounds of his own family, he was apt to feel for people. A few friends were, of course, excepted; but the great mass of humanity was hostile or antipathetic, particularly, in foreign countries; and every time he visited the Continent, the reports that he sent home were more disgusted and discouraged. Thus, from Lisieux, in 1848, he had written that the "mental and moral degradation" of post-revolutionary France was "beyond all I conceived—it is the very reign of sin, and of idiotism." No less deplorable, he soon discovered, was the state of modern Italy; and the spleen which this spectacle engendered presently overflowed into one of the most sumptuous and ambitious passages that diversified his new book—the celebrated outburst of eloquence that beckons the traveller, whom he is guiding, from the gloom of the "Bocca di Piazza" towards the radiant expansion of St. Mark's Square.

Three themes compose this passage, themes as dramatically contrasted, yet as harmoniously reconciled, as separate themes in music. An immense paragraph is devoted to St. Mark's itself. Ruskin's description ascends from detail to detail: from the "five great vaulted porches," lined with "pillars of variegated stones, jasper and porphyry, and deep-green serpentine," and "beset with sculpture . . . clear as amber and delicate as ivory,—sculpture fantastic and involved, of palm leaves and lilies, and grapes and pomegranates, and birds clinging and fluttering among the branches, all twined together into an endless network of buds and plumes": past the "breasts of the Greek horses" blazing above the archivolts "in their breadth of golden strength": beyond St. Mark's lion on its star-covered blue field: "until at last, as if in ecstasy, the crests of the arches break into a marble foam, and toss themselves far into the blue sky in flashes and wreaths of sculptured spray, as if the breakers on the Lido shore had been frost-bound before they fell, and the sea-nymphs had inlaid them with coral and amethyst."

After this magnificent, if somewhat breathless, flight, an abrupt yet ingenious transition brings us home to England. It introduces a colder and quieter music. Ruskin compares the doves about the porch of St. Mark's, and the "soft iridescence" of their living, changing plumage, with the "restless crowd, hoarse-voiced and sable-winged, drifting on the bleak upper air" above an English cathedral close. But the third theme to appear is of all perhaps the most significant. For Ruskin, the contemplation of beauty, exquisite while it endured, was never long unmixed with bitterness. He swoops from the past to the present, from art to humanity, from the pinnacles raised in an age of faith to the modern crowd below them. ". . . What effect has this splendour on those who pass beneath it? You may walk from sunrise to sunset, to and fro, before the gateway of St. Mark's, and you will not see an eye lifted to it, nor a countenance brightened by it. Priest and layman, soldier and civilian, rich and poor, pass it alike regardlessly." But "the meanest tradesmen" had dragged their stalls into the very recesses of the entry: around the square, in the cafés that lined it, idle Venetians of the middle sort lounged and read their newspapers: at the hour of vespers, an Austrian military band discoursed its brassy music, "the march drowning the miserere, and the sullen crowd thickening round them,—a crowd, which, if it had its will, would stiletto every soldier that pipes to it": while on the steps of St. Mark's itself, in the shadow of its arches, "all day long, knots of men of the lowest classes, unemployed and listless, lie basking in the sun like lizards; and unregarded children,—every heavy glance of their young eyes full of desperation and stony depravity, and their throats hoarse with cursing,—gamble, and fight, and snarl, and sleep, hour after hour, clashing their bruised centesimi upon the marble ledges of the church porch."

During his visit to Naples, several years earlier, Ruskin had felt that in the volcanic activity of that delightful region he recognised a malevolent force, co-existent with, and underlying, the benevolent workings of the natural world; and again and again, throughout his long existence, hints of an evil principle, dimly but dreadfully apparent in the life of man and nature, were to cloud his imagination and darken his sense of sin. Yet these "permitted symbols of evil, unredeemed," if they repelled him, also sometimes fascinated. He was too genuine and too sensitive an artist to fail to recognise a kind of distorted splendour or perverse beauty in a spectacle he loathed and dreaded: and his description of the beggar-children at the doorway of St. Mark's has the characteristic ring of the finest Ruskinian prose, every word heightening the cumulative effect, and the addition of a single epithet—"*bruised*" coupled with "*centesimi*"—triumphantly completing the impression that previous verbs and adjectives have built up. . . . From the façade and its inhabitants, Ruskin now turns to the interior of the church itself. Once more, he had scope for eloquence; but his admiration for that "vast cave"—dimly illuminated by "narrow phosphoric streams" of sunlight, reflected upon polished walls and upon the "waves of marble that heave and fall in a thousand colours along the floor," and lit up with pin-point brilliance by innumerable lamps and tapers—gives way to a perplexed and dubious note, when he comes to consider the modern faith of which it forms the background. Could Romanism be ever deserving of praise? Ruskin's own faith, though reinforced by regular religious practises and constant reading of the sacred texts, had often rocked perilously since he first attained to manhood. Thus, in 1848, writing to his father, he had admitted that he found it hard to believe, and suggested that James Ruskin experienced the same difficulty: ". . . You, as well as I, are in this same condition, are you not, Father? Neither of us *can* believe, read what we may of reasoning or of proof; and I tell you also frankly that the more I investigate or reason over the Bible as I should over any other history or statement, the more difficulties I find, and the less ground of belief; and this I say after six years of very patient work . . . at least in those hours set apart for such study. Now, this " (he remarked) " is very painful—especially so, it seems to me, in a time like the present . . . in which wickedness is often victorious and unpunished; nothing but sorrow can come from a doubtful state of mind. . . ." It was, therefore, with redoubled earnestness that, having been moved and touched by the sight of Catholic believers who constantly slipped into the gloom of St. Mark's, abased themselves before an altar, and " rising slowly with more confirmed step, and with a passionate kiss and clasp of the arms given to the feet of the crucifix, by which the lights burn always in the northern aisle," left the church " as if comforted," he repulsed the idea that the consolation they had received had been of any real or lasting value. ". . . We must not hastily conclude . . ." (he felt bound to warn his readers) " that the nobler characters of the building have at present any influence in fostering a devotional spirit. . . . Darkness and mystery; confused recesses of building; artificial light . . . maintained with a constancy which seems to give it a kind of sacredness; preciousness of material easily comprehended by the vulgar eye; close air loaded with a sweet and peculiar odour . . . solemn music, and tangible idols or images having popular legends attached to them,—these, the stage properties of superstition . . . are assembled in St. Mark's to a degree, as far as I know, unexampled in any other European church. . . . The popular sentiment which these arts excite is to be regarded by us with no more respect than we should have considered ourselves justified in rendering to the devotion of the worshippers at Eleusis, Ellora, or Edfou."

Pondering the problems of faith as he roamed around St. Mark's Square, abroad on the canals sketching the ornament of some crumbling balcony or palace window—before that too, like so much else, was defaced or devoured by modern greed and ignorance—at home in his secluded work-room where he spent the evening hours committing the results of the day's labour to his closely-written note-books, Ruskin would have led the life of a devoted and impassioned hermit, had it not been for the fact, inconvenient yet inescapable, that the hermit was a married man. True, he saw Effie comparatively seldom; and, less patiently than in the past, Effie commented to relations and friends on the widening gulf between them. John had shut himself up in his room, had breakfasted alone and intended to remain there all day, " knowing he cannot be disturbed by us, as he has heated his stove to such a degree that when I went to see what had become of him I could not remain a moment . . . although he considerately hoped I would stay if I liked." Elsewhere she supposed that, now his health had improved, he would " also feel more amiable "; and, as she, too, was stronger, she hoped they would be better friends. For all she cared (added Effie, with somewhat acid emphasis) his parents might have him as much as they pleased: " I could hardly see less of him than I do at present. . . ." She had resolved that they must lead their own lives, and had herself the consolation of various kindly new acquaintances. For example, there was a Mr. Rawdon Brown, one of those well-to-do cultured Englishmen who, happening to find themselves in a foreign city, sink deep roots into its alien soil and resist every effort subsequently to transplant them. Having reached Venice fifteen years earlier, in search of the tomb of Shakespeare's " Banished Norfolk," he remained there for half a century and acquired an expert knowledge of its antiquities and customs. To both the Ruskins he was a serviceable companion; for, besides advising John on numerous difficult problems of history and architecture, he acted as escort and guide to Effie when she wished to go out sight-seeing. This she could scarcely have done alone, so importunate was the admiration she aroused in amorous Venetian citizens and gallant Austrian officers: " they pass me " (noted Effie) " and say ' dear creature ' and lots of things like that and throw bouquets at me." Effie no doubt averted her eyes: certainly she did not stoop to pick up the fallen bouquets. But one may hazard a guess that she was amused and stimulated. Her husband's temperament was compact of contradictions—fiery yet icy, expansive yet secretive, demanding yet neglectful. She responded to the touch of normality, and to the comforting suggestion of commonplace thoughts and passions.

Yes, in Venice, she was happy and calm enough. But back in England, meanwhile, guerrilla warfare had again broken out between the Gray and Ruskin families. The immediate cause was an anonymous letter. This scurrilous and illiterate missive, which asserted that a plot was on foot to separate John from his parents and that Miss Ker had "laid plans with flattering lips," old Mr. Ruskin had forwarded to Mr. Gray, who replied, sensibly and moderately, that in his view anonymous communications were better disregarded. Mr. Ruskin's reception of the hint was decidedly unhelpful. It had needed (he wrote) no anonymous letter to convince Mrs. Ruskin and himself that "there seemed to be an amazing effort made to withdraw our son as much as possible from the influence and society of his parents." Effie's attitude had surprised and wounded them. Was it likely they could feel otherwise than hurt "at seeing a creature who came to us so readily . . . at once change on becoming our daughter-in-law and evince a repugnance both to ourselves and to our house so marked that the French people who were here and who saw Effie, in place of staying to help Mrs. Ruskin with her visitors, hurry my son away . . . gave expression to their sympathy by declaring they would become our children themselves?" John, of course, had sufficient strength of mind "not to become the altered man towards his parents which it was sought to make him—towards his mother, especially to whom, under God, he owes all that he now is or ever will be." But, should his resistance at length be overwhelmed, and should he consent to disregard "maternal influence and authority," he would lose as much as he gained; for, "let him turn out as fine a character as he may he will not surpass . . . that single-hearted and simple being he was when he left his mother's side."

Such were the dispositions of Denmark Hill when, during the spring months of 1850, the Ruskins finally returned to No. 31 Park Street. If, in Venice, Effie had still expected that her husband might one day learn to disentangle himself from his mother's cumbering apron-strings, she soon admitted her mistake and resigned herself to solitude. John was to be busier than ever (she wrote to tell Rawdon Brown) and had just announced that every morning after breakfast he would leave for Denmark Hill, where he intended to remain till six o'clock, at which time he would drive back to join her at the dinner-table. She had endeavoured to dissuade him, pointing out that he might take refuge in his study in his own house, " and then I might see him sometimes during the day "; but he had retorted that he had " no light in town nor his Turners and that I will soon find acquaintances and can take care of myself (which I think you rather doubt)." Yet advantages she certainly had, and profited by them with all the elasticity of a young and sanguine spirit. Once again there were the amusements of a London season, the parade of dresses and faces in drawing-rooms and ball-rooms, the stimulating rattle of conversation and the satisfying flow of compliments. In the month of May she was presented at Court, and there observed her middle-aged sovereign looking " immensely stout and red but very calm. I kissed her hand which was fat and red too. . . ." Around the unattached beauty collected an enthusiastic circle of rakish men of the world; but though she did not repulse these admirers, she held them at arm's length with considerable self-possession; and, having eluded the assiduities of Clare Ford, a young and dissipated guardsman, she set about his reformation in a motherly or sisterly style, advising him to save money, and to give up " drinking brandy with his coffee and smoking till three in the morning ": with the result that, as he seldom slept, he spent the midnight hours writing her long and grateful letters " on the fallen Nature of Man and his weakness . . . most strange productions," and a friend observed that her house in Park Street should be renamed " The Reform Club."

Some gossip she could not escape. But Effie assured her mother that the stories she might have heard were utterly unjustified. ". . . I am so peculiarly situated as a married woman that being left much alone and most men thinking that I live quite alone I am more exposed to their attentions. But I assure you—I never allow such people to enter the house and stop everything of the kind which might be hurtful to my reputation. . . ." Clare Ford, who in a moment of baffled desire had informed her that she might expect to "die of propriety," at length accepted his dismissal and joined the Diplomatic Service;[1] and Effie, who would appear, temporarily at least, to have regarded the romantic and irresponsible young soldier with a somewhat greater degree of interest than had yet been aroused by any of his fellow-rakes, continued to play the solitary and equivocal part to which her husband had assigned her. After a summer of social annoyances and a "little useless trip" to Cambridge which took place in the autumn months, Ruskin had settled down to the preparation of his first volume, eventually published at the beginning of March, 1851. The reception of his book was, as usual, flattering. Professional critics wrote in enthusiastic terms; and fellow-authors expressed their approval with unstinted generosity. Charlotte Brontë (whom Ruskin did not know) declared that "the *Stones of Venice* seem nobly laid and chiselled"; and Carlyle (whom he had recently met) thanked him at length for a presentation copy, which he called "a strange, unexpected, and I believe, most true and excellent *Sermon* in Stones—as well as the best piece of schoolmastering in Architectonics; from which I hope to learn much in a great many ways. The spirit and purport of these critical studies of yours are a singular sign of the times to me, and a very gratifying one. Right good speed to you, and victorious arrival on the farther shore."

Carlyle's conclusion was singular and characteristic. "It is a quite new 'Renaissance,'" (he wrote) "I believe, we are getting into just now: either towards new, *wider* manhood, high again as the eternal stars; or else into final death, and marsh of Gehenna. . . ." No less prophetic was Ruskin's mood; and it was with a solemn sense of the

[1] Clare Ford became British Ambassador at Madrid, Constantinople and Rome, dying in 1899.

importance of the work in hand, and of the moral obligations inseparable from the author's task, that on the morning of May 1st, 1851, he recorded how, sitting in his quiet room at Denmark Hill, while the birds sang in the garden and London stirred beneath him, he was preparing to undertake the second half of his Venetian labours: "May God help me to finish it—to His glory, and man's good." That autumn he must revisit Venice. But in the meantime some aspects of English art and English society were claiming his attention. For example, there was the embittered dispute that had broken out over the productions of a group of young and hopeful painters who had elected to denominate themselves "the Pre-Raphaelite Brotherhood." Ruskin's response to their pictures had at first been hostile or indifferent. Millais' "Carpenter's Shop" he had "passed disdainfully" when it had been exhibited a year earlier, till Dyce, the Academician, had dragged him back and obliged him, against his will, to scrutinise its merits. With the Pre-Raphaelites themselves he had not yet made acquaintance. Founded in 1848, the Brotherhood now consisted of three leading, and four subsidiary, members. Only the leaders need concern us here—three spirited young men of widely varying temperament: Holman Hunt, solemn and conscientious, with his square, rather heavy face and short tip-tilted nose: his protégé and pupil, Dante Gabriel Rossetti, at that time "a young man of decidedly Southern breed and aspect," whose long brown hair swept his shoulders as, in his unfashionable brown overcoat and creased and spotted black suit, he slouched moodily through the streets of London, "pouting with parted lips, searching with dreaming eyes": and John Everett Millais, once the youthful prodigy of the Academy School (where Holman Hunt had encountered him), now the chief butt of those numerous and ferocious critics whom the mere mention of the Pre-Raphaelite Brotherhood whipped into a kind of frenzy.

Of the three Millais was, from an executive point of view evidently the most gifted, and, as regards worldly ambition, perhaps the most determined. It was recorded of him that, when he visited a phrenologist, under an assumed name, concealing his profession, he had been informed that, while the shape of his head gave no indication of any particular aptitude for the liberal arts and sciences, he had a considerable fund of commercial acumen and should succeed in business. That side of his nature had not yet declared itself. In 1851, he was a remarkably handsome youth, whose large eyes beamed with "angelic" fervour and whose coronal of "bronze-coloured locks" completed a forehead of classic breadth and symmetry. His manners were impulsive and charming; and "he dressed" (we are told) "with exact conventionality so as to avoid in any degree courting attention as a genius." In the doctrines that the leaders professed, there was much to appeal to Ruskin's favourite prejudices. As a very young man, Hunt had sat up the greater part of the night reading *Modern Painters*, possessed by the feeling that it had been "written expressly for him"; and, if Ruskin had not directly inspired the foundation of the Pre-Raphaelite Brotherhood, one of the Brothers at least was deeply indebted to his influence. The contemporary value of that influence could scarcely be exaggerated. For any young man of the period, whose love of art was a burning passion, and to whom the manifestations of academic art seemed vulgar, conventional and passionless, Ruskin's book had opened gigantic horizons: sweeping aside the viscous dark-brown haze with which second-rate imitators of Sir Joshua Reynolds were used to shroud their canvases, he had revealed skies of vivid Italian blue and pointed the way to a fresher, earlier, more spiritual epoch in the history of European painting. *There* was innocence, *there* was simplicity. As the Pre-Raphaelites turned over a collection of prints, "we appraised as Chaucerian the sweet humour of Benozzo Gozzoli . . ."; and this spirit (which struck them as peculiarly English; for the leaders of the movement were not only enthusiasts but patriots) "we acclaimed as the standard under which we were to make our advance." Nature was to be their guide. But "our original doctrine of childlike submission to nature" did not imply any harsh or slavish realism. "Despite differences," Rossetti and Hunt agreed "that a man's work must be the reflex of a living image in his own mind, and not the icy double of the facts themselves. . . . We were never realists" (wrote Hunt). "I think art would have ceased to have the slightest interest for any of us had the object been only to make a representation, elaborate or inelaborate, of a fact in nature." It was one of the chief beauties of Ruskin's gospel that he should have sought to raise the plastic arts from the level of mere dilettantism to which, in his opinion and in the view of the Pre-Raphaelites, they had temporarily descended. A work of art was no longer to be considered as a successful piece of virtuosity, the product of an expert craftsman, doomed to be the treasure-trove of some rich and cultured amateur. It had endless references to the life of man, subtle connections with the highest human faculties. Since the temper of the age was ethical, the Pre-Raphaelites, in their interpretation of the artist's task, were inclined to enlarge, with all the eloquence at their command, upon the purely moral aspect. Art was the "handmaid . . . of justice and truth"; and the inward excellence of a composition must be seconded by the stirring and elevating qualities of the story it unfolded. Hence their choice of dramatic subjects—"Lorenzo and Isabella," with a bully, from whom Millais had suffered at the Academy School, spurning Isabella's greyhound: "Rienzi," its central figure lifting his clenched fist towards the sky in a furious protest against despotism: or "Christians escaping from persecuting Druids." Hence, too, the curiously poetic skill with which they loved to weave a glittering symbolic thread into the smallest details of their pictures. Not a blade of grass was trampled down, and not a twig snapped, unless it somehow enhanced the effect of the theme they were developing. Nourished on romantic poetry—more especially on the work of Keats—the literary imagination they displayed was often considerably ahead of their æsthetic sensitiveness.

Ruskin's sympathies fluctuated—and would always continue to fluctuate—between ethics, art and literature;

and a passage in *Modern Painters*, which, throughout his life, Holman Hunt remembered with admiration and affection, was the critic's celebrated and ingenious analysis of the symbolism underlying a huge canvas by Tintoretto in the Scuola di San Rocco. Why has the Virgin of the Annunciation been placed by the painter in an ancient ruined building? As happens so frequently when we are reading Ruskin's criticism, our first response to the explanation he provides is a movement of impatience. His discovery that "the ruined house is the Jewish dispensation," a half-built house the Christian, while the stone, rejected by the builders but destined to become the head-stone of the corner, is represented in the foreground, does little enough to further our appreciation of Tintoretto's genius. Yet, amid his unravelling of the learned riddle—solved with an authoritative neatness that must have delighted Denmark Hill—he suddenly out-soars the immediate problem he has set himself, carried away on one of those gusts of feeling that, when his imagination was stirred to its depths, sweep across Ruskin's style like some primitive natural force. He is comparing the point of view of the sixteenth-century painter with the beatific Annunciation conceived by Fra Angelico:

> "Severe would be the shock and painful the contrast if we could pass in an instant from that pure vision to the wild thought of Tintoretto. For not in mute reception of the adoring messenger, but startled by the rush of his horizontal and rattling wings, the Virgin sits not in the quiet loggia, not by the green pasture of the restored soul, but houseless under the shelter of a palace vestibule ruined and abandoned, with the noise of the axe and the hammer in her ears, and the tumult of the city round about her desolation."

It was in the poetic hardihood of such passages as this that Ruskin revealed himself to the Pre-Raphaelites—and reveals himself even now to the sympathetic modern reader —as a master of imaginative criticism whose sensibility enlarges and illuminates every subject that engrossed him. As in Tintoretto's Annunciation, impressions of beauty and impressions of terror are sometimes strangely intermixed: the contemplation of beauty surprises and alarms him: and, as if dismayed by the vividness of his vision, he often proceeds to take refuge in prejudice or pedantry. But the moment of illumination, however brief, is dazzling. Ruskin, during his early middle age, occupied the odd and enviable position of a critic who not only enchanted the young, but was accepted with admiring approval by their academic elders. He was, in fact, the perfect defender of Pre-Raphaelitism. Since 1848, journalistic abuse of the Brotherhood had swelled into a "hurricane"; and to the angry chorus of professional critics, who stigmatised their "morbid infatuation," "conceit," "mannerism," "eccentricity," were added the voices of non-professional detractors—Dickens, Kingsley, Macaulay, the last of whom observed that he was glad to notice Pre-Raphaelitism spreading, in as much as it was by spreading that affectations perished. Among their younger champions was Coventry Patmore. Ruskin knew and enjoyed his poems; and to Patmore, it would seem, must go the credit of persuading Ruskin to write two letters to *The Times*, defending Hunt and Millais. Ruskin's first letter on May 13th, 1851, came (Holman Hunt records) as "thunder out of a clear sky." He dwelt at length upon individual merits, declaring that in the whole Academy exhibition there was "not a single study of drapery . . . which for perfect truth, power, and finish could be compared for an instant with the black sleeve of the Julia or with the velvet on the breast and chain mail of the Valentine of Mr. Hunt's picture; or with the white draperies on the table of Mr. Millais' 'Mariana,'" and expressed his conviction furthermore that, "as studies both of drapery and of every minor detail, there has been nothing in art so earnest or so complete as these pictures since the days of Albert Dürer. This I assert generally and fearlessly."

His second letter was slightly more measured. Besides paying a generous tribute to the "marvellous truth in detail and splendour in colour" displayed by Holman Hunt's "Valentine defending Sylvia," he took the Pre-Raphaelites to task for the unpleasing and unsuitable type of human physiognomy they often chose to represent: a distinct "commonness of feature" was to be detected in many of their personages, and the kneeling figure on the right of Mr. Hunt's canvas, though it depicted an incident in the *Two Gentlemen of Verona*, was certainly no gentleman. . . . Nevertheless, he wished the Brotherhood, all of them, "heartily, good speed, believing, in sincerity, that if they temper the courage and energy which they have shown in the adoption of their system with patience and discretion in framing it, and if they do not suffer themselves to be driven by harsh or careless criticism into rejection of the ordinary means of obtaining influence over the minds of others, they may, as they gain experience, lay in our England the foundations of a school of Art nobler than the world has seen for three hundred years." The Pre-Raphaelites had begun to despair; they were poor, as well as young, men; and the concerted attacks from which they had been suffering threatened, not only to blast their hopes of reputation, but to rob them of their livelihood. After a modest interval, Millais and Holman Hunt wrote a joint letter to Ruskin to thank him for his kindly offices. They wrote under Millais' address; and next day John and Effie drove in their carriage to his parents' house in Gower Street. Their meeting was entirely successful; the Ruskins were delighted with Millais' pen-and-ink drawings, and captivated by his natural charm, his "exuberant interest in human experience" and "child-like impulsiveness in conversation" which "made him in a few days like an intimate of many years' duration." He was soon a familiar of the critic's household. Though "singularly at variance" in their opinions on art, "we are such good friends" (Millais related) "that he wishes me to accompany him to Switzerland this summer."

Millais was obliged to refuse; and that summer he and Holman Hunt, each of them equipped with a heavy palette of white porcelain—only porcelain, they felt sure, would safeguard the pristine purity of the colours they were handling—retreated to the banks of a little stream near Ewell, where Hunt had placed his "Hireling Shepherd" and Millais, among the tall flags and tangled drooping dog-roses, had discovered an exquisite background for his water-borne "Ophelia." Thus it was without a Pre-Raphaelite escort that the Ruskins left England in August, 1851. Before he embarked, Ruskin had completed two pamphlets, *Pre-Raphaelitism*, in which he strengthened and extended his views upon the movement, and *Notes on the Construction of Sheepfolds*, a plea for a united Protestant front, coupled with an argumentative exposition of his own dislike or dread of Roman Catholic dogma. During later years, the tendency of Ruskin's mind was to grow more and more discursive, till a moment came when it was practically impossible for him to focus the whole of his intelligence on any single subject, so insistent was the appeal of half a dozen others, so uncontrollable the excitement that, as his theme developed and expanded, rapidly took hold of him. That tendency was already manifest; but in 1851 the æsthete still predominated over the prophet, sage or visionary. His second working period in Venice, where the Ruskins arrived after their usual leisurely ramble across Switzerland and Northern Italy, continued from September, 1851, to June, 1852, and demanded at least as great an expenditure of concentrated effort. Venice welcomed him blandly. It was "more beautiful than ever," he reported home to Denmark Hill—more comfortable, too, now that Rawdon Brown had helped him to find excellent lodgings in the Campo Santa Maria Zobenigo. For his father's benefit, he gave a pleasing account of the domestic amenities he enjoyed there. He rose at half-past six, was dressed by seven and read till nine o'clock. "Then we have breakfast punctually: very orderly served—a little marmalade with a silver leafage spoon on a coloured tile at one corner of the table; butter very fresh in ice; fresh grapes and figs, which I never touch, on one side; peaches on the other, also for ornament chiefly . . .; a little hot dish which the cook is bound to furnish every morning, a roast beccafico or other little tiny kickshaw; before Effie, white bread and coffee. Then I read Pope or play myself till ten, when we have prayers; and Effie reads to me and I draw till eleven. Then I write till one. . . ." And so the day unrolled itself, studious and carefully ordered, concluding at nine when he finally prepared for bed.

The social gaieties of Venice seemed less wearisome than those through which he had yawned or protested in so many London drawing-rooms. Both the Ruskins were "excessively petted," alike by Venetian society and by their Austrian overlords; the aged Marshal Radetsky presented Effie with his portrait; and, at a party he gave, which the Archduke Charles Ferdinand attended, she "was allowed by every one to be the *reine du bal*." Venice at the time was full of English visitors—Lord Dufferin, "paddling about in the lagoons . . . in one of those india-rubber boats which you may see hanging up at the door of a shop in Bond Street": and Dean Milman, "very fond of hearing himself talk and very positive," whom Ruskin showed over the Duomo at Murano, "making him observe the great superiority of the old church and the abomination of its Renaissance additions," and simultaneously "abusing St. Paul's," so that the Dean was "much disgusted." Altogether, a halcyon interlude. But even at this distance, in this enchanted city, the influence of John's parents was still impossible to shake off. Mr. Ruskin maintained his epistolary warfare, loudly expressing his alarm at the dimensions of John's overdraft, which now amounted to £1000, and lamenting, in a letter to Mr. Gray, that Effie's selection of her wardrobe revealed a certain unladylike preference for gaudy and outrageous hues: whereas "the Highest Ladies in London are remarkably sensitive about quiet colours, especially out-of-doors. They have quite a dread of Red and Yellow and Effie can by her gifts of nature afford to be as quiet as a Quakeress." If Effie appeared extravagant, his son, he was obliged to admit, was never very practical. And his alarm and exasperation were presumably much increased when, during the early months of 1852, he received a series of three letters which John requested that he would read, and then dispatch to *The Times* for publication in its correspondence columns. They breathed a radicalism vehement and unabashed. Not content with advocating universal suffrage (though the electoral system he recommended was to be qualitative as well as quantitative), he declared himself in favour of a graduated income tax, and of the imposition of a super-tax on incomes above a certain figure. His father was puzzled and dismayed. That John, the triumphant product of paternal thrift and industry, should seek, by a letter to *The Times*, to sap the solid foundations on which commercial England rested, struck him as so singularly wrong-headed that the style in which he replied was almost acrimonious. John's books, he declared, were as impregnable to critical attacks as the Eddystone Lighthouse, " whereas your politics are Slum Buildings liable to be knocked down." Thus he declined to forward the letters, which remained unpublished until they were resurrected in book form many years later. But the first ominous signs had appeared. Henceforward the pangs of an exacting social conscience, which derived both from a sense of guilt and a conviction of superiority, were to war against Ruskin's peace of mind, and intensify and exaggerate his fundamental restlessness.

IV

IT WAS not to Park Street that young Mr. and Mrs. John Ruskin returned in the summer months of 1852. That expensive residence had been abandoned; and, as John's and Effie's future home, the elder Ruskins had chosen a small house, No. 30 Herne Hill, next to the house where John had been brought up, and in their own immediate neighbourhood. Both the house itself—a modest red-brick cube—and the furnishings his father had provided, Ruskin found at first sight exceedingly distasteful. He settled down there, nevertheless, and, plunging back into the work that absorbed him, finished the second volume of *Stones of Venice* for publication during the spring of 1853, and by the autumn of that year had satisfactorily completed the whole ambitious project. His parents, meanwhile, could congratulate themselves on having re-established the control of their son that his infatuation for Effie and the influence of life in Park Street had temporarily weakened. The filial tie was as strong as ever; and to maintain it, Mrs. Ruskin expended all her female artifice. Aloof and dispassionate when he was still a child, she had now transferred to John the natural strength of feeling that she had once lavished on her husband. The tone of her letters was almost loverly. During his sojourn abroad, she had written to him of the "heart-sickening impatience" that she felt to see and hear and speak to him; and, besides dwelling upon her own emotions (which, "in justice of herself," she must say that she had not allowed to "operate to the discomfort of others") she returned frequently to the subject of John's health, which (she admitted) still gave her grounds for serious disquietude. Effie's cause, as her mother-in-law must have suspected, was, by this time, a very nearly lost one. Cut off from her friends in London, except on the occasions when she could borrow old Mr. Ruskin's brougham and drive down from the suburbs, Effie resented her servitude to Denmark Hill, and did not enjoy the dull family dinner-parties that almost every night awaited her. There was no pleasing the two old people; and, when the New Year arrived with fog and chill, they began to complain "because I won't visit without John or go to balls alone." What ought she to do? Should she refuse invitations, "they say it is my own fault . . . and that I may go wherever I like or do what I choose provided I don't *degrade* John by taking him into society."

In short (Effie concluded) "they don't care any of them what becomes of me . . . so they are left to enjoy themselves. . . . I never saw such a trio. . . ." In their own opinion "three perfect people," they demanded, by way of return for the kindnesses they were still prepared to throw her, implicit reliance on their superior adult judgment. They treated her "as a fool or a child." And Effie, whose strain of childishness was accompanied and qualified by an unusual degree of unpretending shrewdness, revolted angrily against her subjection, and watched their every movement with an increasingly suspicious eye. No doubt her suspicions were slightly over-coloured. It is also possible that the elder Ruskin's campaign against their daughter-in-law was more than half unconscious. Only John could have hoped to keep the peace: and John, within the last year, had given up any remaining interest in the rôle of Effie's guardian. He was not embittered: he was merely unconcerned. Now that his merits were so suitably recognised, his daily occupations so profitably mapped out, he was not averse from allowing Effie to find her own amusements. His duty was to the public at large —the vast progressive Victorian public, of whose artistic conscience he had made himself the keeper. Every one who had "Turners or Missals"—the art of the medieval manuscript had now been added to his interests—seemed anxious he should visit them. He had been invited to lecture at Edinburgh. But, although he had accepted the invitation, he had been sufficiently tired by writing *The Stones of Venice* to feel that he deserved at least a temporary respite. He decided on a Scottish holiday. Effie, with a friend, a Miss McKenzie, would naturally accompany him; and, since he had renewed his Pre-Raphaelite friendships, Millais, his half-brother, and Holman Hunt were also asked to join the cavalcade.

Hunt declined at the eleventh hour; but both the Millais brothers were of the party when, during the summer of 1853, the Ruskins took up their abode at Callander, deep in a green hollow, among the romantic rainy Trossachs. Effie and John Everett Millais, that engaging, impulsive young man, were by this time already old acquaintances; throughout the spring months Millais had been painting her and, although he had found her head " immensely difficult ", and for the purposes of *The Order of Release*, he had changed her abundant hair from auburn-gold to raven-black, she had left on his imagination a strong and lasting imprint. She, too, had approved of Millais. He was " extremely handsome," she told her parents, and much sought after; which, considering his looks and genius, was not at all extraordinary. Otherwise her attitude towards her husband's friend was equally decorous and cautious. But during the stormy weeks they spent in Scotland she was obliged to see him every day; they climbed and sketched together; she even trimmed his curls; when they were confined to their rooms by the weather, they played at battledore-and-shuttlecock. He began to call her " The Countess," in allusion to some remark by an admiring hotel servant. They were young and sanguine and high-spirited. Ruskin, remote and self-absorbed, loomed benevolently in the middle distance. He was detached but by no means disapproving. " A good fellow, but not of our kind," observed Millais to a London correspondent in tones of strained perplexity.

Towards Effie, " the sweetest creature that ever lived," he was astonished to notice that the great critic, his saviour and benefactor, appeared languidly indifferent. Himself he burned with chivalric passion. Nursed on dreams of the heroic past, weaned on Keats' poetry, Millais had a disposition that did not deal in half-shades. "The Countess," it took no very acute eye to discern, was not as happy as she might be; but the possibility of happiness was there, only waiting to be brought out; and while sheets of midsummer rain thrashed down across the sodden mountain-sides, or an infrequent burst of sunshine glistened upon silky birch-boles and turned the swollen streams to "writhing liquid amber," Millais experienced moods of acute depression, from which he endeavoured to escape by attacking a new canvas. That canvas contained a portrait of Ruskin. Previously Ruskin and Millais had been "pitching into architecture"; and the painter, at the critic's direction, had completed a design for the tracery of a window, full of confusedly-embracing angels, which bears a curious resemblance to the products of nineteenth-century *art nouveau*. The portrait was a more serious project. Henry Acland, Ruskin's Oxford friend, was then paying them a visit; and he, in part, would appear to have been responsible for Millais' choice of background—the Falls of Glenfinlas, where the mountain torrent plunged in a sheet of foam past a black and shining rock-face. The site chosen was peculiarly apt. Than Ruskin, no author has written of hurrying water more eloquently or loved it more consumingly, from the Tay to the sources of the Rhone, from mighty and powerful rivers to sparkling country streamlets. Certainly he applauded Millais' decision, and to his father at Denmark Hill wrote with enthusiasm of "the lovely piece of worn rock" on which the artist wished to place him, and where he was to stand "looking quietly down the stream; just the sort of thing I used to do for hours together. . . . I think you will be proud of the picture, and we shall have the two most wonderful torrents in the world, Turner's 'St. Gothard' and Millais' 'Glenfinlas.' He is going to take the utmost possible pains with it. . . . I am sure the foam of the torrent will be something quite new in art."

So much for the portrait's background. In portraying

the central figure, Millais may have felt that he confronted a far more complex problem. He was still the admirer of Ruskin's moral worth, and listened obediently to the various admonitions with which, when he showed his drawings, he was very often favoured. Ruskin, he wrote, had quite convinced him "that the paltry drawings I may have been in the habit of doing are most injurious to the doer in his moral nature." And, on another occasion: "Ruskin I understand more than I have before; truth and earnestness are his great guides, and no labour of thought or work is wearisome to him." The "intensity" of his friend's religious beliefs also heartened Millais. How disconcerting, then, to be forced to observe that he was evasive, incalculable, even cold-hearted, in the sphere of personal relationships. Married to an enchanting young woman, he appeared to shrug-off his responsibilities with an air of chilly unconcern. Himself as direct and warm-blooded as Ruskin was cool, elusive, complicated, Millais, confronted with the married couple, could not but observe "his hopeless apathy, *in everything regarding her happiness*"; and, when he decided at length to remonstrate, Ruskin "only apathetically laughed and said, he thought all women ought to depend upon themselves for engrossing employment, and suchlike cold inhuman absurdities. . . ." The subject was never mentioned again, for thenceforward Millais dreaded that he might fail to keep his temper; but something of the mystery he apprehended would seem to have crept, brush-stroke by brush-stroke, into his meticulous representation of the lonely figure by the waterfall, rapt and brooding on the weather-worn rock, while the yeasty foam of the cataract goes swirling down before it. The portrait at first sight of a philosophic solitary; but the philosopher is encased from chin to knee in an elegantly-cut and trimly-buttoned frock-coat.

The face, however, chiefly commands our interest. Ten years had elapsed since Richmond had painted the young critic sitting by his writing-desk; and, though the resemblance was still close, the general cast of his features had, during the intervening period, grown thinner, sadder, more authoritative. Ruskin was never regularly handsome—he bore on his lower lip the scar inflicted during childhood by his parents' savage watchdog; but Richmond's vision of him has a certain eager charm which had largely evaporated before he reached Glenfinlas, leaving only the magnetic blue eyes still intense and beautiful. The whiskers were now long, and of an indefinite rusty hue. Altogether it was an appearance that admirers, even the most fervent, sometimes voted disappointing; and when, having left Glenfinlas during the last week of October, he stood forth at the beginning of November on an Edinburgh lecture-platform, the impressions that he produced were a trifle contradictory. Instead of the poetic seer whom they had many of them expected—with " dark hair, pale face, and massive brow "—his audience saw " a thin gentleman," very formally and correctly dressed in a stiff white cravat and dark velvet-collared overcoat, who walked with a slight stoop, whose hair and whiskers were sandy, and whose face was rather red than pale. His mouth (remarked a contemporary journalist) was " well cut, with a good deal of decision in its curve, though somewhat wanting in sustained dignity and strength . . . the eye we could not see . . . but we are sure it must be soft and luminous, and that the poetry and passion we looked for almost in vain in other features are concentrated there. . . ." As for his manner of speaking, that was distinctly odd; for, besides a difficulty in pronouncing his *r's* and the " peculiar tone in the rising and falling of his voice at measured intervals . . . scarcely ever heard except in the public lection of the service appointed to be read in churches," he alternated, with disconcerting abruptness, between the oratorical and the colloquial method, reading aloud a part of his lecture, then pausing to illustrate it with some impromptu commentary. As a rule, decided the journalist, he was more readily intelligible when he adhered closely to the written page before him: ". . . the lectures on Turner and the Pre-Raphaelites, which were almost entirely read . . . certainly had far more unity and compactness than either of the previous ones."

Ruskin himself was well satisfied. He had been flattered to learn that Lady Trevelyan (a new and valued friend, with whom he and Effie had stayed on their way to Scotland) "and others of my friends were coming hundreds of miles to hear me"; and he was glad to be able to tell his father that, whereas most lecturers on Edinburgh platforms were distinguished by their shabby and slovenly clothes, he had worn his "usual dinner dress, just what you and my mother like me best in. . . ." Very different, and considerably more disturbing, had been the effect of their Scottish holiday on Effie and John Millais. Though they may not yet have crossed the delicate borderline that sunders love from friendship, their mutual attraction was evidently strong. But then, equally powerful were the considerations that kept them still divided. Effie's was essentially a cautious character: Millais was ardent and impulsive, but he would appear to have behaved throughout with Tennysonian chivalry: and they were both of them a little afraid of the Ruskins—more especially of the Ruskin parents—whom they were beginning to regard as a league of Machiavellian schemers. Could it be (they now asked themselves) that the whole expedition to Scotland had been part of a deep-laid plot planned with the express intention of compromising Effie? It was obvious that, whatever their private feelings, confessed or unconfessed, they must be very careful; and Millais wrote to Mrs. Gray, advising that one or other of Effie's sisters should be sent to stay at Herne Hill, for such companionship would strengthen her position and safeguard her against the importunities of "these cunning London men . . . gallant rakes, who can always find an excuse for calling, and who look upon Ruskin as a kind of milksop." His own intention was merely to leave cards at Denmark Hill and Herne Hill, and afterwards to decline any invitations. Next summer, as soon as he had completed his great Glenfinlas canvas, he expected to set out on an extended foreign tour. Meanwhile he would cease to write to Effie, though Ruskin throughout had been "cognisant to the correspondence . . . approving of it or at least not admitting a care in the matter. . . ." But the Ruskins were a "brooding selfish lot"; and he was well aware that his one-time friend had punctually reported every development of the situation in letters to the old people.

Thus, by the December of 1854, Ruskin, only a few months earlier a fount of "truth and earnestness," had finally fallen in Millais' estimation beyond all hope of re-arising. ". . . An undeniable giant as an author," he was (wrote Millais to Mrs. Gray) "a poor weak creature in everything else, bland, and heartless, and unworthy. . . ." It was symptomatic of Ruskin's "blandness," of the "provoking gentleness" with which, in spite of every obstacle, he quietly went his own way, that he should have continued, even now, to visit Millais' studio. *The Falls of Glenfinlas* must, of course, be completed; and, while the painter, controlling his aversion, laboured sternly, slowly onward, the critic, surveying an imaginary waterfall, stood poised upon the model's dais and gazed out through abstracted eyes at a row of Bloomsbury chimney pots, as their smoke drifted and threaded across a leaden London sky-scape. What he thought or felt was past Millais' guessing. But at Herne Hill (the painter knew) his beloved and long-suffering "Countess" still struggled in the grip of an intolerable bondage, patronised and scolded and spied upon, between parents-in-law who detested her and a husband who, from the most optimistic standpoint, could not be said to love her. Towards the entire Ruskin trio Effie's emotions were now hardening into hatred. During the previous year she had hoped—a desperate hope, it is true—that she might somehow save her marriage; and (according to her subsequent account) she had reminded her husband of his earlier promise and suggested that, six years having gone by, the alliance on which they had entered should at last become a real one. But Ruskin had refused, and refused conclusively and harshly, declaring—again we must remember that Effie is our only witness—that her intellect was deranged and that she was unfit to bring up children, whom indeed it would be a sin to beget, since he was convinced she did not sufficiently respect or love him. He added—a detail which Effie herself is unlikely to have invented—that, until the night of their marriage, he "had imagined women were quite different to what he saw I was," and that it was to "disgust," neither more nor less, that she had originally owed the preservation of her maidenhood.

In other relations exaggeratedly sensitive, Ruskin was afterwards to admit that the last agonies of his marriage had failed to touch him very deeply. He had had many intense sorrows, he observed at a later period; but that was not among them. It was a "vexation, more than an abiding grief," wrote his biographer, E. T. Cook; and although, during the winter of 1853 and the spring months of 1854, the atmosphere of his family life was becoming almost every day more difficult, while the state of Effie's health seemed more and more precarious, he continued calmly along his accustomed road, adding to his collection of medieval manuscripts and editing for the press his Edinburgh lectures. When he referred to his wife, it was usually in a tone of injured resignation. A final letter was dispatched to Mrs. Gray. "I will write you a word of Effie's health" (he told her in December), "but I fear I shall have little cheering information to give you. She passes her days in melancholy, and nothing can help her but an entire change of heart." How Effie might achieve that change was not exactly specified; and the oddity of John's attitude towards Millais (from whom he had encouraged her to accept a drawing, which upon second thoughts he concluded it was more proper she should send back) increased the suspicion she had already formed that the whole Ruskin family, John included, was resolved at any cost to compromise and ruin her. Nor did her sister's arrival improve the position. To Sophie, a precocious child of ten, both Ruskin and his mother and father would appear to have spoken with a somewhat unbecoming frankness; and from her visits to the household at Denmark Hill Sophie could generally be relied on to bring home some inflammatory scrap of gossip, which was duly reported in the letters sent to Bowerswell. John had informed Sophie

(Effie wrote to her mother) " that he watches everything I do or say. . . . I do not know what on earth they are such fools for especially John as were it not for the pain of exposure I have him most completely in my power. . . ." The Ruskins' main object, she felt convinced, was " to get rid of me, to have John altogether with them again. . . . They seem to wish if possible to disgust me to such a degree as to force me—or else get me—into some scrape —John has been trying again to get me by taunts to write to Millais——" But she had prudently resisted the suggestion, determined to endure as long as she could, and, if at last she were obliged to cut the knot, to cut it at her own time.

Ruskin's intentions remain mysterious. In spite of moments of harshness and petulance when, at least according to Sophie, he spoke of " breaking Effie's spirit "—a story we might be inclined to discount, were it not for the strangely ominous letter which he had written to Mr. Gray during the spring of 1849—it is possible that he had contrived somehow to shelve the whole appalling problem. He had his father's devoted approval, his mother's perfervid love. And then, there were the exquisite, unsurpassable diversions provided by his mental life. Always at hand were his Turners, his glowing new-found manuscripts. Them he worshipped with voluptuous ardour—so voluptuous indeed that the quality of the emotion they aroused soon began to trouble him. Was it *right* to enjoy so keenly? His love of art (he confessed to his father in the autumn of 1853) had been " a terrible temptation . . . and I feel that I have been sadly self-indulgent lately—what with casts, *liber studiorum*, missals, and Tintorets." Unless he eradicated this unruly passion, he might " get to be a mere collector. . . . I am sure I ought to take that text to heart, ' covetousness which is idolatry,' for I do idolise my Turners and missals, and I can't conceive anybody being ever tried with a heavier temptation than I am to save every farthing I can to collect a rich shelf of thirteenth-century manuscripts." As his birthday approached, the pangs of conscience from which he suffered grew correspondingly more painful. His next birthday, he remarked, was the "keystone of my arch of life . . . and up to this time I cannot say that I have in any way 'taken up my cross' or 'denied myself' . . . but have spent my money and time on my own pleasure and instruction." His birthday came—he was now thirty-five—but three weeks had still to elapse before he was obliged to record that he had once again succumbed to the insidious temptations that beauty spread around him. The Psalter and Hours of Isabella of France—"St. Louis's Psalter," as Ruskin called them—were not to be resisted. They were the greatest treasure he had ever obtained. Temporarily at least, in the work of a great medieval miniaturist, he found a closed garden of delights, a paradise of burnished gold and delicate lapis blue, from which the rumours of the outer world, even the stern interior voice of conscience, were very rarely audible.

Temporarily—for the more exquisitely he enjoyed, the deeper the misgivings by which his joy was followed. And it was at this period that Ruskin adopted a practice which, it is tempting to suppose, he may originally have undertaken as a means of quietening his conscience. He began to desecrate what he had loved too much. Rather than esteem himself a "mere collector," he deliberately destroyed the value and even diminished the beauty of the objects he had collected. Thus his idolised manuscripts were submitted to the scissors; two or three were dismembered and dispersed, some leaves being given away and others removed for framing; while annotations in pencil, and occasionally in ink, disfigured many pages. "Cut out some leaves from large missal," records his diary on December 30th, 1853; and, on January 3rd: "Cut missal up in evening; hard work." At a later time, friends who noted the fate that had befallen his chiefest treasures occasionally ventured to reprove him. But, evasive and ambiguous as always, Ruskin, then an ageing man, would reply, "with a sad smile," that "these old books have in them an evil spirit, which is always throwing them into disorder," appearing to hint that the evil spirit possessed an inveterate grudge against anything so lovely. The evil spirit was in Ruskin himself, and, like many evil spirits, usually materialised wearing the garments of his good angel.

Among such exalted considerations, Ruskin had, so far as we can judge, no interest or patience to spare for the young woman he had married. Millais had written to Mrs. Gray that if Effie's health was to be saved, "*some steps should be speedily taken* to protect her from this incessant harassing behaviour of the R's"; and by the end of February Effie had at last brought herself to consult her friend Lady Eastlake and had sought the legal advice of Lord Glenelg, both of whom insisted she must demand a separation. On March 7th, therefore, she wrote a long letter to her father, appealing for his help and telling him without reservation the story of her marriage. Yet still the fear of the Ruskins persisted; for she had now begun to regard them with almost superstitious horror. Her parents travelled south, but, until the exact legal position had been established, Ruskin (they decided) should receive no intimation that Effie meant to leave him. Instead, he was informed that she wished to go to Bowerswell; and, since he and his mother and father had planned another foreign tour, in which it was not intended that Effie should participate, he consented with perfect good humour, and politely escorted Effie and her mother when they drove to the northern terminus and took the train for Scotland. Unsuspecting, he bade them good-bye. A letter was already in the post, addressed to Mrs. Ruskin: Effie returned her account books and her wedding ring ("which I return by this means to your son, with whom I can never hold farther intercourse or communication") and explained, lengthily and bitterly, the concatenation of circumstances that had made married life impossible.

Legal proceedings were immediately begun; and on July 15th, 1854, a Decree of Nullity was granted by the Commissary Court to "Euphemia Chalmers Gray falsely called Ruskin." Then, after the lapse of a year, Effie wedded Millais, initiating a married life of unusual peace and fruitfulness. Eight children were born to the Millais.

By becoming the devoted wife of a celebrated Victorian artist, whose extraordinary juvenile gifts soon merged into the *expertise* of a prosperous academic painter, Effie would appear to have achieved just that state of existence and level of contentment to which she was best suited. Worldly both in her strength and her weakness, she was versed in those compromises, those acceptances of the world as it is, which make for mundane well-being. She belonged to, and enjoyed, to-day. For Ruskin, on the other hand, no compromise was possible: the hopes he entertained were too high, his pleasures too unearthly, the standards he had set himself (with which the sensuous side of his nature was perpetually coming into conflict) too rigorous and fine-drawn. Indeed, one may doubt whether Ruskin's failure as a human lover did more than precipitate, in an exaggerated guise, the essential clash between their temperaments. The image he had adored, the young woman he had taken to wife, could have never quite been reconciled; and the discrepancy became yet the more painful because Ruskin had formed the image with all the imaginative skill, all the æsthetic passion, of which his mind was capable. Had he married, as many artists have done, for lust or peace or comfort, his disillusionment might have been less crushing and his conduct more exemplary. In fact, the harshness that he displayed was the measure of his disappointment, the hypocrisy to which he sometimes resorted an indication of the agonised feelings against which he wished to guard himself. The ideal, unreal Effie was to some extent his own creation; and creative artists are notoriously ruthless towards such of their imaginative products as prove illusory and vulgar.

Ruskin dismissed the catastrophe of his marriage as he might have dismissed an ill-conceived and unsuccessful book, once a new and more important effort was growing on his writing-desk. True, for his lawyers' benefit, he described the circumstances of his marriage in a controversial statement; but that statement was never published; and on second thoughts he considered that his best plan was to refrain from any commentary. Let London talk! He preferred to stand aloof. He neither demanded defence nor expected sympathy. "You can be of no use to me at present" (he wrote to one friend more than usually solicitous) "except by not disturbing me, nor thinking hardly of me, yourself; you cannot contradict reports; the world must . . . have its full swing. Be assured I shall neither be subdued, nor materially changed, by this matter. The worst of it for me has long been past." So determined was he to remain unaltered, that it did not at once occur to him that his intercourse with Millais must necessarily be cut short. And on December 11th, 1854, when the portrait begun in Scotland was finally completed and framed, he wrote him an appreciative letter, signed "faithfully and gratefully": "As for the wonderment of the painting" (he observed) "there can of course be no question. . . . On the whole the thing is *right* and what can one say more —always excepting the yellow flower and the over-large spark in the right eye, which I continue to reprobate—as having the effect of making me slightly squint. . . . My father and mother say the likeness is perfect—but that I look bored—pale—and a little too yellow. Certainly after standing looking at that row of chimnies in Gower Street for three hours—on one leg—it was no wonder. . . ."

To Millais, however, the separation of æsthetic and personal concerns came very much less easily. So profound were his surprise and disgust that a week passed before he could bring himself to compose an appropriately indignant answer, in which he stated that he scarcely knew how or why Ruskin could imagine that "I can desire to continue on terms of intimacy with you"; though the "barrier which cannot but be between us *personally* does not prevent me from sympathising with all your efforts to the advancement of good taste in art. . . ." Ruskin, strangely enough—we have, indeed, few clearer indications of his extreme unworldliness—seems to have been almost equally taken aback by the tone of Millais' letter. Beginning "Sir," concluding "Your obedient servant," he remarked that he could only conclude either that Millais believed that he, Ruskin ("as has been alleged by various base or ignorant persons ") had had " some unfriendly purpose when I invited you to journey with me in the Highlands," or that his former friend was engaged in a nefarious plot and involved in the " machinations which have for a long time been entered into against my character and fortune. In either case I have to thank you for a last lesson . . . of the possible extent of human folly and ingratitude." Thus angrily he took his leave; yet, with his customary conscientiousness, Ruskin continued, whenever the occasion offered, to write of Millais' pictures, cordially praising what he admired, condemning what he deprecated. Old Mr. Ruskin, heated to the verge of delirium by the adventures of the last few months, seeing Millais' canvas hung on his walls, wished to stab it with a penknife. John quickly and quietly interposed, removed his portrait from the dangers of Denmark Hill and carried it off by stealth to Rossetti's sheltering studio.

Yet not all Ruskin's restraint and discretion could save him from the horrors that attend a widespread public scandal. Effie's friends were loud in abuse. He was a " blackguard," an inhuman " beast " (the latter an epithet hissed or grumbled out by Lockhart), a " villain " who, if justice were done, should be banished from society. They also concluded that Ruskin was mad. But " some *young ladies* " (they were pained to report) would not hear a word against him; and the Queen, though attempts were made at different times to interest her, refused to extend her approval to any severance of the marriage tie. London reverberated with impassioned gossip; but most interesting, perhaps most significant, of many varying commentaries were the voices that issued—one thunderous and dogmatic, the other light and sharp and quizzical—from Number 5 Cheyne Row. There, in the " valley of the shadow of marriage," further overshadowed at this moment by the apocalyptic production of the history of *Frederick*, Thomas and Jane Carlyle each expressed an opinion, reflecting their own peculiar experience of the difficulties of the wedded state. Carlyle was sonorously downright. Nothing, he said—no degree of neglect or ill-treatment—could excuse a wife's desertion. Jane, on the other hand, was gently and characteristically malicious at the expense of both parties, observing that she knew " nothing about it except that I have always pitied Mrs. Ruskin, while people generally blame her—for love of dress and company and flirtation. She was too young and pretty to be so left to her own devices as she was by her Husband, who seemed to wish nothing more of her than the credit of having a pretty, well-dressed Wife." If there was little obvious similarity between the Carlyle and Ruskin marriages, certain points of resemblance can hardly have failed to strike the restive pair in Chelsea. Supposing Jane had attempted to break away? . . . and that she had once fully intended to desert her husband, throwing herself into the arms of another man, was afterwards the firm belief of Carlyle's executor, Froude, and Jane's confidante Miss Jewsbury.[1] At the last moment she had decided otherwise; and Carlyle, when she told him by what a narrow margin their troubled alliance had escaped complete catastrophe, had replied that, looking back, he did not know that he would have missed her: at the time she contemplated elopement he was so hard at work on *Cromwell*. Neither association had been productive of happiness; and in analysing the personal unhappiness of these two great Victorian soothsayers—and the unhappiness they inflicted on the women whom they married—we seem to be confronted by a far deeper, wider conflict, which makes itself felt again and again throughout the nineteenth century and is exemplified by the careers of most Victorian artists. It is illustrated, with fascinating eloquence, in the work of Tennyson and Arnold. The lives of Carlyle and Ruskin reveal its shattering effect upon the individual's well-being.

For Carlyle, as he came to know him better, Ruskin was to acquire a warm and almost filial sympathy. In the older man he recognised a spirit that, like his own, could

[1]Ruskin, it is interesting to remember, did not join the general outcry against Froude's account of the Carlyles' married life. " By nobody more than by Mr. Ruskin " (writes W. G. Collingwood) " was Carlyle's reputation valued, and yet he acknowledged that Mr. Froude was but telling the truth in the revelations which so surprised the public. . . ."

John Ruskin

find no peace among the conditions that modern life imposed upon it: a temper naturally demanding, naturally dogmatic, shaped by the influence of early parental discipline, which had implanted a respect for authority without preparing the ground for any real submission. He saw a man moreover who, like himself, was the victim of a deep interior discord, who professed to despise the happiness he could not achieve, who, indeed, at the mere mention of the word "happiness" was inclined to flare up angrily, as at the gratuitous introduction of some improper and unworthy subject. And then Carlyle, too, was an artist, however unwillingly, however resentfully, with however many flashes of crude deliberate philistinism. In few English writers have the arts of accurate observation and vivid succinct description been developed to a finer point; and, though his set passages are sometimes overwhelming—for there he assumes the robes and adopts the attitude of the universal pedagogue, thundering out Biblical prophecies with a German-Scottish accent—where he is less didactic and less portentous, as in his brilliant informal sketches of contemporary men and women, he reveals at once his extraordinary command of language and the penetrating psychological insight by which it was directed. Yet that insight did not extend to the character and development of the gifted, unhappy woman who shared his life in Cheyne Row. When, after her death, he read her private papers, he was astonished by the revelation they afforded of his wife's interior shipwreck, of grievances he had scarcely suspected, of miseries and apprehensions with which he had wholly failed to sympathise. Those miseries were partly self-induced. An "ex-spoilt child," to use her own phrase, the darling of her father and mother, a cultivated middle-class girl, equally proud of her Latin and her eyelashes, Jane Carlyle had married the peasant-scholar from Annandale in a spirit of admiration rather than in a mood of passion. Since he was the "*least unlikeable* man in the place" (she latterly informed her cousin) "I let him dance attendance on my young person, till I came to *need* him—all the same as my slippers to go to a ball in, or my bonnet to go out to walk, when I finally agreed to marry him, I cried excessively and felt excessively shocked—but if I had then said *no* he would have left me. . . ." As a disillusioned invalid, Mrs. Carlyle may well have underestimated the quality of her own generous youthful motives. She had had a deep regard for the man she married (if little or none of the romantic enthusiasm once inspired in her by Edward Irving), and the sacrifice of her "position" and prospects was neither rash nor casual. But though she had made the gift readily, she could not forget that she had made it, and could never quite forgive her taciturn husband because, as year followed laborious year, and one after another the painful books were hammered out, she could not overcome the suspicion that he took her gift for granted. Jane Carlyle was intensely a woman, endowed with a degree of feminine fascination which triumphed to the end of her life over age and fading looks and ill-health; and, whatever the fate of his sexual instincts, the element of sexual sympathy—that instinctive appreciation of the opposite sex which quickens the imagination even as it warms the senses—in Carlyle's composition was conspicuously absent.

Hence the harsh atmosphere of personal frustration which, like a breath of suffocating London fog, seems, when we read Jane's letters, to have filled the house in Cheyne Row. Carlyle may not have been sexually impotent—on this curious and distressing problem the evidence Froude brought forward, though undoubtedly suggestive, is somewhat inconclusive; but emotionally impotent we can scarcely doubt that he was, a man incapable either of stimulating or of satisfying emotionally the woman whom he lived with, so difficult was it for him to part the thick veils of depression wherein he dwelt enshrouded, so seldom could he approach others on day-to-day terms of human equality and intimacy. Himself he suffered from this life-long deprivation. But more acute and more prolonged were the sense of loss and the pangs of emotional starvation which Jane Carlyle experienced. The downward lines which enclosed her mouth grew deeper and more mournful, the large eyes heavier and darker and sadder, while her wit took on an increasingly acid tone, till none of her intimates —from "Mr. C" himself to the ill-treated but devoted Miss Jewsbury—was spared its biting back-strokes. "She had, when she was angry" (said one of her acquaintances), "a tongue like a cat's, which would take the skin off at a touch." Her letters—wonderful, lengthy, unforced, unpremeditated outpourings, confided to odd scraps of paper, sometimes to the reverse of household bills—were among the chief means that she employed to vent her stifled energies; and in them the figure cut by her husband, irritable and ineffably self-absorbed, cross-grained and inconsiderate, petulant, morose, bilious, is usually absurd, and, on occasions, almost sinister. Yet—and here we reach the crux of the Carlyles' tragedy—in her tormented way she loved him, not with passion nor even with tenderness, but with a grim, unwavering, fundamental loyalty, the tribute of egoist to egoist, of a proud, opinionated and lonely woman to a man who, during the course of his intellectual wanderings, had plumbed the depths of solitude. Worse misfortunes were still to befall them. In 1854 and 1855, when the Ruskins drifted apart as irrelevantly as seven years earlier they had chanced to come together, Mrs. Carlyle, her nervous system undermined by the huge doses of morphine and henbane with which she strove to ward off sleeplessness, was rapidly approaching a major moral crisis. She was becoming bitterly, incurably, perhaps unreasonably jealous of her husband's patrician patroness, the Junonian Lady Ashburton, a woman as clever as she was attractive and (which, no doubt, from Mrs. Carlyle's point of view was particularly galling) certainly far too worldly-wise to give Mrs. Carlyle cause for any obvious grievance. Yet it was clear that she had ensnared the prophet, and that time he would not spend at Cheyne Row was spent gladly at Lady Ashburton's feet in Bath House, Piccadilly. Mrs. Carlyle learned to detest the house—"Oh, good gracious!" (she wrote in her journal) "when I first noticed that heavy yellow house . . . how far I was from dreaming that through years and years I should carry every stone's weight of it on my heart"—and to fear and resent, though she could never learn to despise, its capricious fashionable sovereign. But Carlyle remained a devoted courtier; Jane's objections, if he saw and understood them, struck him as gratuitous; and thus the two of them, in spite of the real sympathy, the profound unexpressed attachment, that underlay their married life, retired into separate hells of incommunicable wretchedness—Jane alone in her Chelsea drawing-room, occasionally relieved by the apparition of some admiring caller: Carlyle, when he could not forget himself beneath the chandeliers of Bath House or bury his cares in the exploration of Frederick's endless bloody campaigns, wandering through midnight streets, with Mrs. Carlyle's little dog Nero pattering attentively before him—a "little dim-white speck, of Life, of Love, Fidelity and Feeling, girdled by the Darkness of Night Eternal"—till he could trudge home to the narrow solitary bed that, as he liked to remind his intimates, sleep so seldom visited. . . .

From this "Dark Night of the Ego"—Carlyle, one often suspects, was inclined to mistake the discomfort of a baffled egotism for the writhings of a tormented soul—the moment has come to return to the complementary case of Ruskin. Both prophets were unhappy men—unhappy not so much because the circumstances of their external lives were thwarting and embittering, as because within themselves they could find no peace and quiet, no refuge from a mysterious sense of guilt and no means of establishing a truce between antagonistic private impulses. They were teachers who could not be taught; and, although they pronounced doctrines and promulgated laws, they were unable to discover any law or rule that would ensure their own tranquillity. Each searched in vain for a clue; but to his search Ruskin brought a temperament more elastic, more variously endowed, more feminine than that of Carlyle. For Carlyle's outlook had a peasant harshness. He loved the written word, its sonority and beauty; to other forms of art he was entirely blind; and against the sensuous charm of the physical universe—all those exquisite minor graces to be discovered by the æsthetic eye in the world of man and nature—his imagination was obstinately closed, since his puritan upbringing had taught him that spontaneous, light-hearted satisfaction must be almost always harmful. Ruskin, on the other hand, did not lack light-heartedness. He appreciated the surface of life, derived exquisite sensuous pleasure from a thousand fleeting incidents, and responded, though at a distance and with much reserve, to the shock of human passions. He could not dismiss the belief that mankind in general, himself included, might still be free and happy.

V

TRUE to his determination that his friends should find him " neither . . . subdued, nor changed " by Effie's disappearance, and that towards the hostile and inquisitive public he must continue to present an attitude of cool, unruffled dignity, Ruskin, as he had previously planned, crossed the Channel with his parents in May, 1854, and remained abroad, quietly and commendably occupied, till the following September. No word of remorse or recrimination, no Byronic apostrophe to an unworthy wife, was uttered from the packet-boat. The voyage would seem to have been smooth and pleasant; for on deck Ruskin noted with enthusiasm the interesting curve of the ancient vessel's stay-sail, and sat down to make the careful drawing which was afterwards engraved as frontispiece to the second volume of *Praeterita*. How fascinating was the world of nature, how absorbing the contemplation of man's ingenious handicraft! At one moment, in the bows of the little steamer, as he watched the " magical division of the green waves between Dover and Calais," it was a scrap of weather-worn sail-cloth, patched and seamed and stained, " warped like a piece of wetted paper," that caught and fixed his interest. But no sooner had he set foot on dry land than the tower of Calais Church, a familiar, friendly sentinel, rose delightfully before him; and that, too, proved an imaginative outlet, first stimulating his sensuous apprecia-tion of colour, mass and texture, then bringing a comforting suggestion of some underlying moral import. For not only " the large neglect, the noble unsightliness " of the venerable building had to be considered—" its stern wasteness and gloom, eaten away by the channel winds, and overgrown with the bitter sea grasses; its slates and tiles all shaken and rent . . . its desert of brickwork full of bolts, and holes, and ugly fissures, and yet strong, like a bare brown rock." But its unpretending gravity and solidity of demeanour also claimed attention—"its carelessness of what any one thinks or feels about it, putting forth no claim, having no beauty or desirableness, pride, nor grace . . . not, as ruins are, useless and piteous, feebly or fondly garrulous of better days; but useful still, going through its own daily work . . . in blanched and meagre massiveness and serviceableness . . . the sound of its bells for prayer still rolling through its rents; and the grey peak of it seen far across the sea . . . above the waste of surfy sand and hillocked shore. . . ."

Here, as elsewhere, Ruskin's processes of thought and methods of criticism are not entirely straightforward. His imagination fastened on the old tower almost as affectionately and greedily as it had fastened on St. Mark's church; but that it was "beautiful" he felt obliged to deny, and concentrated instead upon its underlying symbolism. Indeed, Ruskin's critical approach, though directed and sustained by an acute intellect, was not primarily intellectual. It is in his ability to convey the keenness of his own sensations, the exquisiteness of his own adventures among landscapes, pictures, monuments, rather than in his attempts to explain why he felt as he did or to rationalise the pleasure he was half ashamed of feeling, that we recognise most clearly the operations of his genius. Ruskin himself, though he clung to the rôle of teacher, was prepared to admit that the conclusions he reached were sometimes inconsistent; and with the strain of feminine sophistry that very often characterised him—more especially when he apprehended that unfair and uncharitable efforts were being made to pin him down—he elaborated a theory, designed to explain why he had every right, should he choose to do so, to enunciate with equal zest two conflicting propositions, and proceeded to support it with the evidence of Holy Writ. Than the Bible, one must perforce agree, few books appeared at first sight to contain more contradictory statements. One was enjoined to be humble and proud, violent and pacific. Yet, during the struggle which he still maintained to accept the sacred text uncritically and literally, Ruskin had noticed that, just as Mont Blanc was "set between opposite fan-shaped strata," so in the spiritual geology of the Bible "two opposite groups of texts" might enclose and uphold a central intermediate truth—an arrangement that, "while it betrays the careless, rewards the faithful reader," who, having been commanded to "*Rejoice evermore*," and subsequently instructed, "*Blessed are they that mourn*," achieves peace and certainty at last when he arrives at the central proposition: "*But and if ye suffer for righteousness sake, happy are ye.*"

With such authoritative backing, Ruskin did not hesitate to build up his critical edifice from as many opposing strata as the involutions of his argument momentarily suggested. The charge of self-contradiction was never one that vexed him, and latterly he was to declare that he meant henceforward "to put my self contradictions in short sentences and direct terms, in order to save sagacious persons the trouble of looking for them." Whatever we may think of the theory of "polygonal truth," Ruskin, it is obvious, formed at times a far more accurate impression of the nature of his own talent than most of its admirers. He believed (he had written) that he had genius, though he was "*not* clever" in the ordinary sense; but a "strong instinct," which he could not analyse, urged him to draw and describe, to assimilate into his own substance, the things he loved and valued. Thus his prose-style is living and captivating so long as he is content to record his "progressions of discovery," variations of feeling and "oscillations of temper"— for his immediate response, whether to a work of art or to a landscape, is always refreshing, if at times misleading—but loses its freshness when he endeavours to produce a system in which varying and contradictory moods are to be unified and reconciled. His next major work, the three concluding volumes of *Modern Painters* (on the first of which he had already embarked as soon as he reached Vevay), was destined to illustrate both aspects of Ruskin's literary temperament. The opening chapters are alike prosaic and pedantic. Lengthily and unprofitably the critic debates with the spectre of Sir Joshua Reynolds; heavy are the sarcasms with which he overwhelms it; and to little purpose does he consider and reconsider the essential qualities of the "Grand Style." Not that Ruskin's criticism, whatever subject he is discussing, lacks many brilliant flashes; but the flashes are usually unrelated, while the examples of his own taste with which he points his thesis (and which include an admiring preference for "Hunt's great poetical picture of the Light of the World")[1] are frequently perplexing. Yet, only a page or two before his eulogy of Hunt, he has devoted a long, characteristic and splendid passage to the magnificent but wholly un-Christian visions of Paolo Veronese (representative of a period in Venetian art that he had chosen elsewhere to stigmatise as morally corrupt and pictorially decadent) and leaves the ground with a triumphant sweep, casting behind in his flight the lingering traces of pedantry and prepossession, transported by the remembered enjoyment of some gigantic sunny masterpiece.

Here he is attempting to share his pleasure—perhaps for no better reason than that to share or communicate any delight is almost always to increase it. Ruskin's was a naturally withdrawn spirit; yet like many lonely and self-centred men, he never ceased to hanker after that easy, spontaneous communion with his fellow human beings from which his character and upbringing inevitably debarred him. Two factors, as the years went by, tended to encourage his prophetic tendency and to weaken the harmonising influence that might, in happier circumstances, have been exerted by the artist. There was the sense of frustration which he experienced when he observed the complete failure of his efforts to bridge the gulf between himself and mankind: people read and applauded his books, but he remained as solitary as ever, while the world was

[1]In a pamphlet published during the year 1856, however, Ruskin observed that, although "no one could sympathise more with the general feeling in it," he could not have praised Hunt's composition "unless it had been accompanied with perfectly good nettle painting. . . ."

growing visibly an uglier, more unhappy place. And there was the sense of personal unworthiness which made him doubt whether he had any right to enjoy, and caused him to suspect every form of enjoyment until he had proved, at least to his own satisfaction, that it was ultimately derived from his appreciation of a moral truth. In writing alone did these conflicting aspects of his nature—the proud and the humble, the receptively sensuous and the aggressively didactic—find a brief appeasement. He began to write on a surge of enthusiasm; and the conception of a new book was usually prefaced by a glow of moral well-being. Doubt deserted him, and guilt released its hold. The sense of inherited superiority which had been his when he was a child at Denmark Hill came comfortably flooding back.

Thus, during the summer of 1854, at the moment of picking up the intricate thread, dropped ten years earlier, which was to lead at last to the conclusion of *Modern Painters* in 1860, Ruskin confessed to having received his "third call from God," the first having apparently occurred in 1841 when he discovered that he was destined to survive the disappointment of his love for Adèle Domecq, the second, it would seem, in 1845, again after a nervous illness, when a conviction that his prayers were answered suddenly descended on him. Each was the sign of a crisis surmounted. Now, as he climbed above Interlaken, reached the "pure green pasture of the upper mountains" and saw "the Jungfrau and the two Eigers . . . clear and soft in the intense mountain light," while a "field of silver cloud filled the valley above the lake of Brienz," he "stood long, praying that these happy hours and holy sights might be of more use to me than they have been, and might be remembered by me in hours of temptation or mortification." The "call," however, which came, he tells us, "in answer to much distressful prayer," was not heard till July 2nd, the third Sunday after Trinity. It left him strengthened and uplifted. He was (he wrote from Sallenches on August 13th) "stronger in health, higher in hope, deeper in peace, than I have been for years . . . I cannot be thankful enough, nor happy enough." The mood of spiritual illumination in which every day he seemed to "see further into nature, and into myself—and into futurity," continued to support him throughout the summer months, and was reflected by a letter written to his friend Lady Trevelyan on the eve of his return home: "I have got over my distress and darkness now, thank God" (he remarked), "and I am very full of plans, and promises, and hopes . . . I am rolling projects over and over in my head." These plans denoted not only an influx of fresh hope but a general change of attitude. Hitherto, though he had appeared on lecture platforms, and, with one excuse or another, had often lectured the public through the medium of the printed word, he had had little experience of a life of action and had remained always at a cautious distance from the world of toil and poverty. Now he determined that the standard he had held up on high must be taken down into the market-place. It was not enough to lecture and write, no matter how graceful his prose or how forceful his exposition. Like the Pre-Raphaelites, those ardent young men, he must preach the gospel of true art and spread the light of a true faith with apostolic energy, devoting his time and talents and wealth not to the edification of a leisured few but to the instruction of the vast masses of laborious mankind, of whose habits and needs and problems he was as yet but dimly cognisant.

It was a courageous, if injudicious, resolve. He wished (he informed Lady Trevelyan) "to give short lectures to about 200 at once in turn, of the sign-painters, and shop-decorators, and writing-masters, and upholsterers and masons, and brick-makers, and glass-blowers, and pottery people, and young artists, and young men in general, and school-masters, and young ladies in general, and schoolmistresses." The sign-painters and "the younger ladies" were to be taught to illuminate manuscripts in the correct medieval fashion; for—a significant point—he was anxious to produce prayer-books "all *written* again" (with a somewhat altered liturgy), thus striking a first blow at the "abominable art of printing," which, together with gunpowder, was one of the great curses of the age and "the root of all the mischief." Meanwhile he proposed to "lend out *Liber Studiorums* and Albert Dürers to everybody who wants them; and to make copies of all fine thirteenth-century manuscripts, and lend *them* out—all for nothing, of course; and to have a room where anybody can go in all day and always see *nothing* in it but what is *good* . . . and a black hole, where they shall see nothing but what is bad, filled with Claudes, and Sir Charles Barry's architecture . . ." In addition to these extensive schemes, he would like to establish a "little Academy of my own in all the manufacturing towns, and to get the young artists—Pre-Raphaelites always—to help me," besides an "Academy exhibition, an opposition shop, where all the pictures shall be hung on the line—in nice little rooms decorated in a Giottesque manner—and no bad pictures let in, and none good turned out. . . ."

Ruskin's projects, in their entirety, were never fully realised; but they formed a master-plan, subsequently enlarged, by which for several decades he was to regulate his public life. Little strongholds of enlightenment were to be set up here and there, preferably where the gloom of nineteenth-century England was heaviest and most oppressive, that is to say in the neighbourhood of the great industrial centres; and each was to be stocked with cultural ammunition, including some of the exquisite objects he had himself collected. Meanwhile, by way of a preliminary exercise, having returned to London during October, he joined the Working Men's College in Red Lion Square, which had been founded in 1851 by Frederick Denison Maurice, the Broad Churchman and celebrated social reformer, whose aim was to put some of the benefits of a higher education within the grasp of the skilled but semi-literate workman. He was followed by Rossetti, Ford Madox Brown, and a new adherent to the Pre-Raphaelite gospel, Edward Burne-Jones. Rossetti taught the life class every Thursday evening, and Ruskin held a class devoted to landscape art and elementary draughtsmanship. His audiences certainly admired and respected him, if they did not altogether understand him. During recent years, the idea of popular education had been making rapid progress. Since the relatively prosperous 'fifties had succeeded to the fierce and hungry 'forties, the wave of revolutionary feeling which culminated in the fiasco of 1848 had been replaced by the emergence of a more moderate and conciliatory spirit among the British labouring classes. Some of the subversive zeal of the early Trade Unionists had been diverted into schemes of co-operative self-help. The proletarian was to improve his status, not by direct political action, but by strenuous and patient efforts to raise his intellectual standards; and simultaneously the upper and middle classes, relieved of the apprehensions that had beset them while the revolutionary happenings of 1848 were still a fresh and painful memory, were well pleased to reach down a helping hand and assist his upward progress, provided, of course, he did not endeavour to rise too violently or hurriedly. Such a mood had produced the Working Men's College, and brought Ruskin and his Pre-Raphaelite assistants, stepping out of their dreams of a splendid medieval past, to its crowded gaslit classrooms.

Ruskin's efforts there, as he moved to and fro among his pupils—so unlike them in his soberly elegant garb, the neutral tones of the frock-coat set off by a dandified blue neck-cloth: unlike them, too, in the touch of irresponsible fantasy that he was accustomed to permit himself whenever he talked or lectured—were according to contemporary accounts equally unselfish and imaginative. How to explain something of the essential quality of great art, something of the unending beauty of the natural universe, to men exhausted by their day's work, who had been born, brought up and were to spend their lives in a labyrinthine wilderness of shabby bricks and mortar? Characteristic of Ruskin's philosophy was his belief that art was a form of language which should appeal not only to the collector and the expert, but to the whole of humanity—if humanity could be persuaded to recover its pristine clarity of hearing. One must begin with the simplest principles; but as soon as a small start had been made—

for example, by interesting a sign-painter in thirteenth-century manuscripts, or teaching a journeyman stone-cutter to distinguish between good and bad detail—the movement might surely spread, till the artisans of Leeds and Liverpool were voicing their demands for Turners and Albert Dürers (readily supplied from Denmark Hill) and the inhabitants of London filing quietly and reverently through a succession of "nice little rooms decorated in a Giottesque manner" and hung with the finest examples of modern English painting. What was needed was the initial impetus; nor did Ruskin, during the mid-fifties, seem seriously to have doubted that he could at length supply it. He had the knowledge: he had the material. And, a somewhat erratic *genie*, every week, month after month, he flitted down to Red Lion Square, his arms heaped with books and prints or precious mineral specimens, which he dispersed among his class, looking hopefully, if now and then a trifle wistfully, for the smallest sign of interest.

Sometimes the trophy would be a case of "West Indian birds unstuffed . . . all rubies and emerald," introduced so that his students might learn to despair of imitating natural colour; and sometimes he exhibited a Gothic missal and set them to counting the leaves in different sprays of foliage. For promising pupils he brought separate gifts: on one desk he would place a cairngorm pebble or fluor-spar in a tumbler of water, bidding his *protégé* "trace their tangled veins of crimson and amethyst"; while "lichen and fungi from Anerley Woods" were carefully chosen and picked for the edification of another. He would go to endless pains correcting sketches, and point out as he did so how and why the tree or rock that they were assumed to represent had acquired such and such a shape or leaned at such an angle. His lectures made an immediate impression: "formless and planless as they were" (we are told), "the effect on the hearers was immense. It was a wonderful bubbling up of all manner of glowing thoughts. . . ." With the men he grew "wildly popular"; and this was the more surprising since Ruskin, whose attitude towards the working-class was distinctly patriarchal, revealed himself as a severe critic of egalitarian theories. So his friends (he remarked to the assembled students) were "all agape . . . for this mighty privilege of having your opinions represented in Parliament? The concession might be desirable . . . if only it were quite certain you had got any opinions to represent. But have you? Are you agreed on anything you systematically want? Less work and more wages, of course; but how much lessening of work do you suppose is possible? . . . Have you planned the permanent state which you wish England to hold? Do you want her to be nothing but a large workshop and forge? . . . or would you like to keep some of your lords and landed gentry still, and a few green fields and trees? . . . Your voices are not worth a rat's squeak . . . till you have some ideas to utter with them."

In his political, as in his æsthetic, views, Ruskin had all the qualities, and some of the demerits, of the intellectual free-lance. Yet this most independent of theorists was also the dutiful son who, when his lecture was finished, must step into the carriage that would take him back to Denmark Hill, where his mother and father engrossed his affection and the haven that sheltered his childhood had been securely re-established. His own house had naturally been given up. He was home again, with the only two human beings of whose love he felt entirely sure, towards whom his allegiance —he was still convinced—could never change or waver. They exulted openly over their recaptured son; and old James Ruskin, whose discretion, once the interests of the family were involved, had at no time been conspicuous, declared to casual acquaintances that Effie was a wicked and designing woman, and had deliberately ensnared John (who "might have married a French Countess") adding in his characteristic style: "Never mind, we shall have to pay for it, and we shall at least have John all to ourselves." It was true, as regards his external life. In spirit (one may conjecture) he had never really left home: Effie, at first an absorbing passion, then a source of shame and disappointment, in the latter period of their relation a mere irritating obstacle, had now vanished like a drawing erased, a page torn from a note-book. Her fatal face would seem to have been wholly forgotten; and, although as long as he lived he continued to preserve the passionate letters she had inspired during their engagement,[1] it may be that he had already invented, and had begun to accept, the comforting legend that at no stage of their intercourse had he ever truly loved her.

The lover, for the moment, was banished or imprisoned. Instead, his friends visiting Denmark Hill saw a perfect son whom the old people had contrived to form, if not in their own image, certainly to their own satisfaction, for their own delight and credit. His background was by now luxurious: the large house was full of well-trained servants, carefully educated in their duties under Mrs. Ruskin's supervision, its walls "glittering with pictures, chiefly Turners," which the critic had chosen and the sherry-merchant paid for. Mr. Ruskin impressed a visitor as a very "fine old gentleman," with a comfortable manner, "a lot of bushy grey hair, and eyebrows sticking up all rough . . ." and a habit of singing John's praises heartily and loudly. As for Mrs. Ruskin, she was a "ruddy, dignified, richly-dressed old gentlewoman"—clearly a "*good* old lady, with the *Christian Treasury* tossing about on the table"—who held strong personal opinions and, much as she adored her offspring, sometimes contradicted him. Ruskin (noted the visitor) received "all her opinions with a soft reverence and gentleness that is pleasant to witness. . . ." In the lecture room, or anywhere away from home, Ruskin could be, and indeed very often was, both abrupt and contradictious. But with his mother and father he was an entirely different being; and his admirer was pleased to remark a "spiritual sweetness in the half-timid expression of his eyes. . . ."

There was nothing timid, however, in the enthusiasm with which he showed and explained and rearranged his pictures. He was constantly running up to his study to fetch a print or water-colour, removing a Turner from a

[1]An interesting account of how these letters were discovered in 1931 beneath the floorboards of the Brantwood dining-room was printed, on January 14th 1948, in the London *Evening News*.

Coast Scene near Dunbar by John Ruskin, 1857

distant wall and putting it in the visitor's hands; "and so he kept on gliding all over the house, hanging and unhanging," pausing now and then to talk with the same infectious eagerness. No man could have appeared livelier, none more fully occupied. His activities were varied and incessant; they increased as he advanced through middle age, becoming at length so uncommonly numerous that in a study of modest length it is almost impossible to chart them. Between 1854 and 1860, besides lecturing at the Working Men's College and completing *Modern Painters* (for which he himself executed many highly-finished drawings), he wrote a regular series of *Academy Notes* (which made and unmade the reputations of rising British artists, and usually contained some judicious reference to Millais' latest products), was concerned in an advisory capacity with the erection of the new Museum at Oxford, and, as Turner's executor, arranged and catalogued the immense accumulation of sketches which, after the old painter's death on December 19th, 1851, had been discovered stacked up in his London house. The extinction of his "earthly Master" had been for Ruskin a less severe blow than he had at first expected. He was (he told his father, who had sent the news to Venice) "perhaps more relieved than distressed by it—though saddened. It will not affect my health, nor alter my arrangements." He had deplored Turner's ultimate period, and, dispensing with regrets for the dead, he now set to work to preserve that part of the great man's achievement which he believed to be immortal. It was by no means an easy task. Under the terms of a singularly perplexing will, Turner had appointed Ruskin one of his executors, bequeathed subject to conditions never subsequently honoured a vast hoard of pictures and drawings to the nation, and left much of the remainder of his property to establish a charitable institution for poor and aged artists. Legal proceedings followed his death; and not until 1856 was Ruskin allowed to begin putting the master's scattered remains into intelligible order.[1] By the time he had examined

[1]There appears to be no basis for the story that Ruskin destroyed some of Turner's sketches of tavern and brothel scenes.

and sorted some nineteen thousand sketches, he seemed to experience (as he confided to his diary) ominous symptoms of an impending nervous breakdown.

Yet the danger passed. There was, at least, no serious interruption in the stream of his activities. He continued to lecture and gather his lectures into volumes; a course delivered at Manchester, for example, was printed as *The Political Economy of Art* (presently renamed *A Joy for Ever and its Price in the Market*), concerning which he afterwards observed that it was "not very dull, and of all the books I have written . . . the only one I'm proud of." Then his missionary spirit fastened upon architectural questions. Oxford was to have a scientific museum; his friend Acland had originally launched the scheme in 1847, and by 1854 it had received the approval of the University authorities. The problem of finding an appropriate style for this important edifice provoked, in Oxford and elsewhere, a resounding controversial hubbub. At the turn of the century such arguments were numerous and impassioned. Its architecture expresses the pride of a race; and, far ahead of their commercial competitors, growing every day both in material stability and a sense of moral dignity, the mid-Victorians felt an intense concern, if not always with the interior design of their buildings or the inward structure of society, at least with the imposing *façade* presented to an onlooker. Should the *façade* be Gothic or Classical? Thus, from 1857 onwards, the submission of plans for a new Foreign Office was to arouse tremendous interest. Gilbert Scott prevailed with a Gothic plan; but Lord Palmerston, who had suddenly returned to power, in his "light, airy and cheerful style" dismissed Scott's romantic project as dark and Jesuitical; at which the *Daily Telegraph* loudly rejoiced over the presumed discomfiture of Mr. Ruskin, "that architectural imperator," and the check administered to "mitre and crozier architects who would convert a public office into a sanctuary loaded with carvings and brasswork, lit by fantastic windows, and expensive without being commodious." But at Oxford Gothic had triumphed after a long and strenuous campaign

—" Veronese Gothic of the best and manliest type, in a new and striking combination," as Acland's biographer enthusiastically described it. Ruskin was delighted with his friend's success, of which he learned by telegram. He was " going to thank God for it and lie down to sleep " (he wrote at once to Acland). " The museum in your hands . . . will be the root of as much good to others as I suppose it is rational for any single living soul to hope to do in its earth-time." Corresponding so accurately to Ruskin's own peculiar blend of interests, and symbolising (as it might certainly be taken to do) the harmonious fusion of the modern and the ancient worlds, the idea of a scientific museum housed in a Gothic shell was bound to captivate and hold him. Here, surely, were glimmerings of a real Renaissance? In defiance of cold Palladian precepts, of the soulless uniformity and depressing symmetry of neo-classic architecture, the Museum should be a monument to man at his most spiritual, and a testimony, by the grace of God, to his communal creative efforts. It was to be the masterpiece of a band of happy labourers, working together upon a single selfless impulse, blithe and pure of heart, like the cathedral-builders of the Middle Ages.

This happy band was recruited from Ireland, where they had previously been employed by the architect Benjamin Woodward about the decoration of the new engineering school of Trinity College, Dublin, a building in the Venetian-Byzantine style, of which Ruskin was to declare that it had given him, for the first time, the joy of seeing his æsthetic principles carried into practice. All good design (Ruskin was fond of repeating) must be based upon Organic Form, upon the close and reverent observation of the natural world around us—a precept of particular value to architectural masons, for whose benefit he elaborated his convictions in one of the public addresses collected in *The Two Paths*:

> " From visions of angels (he exclaimed with a characteristic surge of wide and gusty eloquence) down to the least important gesture of a child at play, whatever may be conceived of Divine, or beheld of Human, may be

dared or adopted by you; throughout the kingdom of animal life, no creature is so vast, or so minute, that you cannot deal with it, or bring it into service; the lion and the crocodile will couch about your shafts; the moth and the bee will sun themselves upon your flowers; for you, the fawn will leap; for you, the snail be slow; for you the dove smooth her bosom, and the hawk spread her wings toward the south. All the wide world of vegetation blooms and bends for you; the leaves tremble that you may bid them be still under the marble snow; the thorn and the thistle . . . are to you the kindliest servants. . . ."

Ruskin's dream had been partially realised in the ornamentation of the school that Woodward—soon one of his "truest and most loving friends," and "one of the most earnest souls that ever gave itself to the arts"—planned and executed for Trinity College. Glowing "eyes of coloured stone" were inset in the fabric; and the edifice was further embellished by the addition of "numberless capitals delicately carved over" (a contemporary admirer noted) "with holly leaves, shamrocks, various flowers, birds, and so on." Dublin having set the example, Oxford must not be backward; and Ruskin decided that he would endeavour to enlist the support of the more prominent Pre-Raphaelites. Why not Millais as well as the others? He hoped (he told Acland) "to be able to get Millais and Rossetti to design flower and beast borders—crocodiles and various vermin—such as you are particularly fond of . . . and we will carve and inlay them with Cornish serpentine all about your windows . . . *such* capitals as we will have!" Millais—rather unexpectedly, since as a general rule he failed to recognise the fine distinction Ruskin drew between the public and the private life—would appear to have produced a design of field-mice nibbling wheat-ears; but Rossetti, notwithstanding his brilliant gifts an idle and procrastinatory personage, was of no help to Woodward's assistants, though his protégée Elizabeth Siddal, made "some lovely designs," one of which was carried out

—"an angel with some children and all manner of other things. . . ." Ruskin himself designed a variety of details, including a whole ogival window, and by his own unaided efforts constructed an entire brickwork column. He was at the time staying near Oxford, "in a farmhouse in the middle of a field," surrounded by a garden full of gooseberries and orange lilies; and, with Acland as his tutor, he had started to learn bricklaying; for "half my power" (he wrote) "of ascertaining facts of any kind connected with the arts, is in my stern habit of doing the thing with my own hands till I know its difficulty."

In this respect—as indeed in most respects—he differed from Rossetti, who, having visited Oxford during the summer of 1857 to inspect the new Museum, was so deeply impressed by the architectural charm of another of Woodward's achievements, the new Union building, that he offered to decorate the interior of the Debating Hall (nowadays the Library) and without more ado enlisted the services of seven friends, among them William Morris and Edward Burne-Jones, all more or less PreRaphaelite, all brimming over with the love of art and devotion to the Middle Ages. The story, often told, of their heroic but futile labours is equally saddening and diverting. Damp bricks, thinly distempered, declined to accept the vivid incrustation of paint with which Pre-Raphaelite brushes strove to overlay them. The eight young artists had none of Ruskin's grasp of the practical difficulties inherent in every real creative problem; and their dream-like projection of the *Morte d'Arthur* faded like a dream, as swiftly and inconsequently. Meanwhile the Venetian Gothic Union building, and the hushed streets of summer-time Oxford, resounded to their merriment. "What fun we had!" (one of them remembered) "What jokes! What roars of laughter!" Ruskin was appreciative, but a little dubious. He admired the Pre-Raphaelite zeal: he never quite learned to participate in the Pre-Raphaelite sense of humour, which ran to nicknames and preposterous buffooneries, and led them to diversify a serious composition by slipping in, as the fancy took them, a caricature of Morris or a playful sketch of Rossetti's favourite animal, the "obtuse and furry" wombat. "You know" (he complained to William Rossetti), "the fact is they're all the least bit crazy, and it's very difficult to manage them." Meanwhile the Museum arose; and there, too, some of the artists concerned proved incapable of management. The Irish masons, headed by two brothers named O'Shea, both handsome and both red-bearded, were genial and sympathetic but excessively temperamental. From the Botanic Garden they would bring bouquets of flowers and foliage which they translated into sculpture, thus exemplifying Ruskin's doctrine of Organic Form at its purest and correctest; but, perhaps under the spell of Ruskin's evening addresses delivered at the workmen's institute, they also launched into the animal kingdom, and disturbed Members of Convocation by portraying parrots, owls and monkeys. "The unnecessary introduction of cats" was observed by University critics, and voted frivolous and scandalous. O'Shea would rush into Acland's house, half demented with Hibernian choler, having been discovered in the production of monkeys and ordered from his scaffold by some angrily squeaking don.

Yet the project continued to develop—not as Thebes grew to the sound of Amphion's lyre, but encouraged at every stage by the circulation of Ruskin's quickening influence. He counselled; he admonished; he gave without stint of his interest, time and money. Between 1855 and 1859, the vision he shared with Acland and Woodward gradually materialised. Over the main entry of this shrine of learning, an angel displayed in his right hand the open Book of Nature, while in his left he supported a cluster of "three living cells," symbolic (it was understood) of Life's mysterious origins. Within an imposing quadrangular hall, columns of cast iron soared up towards the glass roof, bursting, as they completed their ascent, into a wealth of wrought-iron foliage. Organic Form again predominated; arching over the student's head were spandrels twisted into the shape of interwoven forest-boughs; the angularity of brackets and girders was softened by the profusion of leaves and blossoms and fruit that had somehow curled among them. Here were the elm, the holly, the briar, the passion-flower and the water-lily. In the main court, with its double arcade, polished shafts of stone (chosen by the Professor of Geology as representative specimens of the principal British rocks) had capitals and bases enwreathed with the forms of numerous plants and animals, disposed in a manner at once æsthetically pleasing and scientifically enlightening.

A year before the completion of the Museum, Ruskin's efforts were rewarded by an Honorary Studentship at Christ Church. It was an acknowledgement that pleased him much; and in 1859, when the new building was finally opened to the public, he helped to prepare an explanatory booklet entitled *The Oxford Museum*, in which he himself defended its Gothic plan and elucidated the system adopted by its decorators. A notable task nobly performed. And yet—across the happiness that he felt, or that he should have felt, there crept a lengthening shadow. The intention had been good, the execution honest. He had been stimulated by the task on hand: now that it was finished and he could at last stand back, so sensitive a lover of the best in art must needs admit that the Oxford Museum, as it had risen, was not entirely beautiful. He did not see it, let us piously suppose, even for a second of horrible illumination, in all its true alarming ugliness. But he was obliged to confess—after Woodward's early death of consumption in 1861—that the building had, from some points of view, "failed signally of being what he hoped." Somehow the plan had miscarried; a malicious spirit was abroad—the spirit of an age he hated and despised and feared—which came always between himself and the satisfaction that he coveted. At its touch the flowers and fruit he had designed, losing their virginal freshness, shrivelled into curlicues of tormented cast-iron: a chemical laboratory in the shape of an abbot's kitchen seemed unsuitable and awkward: his visionary fabric shed its lustrous antique patina and was revealed, beneath one of those lowering skies that often weigh on Oxford, as a mere pretentious accumulation of livid modern masonry.

Dissatisfied he may have been: he was still by no means desperate. His letters written at this period are full of hope and energy, and reflect both the breadth of his interests and the immense variety of his acquaintances. To some correspondents he was the admiring disciple, to others a kindly and understanding patron. Ruskin, though during his early manhood he had shown touches of misanthropy, in middle life usually impressed those who encountered him for the first time as the most benevolent of great writers. He was simple, charming and affectionate. Thus, in 1853, we find him engaged in lengthy correspondence with a young Scottish architect named J. J. Laing, afterwards promoted to be his private copyist, advising him not only on his artistic ambitions but on his moral problems. A little later, he had begun to interest himself in the fortunes of Miss Elizabeth Eleanor Siddal, the exquisite and mysterious virgin whom, at the age of eighteen, while she was working in a milliner's shop, the Pre-Raphaelite Brotherhood had collectively discovered, but whom Rossetti had since elected as his own especial *inspiratrice*. So wholeheartedly did the friends adopt her that besides attempting again and again to imprison her remote and fascinating beauty on the surface of their canvases they allotted her a Pre-Raphaelite pet name, hesitating first at "The Sid," advancing to "Liz" or "Lizzie," finally handing her down to posterity under the endearing style of "Guggums." Ruskin, however, with his usual mistrust of Pre-Raphaelite whimsies, when their increasing friendship authorised a familiar approach, was content to call her "Ida," with reference presumably to Tennyson's *Princess*. She was "beautiful" (he declared) "as the reflection of a golden mountain in a crystal lake." She was also ill and poor and despondent, a frigid, silent, unsmiling creature, whom not all Rossetti's romantic enthusiasm could impregnate with warmth and energy. No doubt she was silent because she had little to say: it was not impossible that her extreme passivity which fascinated the Pre-Raphaelites—themselves, in spite of their other-worldly preoccupations, so sanguine and so boisterous—sprang from an almost complete lack of any genuine feelings. Yet there was about her an air of unearthliness that Ruskin, whose experience of earthly love had been peculiarly ill-starred, found more refreshing, more stimulating than the ordinary sensual radiance. He did not fall in love; but it is clear that the ethereal Ida, the incomparable Liz, the wonderful and lovely Guggums, moved and interested him deeply: with the result that as her health grew gradually worse—she was believed to be consumptive—he abounded in helpful suggestions and delicately kind attentions, praising her poems, purchasing her drawings—for she vaguely dabbled in the arts under Dante Gabriel's influence—and imploring that she would become his pensioner until her health recovered. "Perhaps" (he wrote) "I have said too much of my wish to do this for Rossetti's sake. But, if you do not choose to be helped for his sake, consider also that the plain *hard fact* is that I think you have genius; that I don't think there is much genius in the world; and I want to keep what there is, in it . . . Utterly irrespective of Rossetti's feelings or my own, I should simply do what I do, if I could, as I should try to save a beautiful tree from being cut down, or a bit of a Gothic cathedral whose strength was failing. If you would be so good as to consider yourself as a piece of wood or Gothic for a few months, I should be grateful to you. If you will not, it shall not be." Prevailed on to accept her admirer's help, Elizabeth Siddal survived and at length became Rosetti's wife—after a protracted and unhappy engagement during which Rossetti had learnt to take his pleasures elsewhere, with the elephantine Fanny Cornforth and other model-mistresses—dying in 1862, it was rumoured, by her own hand.

This friendship may have been tinged with love; but Ruskin's relationship with Rossetti was founded on a solid basis of loyalty and admiration. He was loyal, that is to say, to his conception of the painter's genius; and, since the genius was more important than the man, towards Rossetti himself he often adopted the attitude of a well-intentioned task-master, concerned to goad or wheedle the recalcitrant artist along the path of duty. If Ruskin were to put up the funds, could Rossetti be " ready on Wednesday morning to take a run into Wales, and make me a sketch of some rocks in the bed of a stream, with trees above, mountain ashes, and so on, scarlet in autumn tints? If you are later than Wednesday, you will be too late. . . ." Rossetti declined or delayed, only to return to the attack on Ruskin's pocket-book with an alternative proposal. He was unlucky. " You are a *very* odd creature, that's a fact," his patron somewhat wryly commented. " I said I would find funds for you to go into Wales to draw something I wanted. I never said I would for you to go to Paris, to disturb yourself and other people, and I won't. To-morrow (D.V.) I will bring you Ida's money—about half-past two to four. . . ." On such occasions he was prompt in refusal. Nor did he hesitate, if a drawing or painting displeased him, to send it back, as a coat is returned to the tailor's, for immediate alteration.[1] Rossetti was to " take all the pure green out of the flesh in the *Nativity* . . . and try to make it a little less worsted-work by Wednesday." He was to pack his drawings with appropriate care, between sheets of " *smoothest* possible " paper and multiple layers of brown paper, wood and cardboard, address the completed package to his patron in the country, and finally " take it to London Bridge station yourself and be sure to say it is to go by fast train." Shrewdly suspicious of Rossetti's personal habits, Ruskin begged that he would endeavour to keep his room tidy and go to bed at reasonable hours. Alas, to the other's exacting idealism Rossetti continued to oppose a hard-wearing southern cynicism. Ruskin was a convenient provider of " tin," but in questions of art (he sometimes confided to his fellow Pre-Raphaelites) little better than half-educated . . .[2]

[1]These revisions did not always please. " I don't at all like my picture now; the alteration of the head from the stoop forward to the throw back makes the whole picture quite stiff and stupid. . . ." Ruskin to Rossetti, ?1857.

[2]Ruskin, on the other hand, continued to uphold the superiority of a critic's judgement. " You are a conceited monkey, thinking your pictures right when I tell you positively they are wrong . . . You'll find out in six months what an absurdity that ' St. Catherine ' is." Ruskin to Rossetti, ?1857.

Towards the work of other contemporary artists, Ruskin's method of approach was no less paternal and proprietary. He was determined that they should do their best not for him alone but for the world at large, or rather, for himself, not as a patron and collector, but for Ruskin the chosen representative of certain lofty ideals. Thus, during the course of preparing his *Academy Notes*, he had paid special attention to a meticulously accurate panorama of the Surrey downs, entitled *The Stone-breaker*, by John Brett. " In some points " (he announced joyfully) " it goes beyond anything that the Pre-Raphaelites have done . . . I know no such thistledown, no such chalk hills and elm trees, no such natural pieces of faraway cloud, in any of their work . . . It is a marvellous picture, and may be examined inch by inch with delight; though nearly the last stone I should have ever thought of any one's sitting down to paint would have been a chalk flint. If he can make so much of that, what will Mr. Brett not make of mica, slate and gneiss! If he can paint so lovely a distance from the Surrey downs . . . what would he not make of the chestnut groves of the Val d'Aosta! " By 1858 his aspiration had been realised. Packed off abroad under Ruskin's guidance, Brett had embarked on his *Val d'Aosta*, a large, ambitious landscape of the most realistic type, which Millais styled " a wretched work " and Ruskin warmly praised. But Brett, too, was difficult and moody. Like Rossetti, and like J. W. Inchbold, whom Ruskin befriended at the same time, he required constant supervision and much keen but friendly criticism; and, during a holiday round about Switzerland and Italy in 1858, Ruskin laboured indefatigably to keep him to the right track. Inchbold, his travelling companion for a part of the way, had " got entirely off the rails at Chamouni " and his drawing of cottages were failures. To save Brett from a similar catastrophe, he summoned him to Turin. " I sent for him " (he told his father) " because I didn't like what he said in his letter about his present work, and thought he wanted some lecturing . . . He is much tougher and stronger than Inchbold and takes more hammering; but I think he looks more miserable every day, and have good hopes of making him completely wretched in a day or two more. . . ." The sequel came when they had both returned to England, and Brett ventured to dispute some statement made by the older man upon a scientific subject. He asserted that Ruskin was talking "bosh"; at which Ruskin called him a fool, and he incontinently stormed out.

Ruskin's paternal reproofs, however, were not reserved for young and dependent or comparatively little-known artists. The celebrated also received their share; and to the authoress of *Aurora Leigh* (whose latest work, as he told her husband, he considered "the greatest *poem* in the English language, unsurpassed by anything but Shakespeare—*not* surpassed by Shakespeare's *sonnets*") he had no hesitation in pointing out a number of "sharp blemishes." The Brownings, who had first encountered Ruskin during a visit to London in 1852, and who found him "gracious and generous," and "very gentle, yet earnest," were delighted by his praise and took his criticisms with good humour. They, too, reverenced the Middle Ages; and it was no doubt gratifying to learn that, among his other efforts to revive the lost art of illumination, Ruskin had instructed a skilled workman, "who had recovered thoroughly the art of laying on the gold," to copy "the beginning of the Caterina to Camoens, which, on the whole, is my favourite" and which he meant to make "one of the most glorious little burning books that ever had leaf turned by white finger." Before long they had joined the ranks of his favoured correspondents. To them, as to Henry Acland and to the American scholar, Charles Eliot Norton, who had arrived at Denmark Hill with a letter of introduction in 1855, he wrote a long series of letters, full of detailed self-analysis, chronicling his changes of mood, describing his hopes and his disappointments, defining—or attempting to define—both the nature of his artistic talent and the intricacies of his personal character. As his fortieth year approached, a note of dissatisfaction grew more and more insistent. Yes, he was busy, and supposed that he could lay claim to a certain sort of usefulness. "... I'm truly benevolent, miserably benevolent"; yet, as he had admitted earlier, "I find trying to be of use to people the most wearying thing possible." Elsewhere he had suggested that he wrote with little effort; but now writing had become a vexatious task, "for I never write with pleasure to myself—nor with purpose of getting praise to myself—I hate writing . . . but I write to tell truths which I can't help crying out about—and I *do* enjoy being believed and being of use." Was he of real and lasting use though?—it was a question that often returned—and how was his duty towards his neighbour to be reconciled with the duty that he felt that he owed himself? Would it not be better to "bolt one's gates, lie on the grass all day, take care not to eat too much dinner, and buy as many Turners as one could afford"? Artists of genius were a troublesome race. He had known five of them—Turner, Watts, Millais, Rossetti and now the lovely wayward Ida—"and I don't know which was, or which is, wrongheadedest. I am with them like the old woman who lived in the shoe, only I don't want to send them to bed, and can't whip them. . . ." As for the ordinary breed of mankind—it was sometimes more than he could do, to believe that they were destined for the personal immortality that the Christian scriptures promised. "As I read the Bible my main result in way of belief is that those people are to be exalted in eternity who in this life have striven to do God's will, not their own. And so very few people appear to me to do this in reality that I don't know what to believe—the truth as far as I can make it out seems too terrible to be the truth." At moments he was inclined to give up the struggle. Surely (he wrote to the Brownings in January, 1859) "people were never meant to be always howling and bawling the right road to a generation of drunken cabmen. . . . I hope to get just one more howl executed, from which I hope great effects—upon the Moon—and then, see if I don't take to Kennel and Straw, comfortably. . . ."

Thus the fourth decade of Ruskin's life, in its middle years a period of hope and vitality, suffered as it drew towards its close a gradual overclouding. All the obvious benefits of maturity seemed somehow to have escaped him: he combined the extreme sensitiveness of youth with the disillusionment of middle age. Nearly forty years in the world had failed to teach him stoicism: he was still shocked by the world's ingratitude, astonished by the repeated evidences of human perversity and idiocy: yet even when his fellow human beings most disappointed and disgusted him, and he longed to lose himself in the placid contemplation of rocks and trees and flowers, among which he moved with the assurance of a lover and a master, some trait of human beauty would bring him quickly swerving back. Often he had wished it were otherwise, and that he could devote all his attention to natural history and landscape; "but men" (he lamented to Elizabeth Browning) "are too beautiful and too wicked—the moment I begin to draw them . . . I care for nothing else; a girl's hair and lips are lovelier than all clouds; a man's forehead grander than all rocks. If I begin to think and write about the creatures, I get miserable and enraged. If I don't, I feel like a baby and a brute." Now and then he was content to observe. In Turin, for example, where his personal habits, after a long spell of rustication, became modestly luxurious and he confessed to "much contentment in a large room . . . a note or two of band, a Parisian dinner, and half a pint of Moet's champagne," he had been fascinated by the "daring treatment" which a young Italian woman imposed upon her braids and bonnet, fastening her hair "with a golden pin, with a ball of chased gold nearly an inch in diameter, thrusting the pin right through the bonnet and so nailing it to her hair; of course the imagination went straight to her hair, and the bonnet went for nothing"; while, in the same city (he wrote to inform his father) "one of the finest things I saw . . . was a group of neglected children at play on a heap of sand—one girl of about ten, with her black hair over her eyes and half-naked, bare-limbed to above the knees, and beautifully limbed, lying on the sand like a snake; an older one did something to offend her, and she rose with a spring and a shriek like a young eaglet's. . . . I don't, of course, think it proper for girls to lie bare-legged on heaps of sand, or to shriek when they are displeased; but it was picturesque if not pleasing. . . ." Reading this passage, which occurs in a letter of September, 1858, one remembers the vagrant children whom he had examined with a mixture of attraction and repulsion as they sprawled around St. Mark's porch. Strange how some of his vividest impressions proved most difficult to reconcile with belief in any moral order. Stranger still that he should be obliged to confess that "whenever I work selfishly—buy pictures that I like, stay in places that I like, study what I like, and so on—I am happy and well; but when I deny myself, and give all my money away, and work at what seems useful, I get miserable and unwell. The things I most regret in all my past life are great pieces of virtuous and quite heroical self-denial; which have issued in all kinds of catastrophe and disappointment, instead of victory. Everything that has turned out well I've done merely to please myself, and it upsets all one's moral principles. Mine are going I don't know where."

Ruskin's perplexity was deep and genuine: his despondency, as it turned out, to a large extent unwarranted. Although the moral principles on which, when he first adventured into adult life, he believed he had so firm a grasp, again and again during middle age seemed to be crumbling and vanishing, they were too deep-rooted, too much a part of his constitution, ever to fall away completely. At times he might question their value: he could not disregard them. And yet, loving the world as he did, sensitive as he was to the surface beauty of existence—to the turn of a young woman's head, the exquisite half-conscious skill with which she pinned her bonnet, to the bare sunburned limbs of a beggar-girl reclined across a sand-heap—he was perpetually tempted in another direction, importuned by glimpses of a forbidden earthly paradise where happiness was its own justification and the senses their own reward. The resultant conflict is hinted at in a succession of strange photographs which record his likeness at this period. The mobility of youth has quite deserted his face; while the contrast which an Edinburgh journalist had noted in 1853 between its upper and lower halves has become increasingly portentous. The blue eyes are still magnetic; but the mouth and chin, which his Scottish critic had observed to be " somewhat wanting in sustained dignity and strength," appear to have dissociated themselves from the more impressive, more masculine and better-balanced features by which they are surmounted. " I can't conceive why I'm so ugly, but I *am* so ugly. . . ." Ruskin was to lament to Mrs. Browning, who had asked him to send her his portrait in 1861. Such ugliness, however, as distinguishes these photographs is confined to the weak lower lip and to the slightly receding jaw. Whereas the eyes are beautiful and alert, alive with restless query, sliding up at the challenge of existence from beneath down-drawn sandy eyebrows, the mouth is markedly loose and relaxed: indecisive and unhappy, it is also somewhat peevish.

VI

HAD RUSKIN been by temperament more cynical or more sensual, the problems that beset him might have been resolved, or thrust aside, very much more easily. Had his outlook been narrower and his disposition colder, he might have taken refuge, like many of his contemporaries, in a stern unbending puritanism. But although by training he was a puritan, he could never reconcile himself to that deliberate limitation of sensibility which a puritan creed demands from the lover of art and nature. His eyes were among his greatest assets; and, the most seeing of men, he could never learn to close them. How often did the harvest of sight prove to be full of strange and dangerous treasure-trove! For alas, though ugliness was always wicked, wickedness (or what he would have preferred to consider such) was by no means always ugly. Nor was virtue (or what he wished to esteem as virtue) invariably attractive. Thus, one day, at Turin, sitting in a Protestant chapel, listening to a very dull and ill-conducted service, he had been horrified by the contrast between the " little squeaking idiot " who occupied the pulpit, presiding over a congregation which consisted of " seventeen old women and three louts," and the majestic Venetian artist, Paolo Veronese, whose radiant *Queen of Sheba* he had spent the previous day examining. He loved its humanity; he adored its sensuous warmth. " Paolo's as full of mischief as an egg is full of meat " (he had written to Norton in November, 1858)—" always up to some dodge or other—just like Tintoretto. In his Solomon receiving the Queen of Sheba, one of the golden lions of the Throne is put into full light, and a falconer underneath holds a white falcon, as white as snow, just under the lion, so as to carry Solomon on the lion and eagle . . .; the Queen's fainting, but her dog isn't,—a little King Charles spaniel, about seven inches high,—thinks it shocking his mistress should faint, stands in front of her on all his four legs apart, snarling at Solomon . . .; Solomon all but drops his sceptre, stooping forward eagerly to get the Queen helped up—such a beautiful fellow, all crisped golden short hair over his head and the fine Arabian arched brow—and I believe after all you'll find the subtlest and grandest *expression* going is hidden under the gold and purple of those vagabonds of Venetians."

Must he try to convince himself, then, that " this mighty Paolo Veronese, in whose soul there is a strength as of the snowy mountains, and within whose brain all the pomp and majesty of humanity floats in a marshalled glory . . . this man whose finger is as fire and whose eye is like the morning," was condemned to perdition as a " servant of the devil "; whereas the " poor little wretch in a tidy black tie . . . expounding Nothing with a twang," to whom he had listened so impatiently, was a member of the Elect and a servant of Almighty God? By comparison with Titian and Veronese, the earlier Italians, " Francia and Angelico, and all the purists, however beautiful," were but " poor, weak creatures. I don't understand it; one would have thought purity gave strength, but it doesn't." He would go further: the greatest artists were all of them " boldly Animal ": " to be a first-rate painter—you mustn't be pious; but rather a little wicked, and entirely a man of the world." And again: " A good, stout, self-commanding, magnificent Animality is the make for poets and artists "—a conclusion which he would sometimes contradict, but which remained nevertheless one of the opposing " fan-shaped strata " built into the volcanic substance of his critical Mont Blanc. Meanwhile it was clear that, much as he might respect the robust animality of the great Venetian painters, this was a quality that in the management of his own existence he could not hope to emulate. He was unsure of his own direction, doubtful of his aptitudes. Pleasure might call to him, but Duty nagged at him. There were moments when he dreamed of retiring "to Paris or Venice and breaking away from all modern society and opinion," of cultivating himself alone and seeing what would come of it; but from these dreams he was invariably recalled by a recollection of the thousand-and-one tasks that urgently required him. He wished to destroy as well as create; for besides gathering "all the Titians, Tintorets, Paolo Veroneses, Turners and Sir Joshuas in the world into one great fireproof Gothic gallery of marble and serpentine," drawing "all the subjects of Turner's 19,000 sketches in Switzerland and Italy," and, in the sphere of immediate social reform, getting "everybody a dinner who hasn't got one," he would have liked to "macadamise some new roads to Heaven with broken fools'-heads" and "hang up some knaves out of the way. . . . I think it would be wholesome for them, and for other people, and . . . they would make good crows' meat." Yes, he must fight. But where should the battle begin? He had not yet made up his mind (he complained to Norton in August, 1859) what he ought to fight for—"whether, for instance, people ought to live in Swiss cottages and sit on three-legged or one-legged stools; whether people ought to dress well or ill; whether ladies ought to tie their hair in beautiful knots; whether Commerce or Business of any kind be an invention of the Devil . . .; whether Art is a crime or only an Absurdity; whether clergymen ought to be multiplied, or exterminated with arsenic, like rats; whether in general we are getting on, and if so where we are going to. . . ."

In which direction was he bound himself? Months slipped by; a new decade had opened; he seemed as far as ever from alighting on a satisfactory answer. He persevered in his work—not because he over-estimated its value: "my work" (he told the Brownings) "does no one much good"; but because the mechanism of his incessant activity was "becoming too strong for any hope of resistance, and what of worth can be done must be done by accepting that spirit (or that spring, I had better have said), and out of wheels and spindles bringing what whirring results one can, till they have had their day. . . ." So let them revolve! To accelerate the process, there was a growing conviction that unless he made haste, all that he prized in the world would be ruined and obliterated. With the return of interest in Gothic architecture, insensitive and impious hands were being laid upon the cathedrals of Europe. The "restorers" were at work, scraping, rebuilding and demolishing. During September, 1858, Ruskin had wandered forth among the fountains of the Place de la Concorde—"beautiful beyond description in the golden twilight"—having satisfied himself that the fabric of Nôtre Dame was now a total loss; and reports continued to arrive of further depredations. The catastrophe, he felt, showed a malicious sense of timing; for it was just as he had persuaded his readers "to look a little at thirteenth-century Gothic," that the hordes of the vandals had swooped down, and "*every* cathedral of importance" had been destroyed by restoration. The same fate was overtaking the pleasant towns of Switzerland: every place that he had once loved was to-day a railway station or a rubbish heap.

So vexed and perplexed was the mood in which Ruskin set foot upon the slope that leads gradually downhill from forty towards old age. Meanwhile, between 1858 and 1860, two events had occurred—events at first sight of disproportionate significance: he had encountered a little girl to whom her mother had begged that he would teach the rudiments of drawing, and he had produced and published a forthright attack directed against the entire system of modern economics. Each event was to introduce a momentous chain of happenings, and each corresponded to one of the main aspects of Ruskin's personal character. The lover had been long in abeyance. Since the failure of his love for Effie, there is no record that he had experienced any private passion. Perhaps his senses were troubled, but his heart remained unmoved. Then, in 1858, some months before his period of "unconversion," the weakening of his early Evangelical faith, which he himself dated from the holiday he spent in Turin, where the Protestant pastor had been compared unfavourably with Paolo Veronese, and he had gazed at the half-naked limbs of the swart Italian beggar-child, a new excitement began to enter his life, an intense emotional preoccupation, destined, as time went on, to master his feelings more and more completely. Rose La Touche was only nine years old, when she and her forty-year-old admirer came for the first time face to face. Their encounter was strangely fortuitous. Ruskin always enjoyed praising the work of gifted amateurs—in one generation his protégée was Miss Elizabeth Siddal, in another Miss Kate Greenaway—and among those upon whom he lavished encouragement during the late 'fifties, besides Thomas Dixon, an ambitious cork-cutter who wrote to him from Sunderland, were the future Lady Ashburton, Lady Canning, and her sister Lady Waterford. Of both sisters he had a high opinion. Lady Canning's floral sketches, so he informed her mother, were "the grandest representations of flowers he had ever seen"; while, to describe Lady Waterford's "Charity Girl," he borrowed from Pre-Raphaelite terminology and declared that she was "stunning!" Among Lady Waterford's friends was a certain Mrs. La Touche, the wife of a rich Irish banker, former Master of the Kildare Hounds, who had recently found the light and had been converted and re-baptized by that fire-breathing evangelist, the Reverend C. H. Spurgeon. Their home was at Harristown, Kildare; but Mrs. La Touche, an intelligent and cultivated woman, often came to London; and it was during one of these periodical visits that she enlisted Ruskin's sympathy, explaining that she was anxious that her three children—two girls and a boy—should begin their education in art under Mr. Ruskin's guidance. Would he visit them? Ruskin agreed, and presently appeared in Mrs. La Touche's drawing-room "somewhere near Green Street." His hostess pleased him; "extremely pretty still," she was all that he had expected, "but a good deal more than I expected, and in all sorts of ways." She was vivacious, impressionable and seemed eager to learn. Plainly, her visitor may have assumed, another Lady Waterford! Her main anxiety, however, was for the education of her children; and in her younger daughter Rose (as had already been suggested by her introductory letter) Mr. Ruskin would perhaps distinguish a talent worth developing. Emily was out of the house. But might not Rose be summoned? Ruskin assented. Soon " the drawing-room door opened, and Rosie came in, quietly taking stock of me with her blue eyes as she walked across the room; gave me her hand, as a good dog gives its paw, and then stood a little back." Thus, poised on the verge of an unpredictable gulf, the child in her nursery frock, the middle-aged man with his rusty whiskers, thin and stooping but alert, in the formal clothes to which he always contrived to impart an air of expensive informality, hesitated for an instant while they exchanged observant glances. " I thought you *so* ugly," Rosie told him afterwards. " She didn't quite mean that," he hastened to add; but, her mother having spoken to her again and again of " the great Mr. Ruskin," she had looked forward to meeting the facsimile of one of Garibaldi's portraits or a replica of Theseus among the Elgin Marbles; and their visitor was sufficiently prosaic—enough like any other middle-aged gentleman whom she had encountered in her mother's company—to strike her at the initial glance as extremely disappointing.

Very different was Ruskin's immediate response. More than thirty years later, when every detail of that first meeting was still distinct within his memory—preserved with jealous care, just as a letter that Rosie had sent him, encased between thin gold plates, was hoarded in his breast-pocket—he committed his earliest impressions to the pages of *Praeterita*. Nothing had vanished—neither her way of standing, which was " a little stiff," nor the shape of her mouth, the " lips perfectly lovely in profile; a little too wide, and hard in edge, seen in front." She was of middle height, her eyes " rather deep blue at that time, and fuller and softer than afterwards." The rest of the features were " what a fair well-bred Irish girl's usually are; the hair, perhaps, more graceful in short curls round the forehead, and softer than one sees often, in close-bound tresses above the neck." The ensuing colloquy is unrecorded; but Ruskin tells us that he promised to teach the children, and, since he could not undertake to come every other day so far afield as Mayfair, proposed that his two pupils, suitably escorted, should drive out to him at Denmark Hill. Thither they came one sunny day. During which month seems a trifle obscure; for there is a letter addressed by Mrs. La Touche to Ruskin dated February, 1858, mentioning the pleasure that both she and Rose had derived from this original visit; whereas Ruskin believed that his introduction to the La Touches took place very much later during that "eventful year," soon after his return to England, when, we must assume, he was already "unconverted." He remembered it at least as rich in autumn splendour. The orchard boughs were laden with apples, and peaches glowed behind their netting on "the old red garden wall." Together he and the children explored the farm. Rose's sister, Emily, proved to be "a perfectly sweet, serene, delicately chiselled marble nymph of fourteen, softly dark-eyed, rightly tender and graceful in all she did and said." She excelled in arranging with an exquisite sense of style everything her fingers touched; and if she lifted a handful of flowers, "they fell out of her hand in wreathed jewellery of colour and form, as if they had been sown, and had blossomed, to live together so, and no otherwise. Her mother had the same gift, but in its more witty, thoughtful and scientific range. . . ." The whole family, indeed, appeared to be not only charming and talented, but eminently suggestible. Their first lesson "lost itself . . . in pomiferous talk, with rustic interludes in the stables and pigsty"; but before long the little girls, encouraged by their master, had settled down to serious business, examining Turner's sketches of mountain scenery, learning to draw the "convolvuluses, hollyhocks, plums, peaches, and apples" that he brought in from the garden, absorbing geometrical principles, and making bold expeditions into "the pretty mysteries of trigonometry."

He adored them both; and he liked their mother; but for Rose, as it soon became apparent, the affection that he felt was of a very special quality. The Fates were weaving "another net of Love." Just how quickly he became aware of his entanglement we cannot determine with any hope of precision from the records that he left behind. But if his subjugation was not immediate—or if he did not himself immediately recognise that admiration and affection were merging into infatuation—there is no doubt that his feelings had begun to crystallise during the first few days or weeks. Even more nympholeptic than his previous passions, Ruskin's passion for Rose La Touche partook of several different characters. There are some amorists—Ruskin was one of them—to whom youth makes an appeal far stronger and more dangerous than any adult beauty: on whom the childish body and the childish face, with their suggestions of innocence and inexperience, so strangely shot through by gleams of dawning knowledge, exert an infinitely deeper fascination than the most finely developed of finished human masterpieces. Adèle and Charlotte had been young: Rose La Touche was younger still, while Ruskin himself was proportionately older and, in his attitude towards adult women, more deeply disillusioned. Rose was a child and, for many years to come, could make no demands on his imperfect or intermittent manhood. Yet his love was passionate as well as pure; for to assume that Ruskin was by temperament cold, or fundamentally lacking in the ordinary human instincts, is at once to misunderstand the nature of his genius and to omit an important clue to the origins of the catastrophe that later overwhelmed him. In his own view he was Rose's lover; but for the time being, of course, he was content to remain an adoring friend and master. Love took refuge in an elaborate—an almost too elaborate, too delicately studied—playfulness. Together they inhabited a dream-world of fancies, myths and nicknames. Rose was "Rosie-Posie," her governess "Bun": her sister they named "Wisie," after a dog that Ruskin had loved and lost, "a white Spitz, exactly like Carpaccio's dog in the picture of St. Jerome." Mrs. La Touche was "Lacerta"[1] because she

[1]Used by Ruskin to mean 'serpent', though literally 'lizard'.

had the wisdom and grace of a serpent, without its guile or venom. As for the Master, he was "St. Crumpet," perhaps in reference to his "ugliness," though the saintly title denoted that he was kind to beggars.

Rose herself, the centre of his cult, the midmost flower of his *hortus conclusus*, that haven of the inner life to which, since his boyhood, he had so often fled for refuge, had, even at the age of nine or ten, not a few of the mysterious attributes we associate with a cult-object. She had nothing of Ida's romantic nullity; nor was she a perfectly commonplace, well-balanced female-in-miniature of the type of Adèle Domecq. It is obvious that she was an exceedingly clever girl. She had a quick brain and, as Ruskin presently discovered, a strong religious tendency. Emotional and responsive to love, she included, nevertheless, in her constitution a certain touch of latent hardness. This aspect of her being was reflected by features that, although singularly attractive, were apparently a trifle sharp-edged; when she was nine years old, Ruskin noted that her lips, seen from the front, were somewhat hard in outline; and, during his later existence, he admitted that her chiselled beauty had been "too severe to be entirely delightful to all people." That she was uncommonly old for her years is demonstrated by a letter which Ruskin preserved to the end of his life and with fond indiscretion printed in *Praeterita*. Addressed to "Dearest St. Crumpet," it shows both an unusual command of language and an altogether precocious grasp of her correspondent's feelings. It is a consoling, yet a cajoling, missive. Rose was abroad at the time—some months after their first meeting Mr. and Mrs. La Touche had decided to pass the spring in Italy—and Rose, who (her adorer remarked with gratitude) was "really a little sorry to go away, and . . . understood in the most curious way how sorry *I* was," writes to describe her sensations on crossing the Channel, her opinion of the pictures in the Louvre, and her introduction to the South of France. She assures Ruskin that she constantly thinks of him and discusses him with her family. Much play is made of his nicknames—"St. Crumpet" and a secondary name, " Archegosaurus," " meant partly to indicate my scientific knowledge of Depths and Ages . . ."; and besides informing him that, during her stay in Paris, she had dutifully admired the Veroneses and the Titians, but had admired the statues almost as much—" Is it wrong, St. Crumpet, to like that noble Venus Victrix as well as Titian? If it is, am I a hardened little tinner? "—she abounds in admonitions and mildly feline *badinage*. He is not to be " Kingfishery "—that is to say, not to sit on a bough in sulky kingfisher-fashion—but to write " packets —trunks " for the whole family's amusement. Of her own central position she seems fully aware, and, dramatising herself as the Rose, she writes to tell him " how my cousins the moorland roses nodded at me as I passed and how they couldn't understand why Irish hedge-roses bloomed in July instead of March." Yet, beneath the femininity, appears now and then an odd and touching sensitiveness. Ruskin's lessons had borne abundant fruit. She, too, had been illuminated by the strange Ruskinian fervour, and even at this stage, when she had not yet reached the brink of adolescence, was learning to discourse in the Master's tone, and to respond to the beauties of a landscape with something of his promptitude. Rose holds the pen, but through her mouth, though remotely and in muted accents, Ruskin's voice is speaking: " It was so pleasant to be running after the sun to the south (Don't be Kingfishery) and awaking at about 5 in the morning to see long plains of greyheaded silvery olives and here and there pink perky peach trees dancing among them. And there were groups of dark cool cypress trees pointing upwards, and hills and grey rocks sloping to the sea—the Mediterranean. So we shook off our sleepiness . . . and saw behind those peaks of craggy hills a pink smile coming in the sky . . . so we watched and suddenly there rose . . . such a sun—' nor dim, nor red ' (you know the verse) and then dipped back again below the hills." A word of sympathy concludes the letter. It is clear that Rose had already begun to carry the burden of Ruskin's private confidences; for she starts her last page by wishing " so very much " that her disconsolate friend were happy. "God can make you so," she reminds him confidently, thus striking a note that, growing by slow degrees louder and more ominous, was, after the passage of more than ten years, to sound their friendship's death-knell.

She returned from Italy, and the relation was resumed. He could not see her as often as he wished; but the idea of Rose, and of the relief and satisfaction she seemed to offer, floated constantly before him. Meanwhile he had finished *Modern Painters*—a task that, together with the other tasks he had recently completed, and the pressure of the troubled feelings under which he had been labouring, reduced him almost to exhaustion. He went abroad, travelling alone; though he was still devoted to his parents, for some time he had begun to fret more and more uneasily against parental government. He no longer shared his mother's religious faith, or could only accept it with many reservations; and simultaneously he felt an increasing distrust of the beliefs, moral and economic, on which old Mr. Ruskin's peace of mind was founded. He had revolted tentatively in 1852, writing a series of letters to *The Times*, which he had first submitted to Denmark Hill and which his father had refused to forward. Now at Chamouni, during the summer months of 1860, he produced *Unto This Last*, of which three instalments were published that summer and autumn in a new popular monthly magazine edited by Thackeray. The *Cornhill* had been launched at the beginning of the year, and from the opening number, which sold one hundred and twenty thousand copies, had proved extraordinarily successful. Its appeal was wide: in the course of six months it printed contributions by Trollope and Thackeray (each of whom provided a serial novel), by Charlotte and Emily Brontë, by Thomas Hood, Washington Irving and Richard Monckton Milnes. Millais was a frequent illustrator; and the February issue had been distinguished by the original apparition of that exquisite and disturbing poem, Alfred Tennyson's *Tithonus*. The Victorian reading public, prosperous, progressive, eager for enlightenment, at once seized upon the *Cornhill*; and here was the readership at which Ruskin aimed, for *Unto This Last* was primarily an appeal to the conscience of the wealthier, more thoughtful and more influential classes, to a stratum of the English world whose prosperity, luxury and sense of security during the years that separated them from the Year of Revolutions had registered a steady increase. British opulence was the wonder of the Continent; and the issue of the *Cornhill* that included Ruskin's third instalment also found room for an essay on *Luxury* which, beginning with the assertion that "there was never, probably, in any age or country, a larger mass of comfortable, respectable people, than is now to be found in these islands," concluded by suggesting that "the atmosphere in which the comfortable classes of modern English society live, is most unfavourable to intellectual and moral stature, and that changes in it are the indispensable condition of growth. Its most unwholesome ingredient is the intense self-satisfaction by which it is pervaded." That spirit of self-satisfaction, coupled with an "exaggerated appetite for solid advantages" on which the anonymous essayist elsewhere gravely commented, in the pages of *Unto This Last* became Ruskin's chiefest target.

Thus the man who at other moments announced that he was tired of trying to do good, and that he contemplated retiring into æsthetic seclusion, there to cultivate his own gifts and endeavour to enjoy his life, in 1860 apparently reversed his decision and took up yet another crusade. "Just one more howl . . ." he had written to the Brownings. But there was less of the howl, less of an aggrieved and girding tone, in this new attack on the public conscience than in any previous prophecy. It is measured, closely condensed, elaborately thought out. It is at the same time extremely personal; for Ruskin's personal situation can never be disassociated from the opinions that he put forward, and he was as inescapably himself as in the rôle of art-critic. The state of society excited his anger, not only because social conditions were theoretically unsound, but because they exacerbated his sense of sin, and, as a lover of beauty and a sensitive human being, it seemed utterly intolerable that he should be called upon to contemplate them. Every drive from Denmark Hill northwards into London took him through regions of slowly darkening squalor, and there was worse—far worse—to be observed in other London districts. Since his boyhood the metropolis he knew had undergone gigantic changes. It had developed beyond all expectation. Between 1800 and 1830 the inhabitants of Greater London had increased from 865,000 to 1,500,000; and by the 'fifties another million laborious citizens had by some means found a home there. How they were lodged and how they obtained a livelihood were problems that the most energetic reformer might well despair of solving; but Henry Mayhew, whose *London Labour and the London Poor* (a much more curious work than Frederick Engel's earlier inquiry into the condition of the English working classes) was first published in 1851 and revised and re-issued on several occasions up to 1865, had made a strenuous effort; and his three massive original volumes contain an extraordinarily dramatic picture of the world's largest, richest city, where the prosperous quarters floated like small trim islands upon a vast surrounding ocean—an ocean of poverty, with depths below depths, in which the off-scourings of one class provided, literally as well as figuratively, a hope of subsistence for the class immediately beneath it.

"Mud-larks," "pure-finders" and "toshers,"[1] scavengers and street-sweepers, pedlars and costermongers, all added to the complexity of the fantastic London landscape; of these a considerable number existed close to the starvation-level; and the conditions in which they were housed were uniformly wretched. Though attacks had been launched on some of London's more pestilential slum quarters, many "rookeries" still existed—dilapidated clusters of ancient filth-encrusted houses, which enclosed populations of unknown extent, and looked down on a

[1] "Mud-larks" lived by scavenging in the mud of the Thames foreshore: "pure-finders" by collecting the droppings of dogs which they sold by the pail to the tanneries: "toshers" by exploring the London sewer system for useful or valuable objects which had slipped down house- and street-drains—a dangerous occupation which called for skill and courage.

courtyard containing a pump, a rubbish-heap and a single common privy. Stumbling up a flight of broken stairs, Mayhew would find himself in a room "about nine feet square" which "furnished a home for three women," one of whom, a girl, "eighteen years old last twelfth-cake day," had been confined and lay on a mattress, on the floor, beneath a patchwork counterpane. The room was thick with the smoke which poured from the chimney: "the place was filled with it, curling in the light, and making everything so indistinct that I could with difficulty see the white mugs ranged in the corner cupboard . . . the ceiling slanted like that of a garret, and was the colour of old leather, excepting a few rough white patches, where the tenants had rudely mended it. . . . Light was easily seen through the laths, and in one corner a large patch of the paper looped down from the wall. . . . They had made a carpet out of three or four old mats. They were 'obligated to it for fear of dropping anything through the boards into the donkey stable in the parlour underneath. But we only pay ninepence a week rent,' said the old woman, 'and mustn't grumble.'"

This interior is only one of many—not a few of them far more squalid—into which Mayhew, a Virgil of the industrial underworld, conducts the sympathetic reader. Besides his visits to the "respectable" poor and his expeditions along the banks of the Thames, where he observed the "mud-larks," young children or old men and women, groping in the inky river-mud for bones, lumps of coal, scraps of iron and other precious refuse, Mayhew found his way to the music-halls and tap-rooms, saw the wild gaiety of a "penny-hop" and watched the "toshers," temporarily rich after a successful foray, spending the spoil of the sewers in some "low" and friendly public-house. But whether "respectable" or criminal, abject as the "mud-larks" and "pure-finders" or relatively prosperous as the "toshers" and the costermongers, the entire London proletariat, according to Mayhew's examination, was alike in one respect: it had neither traditions nor organisation, neither present security nor any hope of betterment: accumulated by chance and necessity, as the demand for cheap labour drew more and more of the population away from the country into the fast-expanding capital, it scraped a precarious livelihood by every means open to it, a miscellaneous, amorphous mass, with no roots in the past or claims upon the future. Philanthropy could merely brush its surface. Its plight (many Victorian critics candidly considered) was a sad but inevitable result of the rate of modern progress.[1]

Into this theory entered much serious conviction, united, now and then, with a certain touch of cynicism. The opponents of Lord Shaftesbury's Factory Acts included not only conservative employers but thoughtful economists, firmly persuaded that any attempt to regulate the supply of labour—for example, by prohibiting the employment of very young children or shortening the hours they worked—would so dislocate the structure of commercial society as to provoke evils far more pernicious than the wrongs it sought to combat. *Laissez faire* was still the predominant doctrine; the views of the Manchester School were still embraced with fervour by such well-intentioned and well-endowed business men as Mr. James Ruskin, who believed in a set of economic laws almost as rigid as those laws, moral and physical, which a benevolent Creator had invented to roll along the universe. Against this belief his son was rebelling. During his weeks of seclusion at Chamouni, he took society to task for all the anguish and perplexity that it heaped upon his conscience —for what it allowed him to see in the London streets and for what it obliged him to read when, cultivated, secure and free, he opened in his foreign hotel an English daily paper. Incidentally he was taking his father to task, both for the evils he deplored but countenanced, and for the state of privileged subjection in which the doting old man had obliged his only son to grow up. *Unto This Last* was a blow for humanity: it was also a blow for spiritual inde-

[1]Commenting on the state of the East End during periods of depression, *The Times* observed in the 'fifties that " there is no one to blame for this ; it is the result of nature's simplest laws."

pendence struck by Ruskin on his own behalf. He wished to emancipate mankind at large from their dull degrading bondage: himself he yearned to escape from a very different form of servitude which, if it had not degraded, had certainly crippled and enfeebled him.

The opening instalment of *Unto This Last*,[1] sub-titled *The Roots of Honour*, appeared in the August *Cornhill*, between Trollope's *Framley Parsonage* and the second of Thackeray's essays on *The Four Georges*, one being an elaborate and affectionate picture of the Victorian social background, the other a glimpse of the bad old times, which modern morality and modern progress had long since superseded. Both were works of comfortable entertainment; but there was nothing comfortable in the enthusiasm with which the author of *Unto This Last* rushed straight upon his subject: "Among the delusions" (he began) "which at different periods have possessed themselves of the mind of large masses of the human race, perhaps the most curious—certainly the least creditable—is the modern *soi-disant* science of political economy, based on the idea that an advantageous code of social action may be determined irrespectively of the influence of social affection." There, at once, is the gist of his argument. Social relations cannot be determined by precepts of expediency: the relation of employed and employee is a relation between man and man, and unless "social affection"—the respect that we owe to our fellow human beings—is considered in the contract, society must become a ruthlessly destructive and, at length, a self-destructive organism. Men, he pleads, cannot be regarded as mere economic units, bound by inexorable laws of supply and demand, which authorised the progressive employer to demand as much labour as he could exact at as low a price as he could pay for it, thereby obtaining "the greatest benefit to the community, and through the community, by reversion, to the servant himself." This might be a praiseworthy means of procedure, if the man employed "were an engine of which the motive power were steam,

[1] "I will give unto this last, even as unto thee."—*Matt.* xx 14.

magnetism, gravitation, or any other agent of calculable force. But he being, on the contrary, an engine whose motive power is a Soul, the force of this very peculiar agent, as an unknown quantity, enters into all the political economist's equations, without his knowledge, and falsifies every one of their results. The largest quantity of work will not be done by this curious engine for pay, or under pressure, or by help of any kind of fuel which may be supplied by the chaldron. It will be done only when the motive force, that is to say, the will or spirit of the creature, is brought to its greatest strength by its own proper fuel; namely, by the affections."

Many of the keenest spiritual torments that afflicted the Victorian epoch were caused, it would now appear, by an unceasing effort to persuade Christian morality and commercial expediency to run in double-harness. The remedies which the Victorians applied were strenuously philanthropic: the system itself must remain unaltered, but its uglier manifestations need not go uncared for; and a hundred-and-one benevolent institutions were set on foot to deal with them. Ruskin did not disdain, and himself practised, philanthropy, but he could not believe that, until the system itself had been revolutionised, these superficial remedies were of any lasting value. "Never" (he had already written in *The Stones of Venice*) "had the upper classes so much sympathy with the lower, or charity for them, as they have at this day, and yet never were they so much hated by them; for, of old, the separation between the noble and the poor was merely a wall built by law; now it is a veritable difference in level of standing, a precipice between upper and lower grounds in the field of humanity, and there is pestilential air at the bottom of it." That had passed; after all, the writer was an art-critic; and there were in his book many superbly decorative, finely eloquent disquisitions to which the nervous reader could resort for intellectual refuge. In his latest essay there were few or none; persistently, relentlessly, even arrogantly, he proceeded with his argument, demanding whether it were true (as the political economists asserted) that wages could never be regulated except by the demand for labour: whether it were right that civilisation, so-called, should oblige vast masses of mankind to support themselves by work in which they could not reasonably be expected to feel the smallest pride or interest: finally, whether the whole structure of contemporary commerce were not at the same time both inequitable and wasteful. His concrete suggestions might, no doubt, be brushed aside. It was more difficult to dismiss his destructive criticism, or the appeal that he made to established Christian ethics. Having insisted that the employer should not only deal fairly with, and respect, but learn to *love* his workmen, he went on to urge that, for a while at least, until others could share in it, the more prosperous classes should curtail their private luxury. Not that he deprecated luxury for its own sake: " Luxury is indeed possible in the future—innocent and exquisite; luxury for all, and by the help of all; but luxury at present can only be enjoyed by the ignorant; the cruellest man living could not sit at his feast, unless he sat blindfold." Even more disturbing than this appeal to compassion —a virtue on which, not without good excuse, the Victorian upper classes felt that they could pride themselves—was his vision of the planned state, in which freedom of individual enterprise would be, to some extent, restricted: " I hold it for indisputable " (he observed) " that the first duty of a State is to see that every child born therein shall be well housed, clothed, fed and educated, till it attain years of discretion. But in order to effect this the Government must have an authority over the people of which we now do not so much as dream."[1]

When the Labour Movement at length became an important force in England, inquiry among its leaders and members established the fact that *Unto This Last* had had a wider and deeper influence upon their way of thinking than any other volume.[2] Yet Ruskin was not an orthodox

[1]Ruskin, on the other hand, believed that " all effectual advancement towards . . . true felicity of the human race must be by individual, not public effort."

[2]Fervent admirers of *Unto This Last* included, according to Mr. J. H. Whitehouse, President of the Ruskin Society, the late Mahatma Gandhi.

Socialist. Unlike William Morris, whom he loved and respected, but with whose life his character and career present at so many points an extremely striking contrast, he refused to yoke his inspiration to any single movement, but continued, in his whimsical and capricious fashion, as it were to dangle his allegiance before several different parties. "Of course I am a Socialist" (he wrote)—"of the most stern sort—but I am also a Tory of the sternest sort." At one moment he was "a Communist of the old school"; at another, a staunch Imperialist. But to this breadth of view there was an important limitation—at no time would he concede that he might ever be a Liberal. "I am a violent Illiberal," he informed the world; for, although many of the opinions he put forward had been developed in deliberate defiance of the opinions held at Denmark Hill, his parents' household still provided the type of the ideal government he wished to impose upon society—paternal, authoritarian, in which men had learned to rule and learned to submit to their rulers with equal grace and good sense. But the touch of Toryism in Ruskin's Socialism could not conceal the essential subversiveness of the measures he was advocating; and, while James Ruskin professed himself deeply pained and, with the emphatic syllable "*Bosh!*" Rossetti slammed the door of his ivory tower behind him, British journalists were loud in condemnation, stigmatising the *Cornhill* essays as "eruptions of windy hysterics" and "utter imbecility." The world, announced a reviewer, did not intend to allow itself to be "preached to death by a mad governess." Particularly repulsive was "the way in which Mr. Ruskin writes of the relations of the rich and poor." It was worse than repulsive: it was actually seditious, an incitement to revolutionary hot-heads to destroy the very fabric of civilised existence. There was a grave danger, the critics apprehended, that his "wild words" would "touch the springs of action in some hearts, and ere we are aware a moral floodgate may fly open and drown us all."

So vehement were the protests it aroused that Thackeray, yielding apparently to the pressure exerted by his publisher, agreed to discontinue *Unto This Last* and declined to print the fifth instalment. Ruskin was hurt and angry: he was yet more dismayed when his essays, in book form, failed to find an audience, and he learned that they had had an adverse effect upon the popularity of his other books. Thus began the "period of reprobation"; and the disappointed prophet signalised his fall from public esteem by several sweeping gestures. He did not break with his parents—that would have demanded a degree of courage and unkindness quite beyond his personal scope; but he made it clear, once and for all, that his father and his father's beliefs had no longer any hold on him. Not an illusion was permitted to survive: neither his own nor his parents' feelings were spared in the singularly ruthless scrutiny to which, during the years that followed, he submitted their relationship. He informed his mother and father, categorically and dispassionately, that he was convinced that they had ruined him. Their early discipline he by no means resented; for "men ought to be severely disciplined and exercised in the sternest way of life . . . but they should never have their hearts broken"—a catastrophe that he now attributed to the various errors of his upbringing, "the two terrific mistakes which you and Mamma involuntarily fell into. . . . You fed me effeminately and luxuriously . . . but you thwarted me in all the earnest fire and passion of life. About Turner you indeed never knew how much you thwarted me—for I thought it my duty to be thwarted. . . . If I had had courage and knowledge enough to insist on having my own way resolutely, you would now have had me in happy health, loving you twice as much (for, depend upon it, love taking much of its own way, a fair share, is in generous people all the brighter for it), and full of energy for the future—and of power of self-denial." As it was, his "power of *duty*" had been exhausted in vain and he was obliged "for life's sake" to resort to self-indulgence "just when a man ought to be knit for the duties of middle life by the good success of his youthful life. No life" (he concluded) "ought to have *phantoms* to lay"; and the phantoms that appeared to surround him were numerous and terrible. Only by work could he hope to appease them; and, since the failure of the prophetic essays, work, though he did not desist from it, was a method of consolation that very often failed him.

These complaints were not limited by the complainant to the immediate circle of his family. He confided also in such friends as Lady Trevelyan and Charles Eliot Norton, expatiating at length on the infinite harm that paternal love had done him. "... I know my father is ill" (he wrote to Lady Trevelyan from Milan during July, 1862) "but I cannot stay at home just now, or I should fall indubitably ill myself.... If he loved me less, and believed in me more, we should get on; but his whole life is bound up in me, and yet he thinks me a fool.... This form of affection galls me like hot iron, and I am in a subdued fury whenever I am at home, which drives all the marrow out of every bone in me." To Norton, he spoke of the "unendurable solitude" that encompassed him at Denmark Hill; and, more and more aroused in his own defence, and more and more embittered against the blind, uncomprehending love to which he attributed all his woes and failures, he proceeded to detect its traces in the attitude towards him of that exceedingly unsentimental person, Dante Gabriel Rossetti. "I am grateful for your love" (he remarked)—"but yet I do not want love. I have had boundless love from many people during my life. And in more than one case that love has been my greatest calamity—I have boundlessly *suffered* from it. But the thing, in any helpful degree, I have never been able to get, except from two women ... and from Edward Jones, is 'understanding.' I am nearly sick of being loved—as of being hated—for my lovers understand me as little as my haters." There is, indeed, about Ruskin's letters to his parents and friends written at this period, a tone that can only be described as one of anguished petulance. The petulance is unmistakable, but so is the anguish. Suddenly cut off from the springs of religious faith, condemned "to live without hope of another world" when he had been "accustomed to it for forty years," having at last declared war against the system of paternal authority in which his youth was moulded, he became as wilfully rebellious as he had previously appeared submissive, and announced that only by respecting his independence could those who professed to love him ever hope to save him. . . . "The *only* thing you can do for me (he explained to James Ruskin) is to let me follow out my own work in my own way and in peace. All interference torments me and makes me quite as ill as any amount of work. . . ." And to Rossetti, in a letter, already quoted, which administered the final shock to their slowly weakening friendship: ". . . I am at present out of health and irritable, and entirely resolved to make myself as comfortable as I can, and therefore to associate only with people who in *some degree* think of me as I think of myself. I *may* be wrong in saying I am this or that, but at present I can only live or speak with people who agree with me that I *am* this or that." As if to emphasise his spiritual isolation, Ruskin again left England during the summer of 1861, and for the next two years made his headquarters abroad, either in Switzerland or in Italy. He wrote to his mother and father at frequent intervals, and, when he returned to England, never failed to see them. But the old bondage had been finally cast off. He was at length a free man—and none the less unhappy.

The perplexed sage, the "disappointed Philanthropist," the rebellious son and revolutionary Illiberal enjoyed, nevertheless, a single gleam of comfort. He was in love with Rose; and Rose, he believed, was not indifferent to his interest. Whatever Rosie might think of "St. Crumpet" —and he calmed himself by remembering that from Ireland, to which the La Touche family had now returned, she wrote to him repeatedly—he acknowledged the immense debt that he owed to her soothing, stabilising influence. Elsewhere all was distress and darkness: "intense scorn" of his previous efforts and "still intenser scorn of other people's doings and thinkings, especially in religion," were coupled with the "perception of colossal power . . . in Titian and of weakness in purism," a feeling of intolerable loneliness at home, " only made more painful to me by parental love . . . which was cruelly hurtful without knowing it," and with " terrible discoveries in the course of such investigation as I made into grounds of old faith . . . I don't in the least know," he admitted to Norton during February, 1861, " what might have been the end of it, if a little child (only thirteen last summer) hadn't put her fingers on the helm at the right time, and chosen to make a pet of herself for me, and her mother to make a friend of herself . . . certainly the ablest and I think the best woman I have ever known. . . ." He could not see the La Touches very often. In the summer of 1861, instead of going to Switzerland as was his wont, he remained at Boulogne, between the ocean and the sandhills, where he looked forward to Rosie's weekly letters, observed the sea and sky, read Greek (because Rose had begun to ask him questions about her Greek Testament) and now and then went out with the local fishermen, admiring their gaiety and courage and robust independence. Would that his own organism were as solidly well-built! He was proud to be allowed to manage the boat, though the captain, soon an old friend, prudently refused to let him bring it into harbour; and he shared in many enchanting expeditions, particularly one warm but windy night when the whole sea was alive with phosphorescence, and, the craft running gunwale under, " currents of blue fire " floated continually over the lower side of the deck. But even here he found subjects of anguish and perplexity. Was it not strange that his " good and thoughtful sailing-master " should be an unlettered Boulogne pilot, and that the supposedly benevolent scheme of creation should permit radiant-hued sea-creatures to go equipped with poisonous prickles?

From Boulogne he returned to England in August—but not at once to Denmark Hill. The La Touches had sent him a " very earnest invitation " to pay them an extended visit; and by the end of the month, passing through Dublin (which " joins the filth of Manchester to the gloom of Modena, and the moral atmosphere of St. Giles's ") he at length set foot in Harristown, where the children—for it was late in the evening when he arrived—hurried out of bed to see him: Percy, " barefooted like a little Irishman . . . Wisie, like Grisi in *Norma*," and Rose, who followed her brother, wearing a " tiny pink dressing-gown." They were " all very happy and very well." Ruskin played and walked with the children, and conversed amicably with their parents; but it was during this visit that a faint shadow of disquietude began for the first time to colour their relationship. Mrs. La Touche had taken alarm at his religious heresies; and, since she could not persuade him to change his views, she exacted a promise that for the space of ten years he would not seek to propagate them. Ruskin had assented, feeling (as he told his father) that " it was the only thing I could do for Mrs. La Touche," who " would do all she *could* for me." Lacerta's solicitude was, indeed, conspicuous. She showed a more than sisterly concern with " poor St. Crumpet's " troubles. " Nothing " (she confessed later to a friend, George MacDonald) " will ever get me right, save getting him right—for somehow if he were holding on to a straw and I to a plank, I must leave my plank to catch at his straw. Still, I don't care what becomes of me so long as anyhow he can be brought to some sort of happiness and life. He knows that very well, and is welcome to know it." She did not, however (as was natural enough), take her friend's devotion to her daughter, now barely adolescent, altogether seriously. Rosie was still a child, she insisted—a fascinating child, no doubt, as she galloped through the park on her pony, her enormous dog beside her, or sat solemnly discussing St. Crumpet or reading the long effusive letters he wrote to her from Boulogne; and Ruskin found that his passionate appreciations of Rosie's influence and importance were apt to be received by her mother, otherwise so sympathetic, with gentle incredulity. At times he accepted her point of view; and then he became conscious of his age, of his despondency, exhaustion and " unfitness for active life," and decided that the glorious plans he had woven around Rosie must sooner or later be abandoned. On leaving England, he carried the problem abroad, where the cogitations it involved detained him till December. He had had (he wrote to James Ruskin) "several things to make up my mind about . . . and under circumstances of some ambiguousness—what my conduct should be to the La Touches was the chief of these: and *that* depended partly on my thoroughly knowing the state of my own health, and partly on my finding out if possible whether Rosie was what her mother and you think her, an entirely simple child, or . . . in an exquisitely beautiful and tender way, and *mixed* with much childishness," the subtle and perceptive being whom he himself imagined.

In fact, she was neither one nor the other, but (we may assume) an unusually intelligent child, gifted with a curious, perhaps an almost morbid, sensitiveness to the feelings of the older persons by whom she was surrounded. Both her mother and Ruskin were demanding and possessive characters; and it seems not unreasonable to suggest that the frequent collapses from which Rose La Touche suffered during the period of her adolescence may have been due at least as much as to psychological strain as to physiological weakness. This was a view of the situation that Ruskin himself had considered but rejected. Rose fell gravely ill during the autumn of 1861; and, writing to his father at the beginning of November with the news that she had recovered, though she was still forbidden to write long letters or make any strenuous effort, he assured him that "Rosie's illness has assuredly *nothing* to do with any regard she may have for me. She likes me to pet her, but it is no manner of trouble when I go away; her affection takes much more the form of a desire to please me and make me happy in any way she can, than of any want for herself, either of my letters or my company." No doubt he hoped that the want would arise. Meanwhile he was prepared to wait; and, having returned to Switzerland, he settled down once more to the studies he now found most consolatory, slowly and carefully driving a path through various Greek and Latin authors, enjoying the grandeur of Livy and admiring "Horace's calm and temperate, yet resolute, sadness." Besides the Augustan poet's attitude towards death, what "weak nonsense" seemed the pontifications of every modern moralist!

Ruskin's existence, then, between the publication of *Unto This Last* and the spring months of 1864, followed a fairly constant pattern. Still industrious yet relatively unproductive, he paid occasional visits to England, but more often was to be discovered moving to and fro across the Continent. Sometimes he was accompanied by friends —by Edward Burne-Jones and his wife: for that engaging young painter now occupied the place in his affections once filled by Rossetti—and sometimes he lived alone, reading and meditating and awaiting Rosie's letters, a "kingfishery" recluse amid some Alpine solitude. His literary output was small. In 1862, however, encouraged by Froude, the editor of *Fraser's Magazine*, who had written to him admiringly at Carlyle's instigation, he embarked on a new series of economic essays. The result was *Munera Pulveris*, a work which repeated and enlarged the message of *Unto This Last*, and his view of what constituted the real wealth of a people, complicated by some odd touches of mythological fancy. Its reception, alas, was equally discouraging. Only four essays had yet appeared when the publisher of *Fraser's*, like the publisher of the *Cornhill*, was struck with sudden panic; like Thackeray, Froude gave way, and the work was discontinued. Ruskin staggered beneath this second blow; he was staying at the time in Switzerland and his companion, George Allen, remembered the mood of intense gloom that had enveloped him as soon as word arrived from England, and how, lonely and angry, he had paced for hours on end up and down a terrace-walk. His sense of isolation was proportionately exaggerated; and in isolation the cult of Rose grew increasingly extravagant. No "rosaceous" detail, no scrap of her handwriting, no anecdote of her behaviour, was too small to hold his interest. But he was never unconscious of the distances that separated them—distance in age and distance in faith; for, although Rose might have been prepared to overlook the fact that St. Crumpet was a middle-aged man (a man moreover who, as he complained bitterly, had never learned to "climb, run, or wrestle, sing, or flirt," and felt at the same time disturbingly young and prematurely antiquated), it was not likely that she would allow herself, or be allowed by her parents, to contemplate marriage with an infidel. And marriage was now his objective. He had come to believe—it was a recurrent delusion—that he might at length, in spite of all his previous disappointments, be normally, completely happy.

To this end, he had promised Mrs. La Touche he would not propagate his doctrinal errors. Mrs. La Touche, on the other hand, most unfairly or most unfortunately, had permitted Rose to discover that St. Crumpet's religious views were not everything they should have been. The little girl was greatly disturbed. Rosie, he reported in December, 1862, was "mightily vexed about my heathenism (her mother has let her see some bits of letters I never meant her to see)—and sends me a long little lock of hair, to steady me somewhat if it may be; of sending which, nevertheless, she won't take the grace—or responsibility—herself, but says, 'Mama cut it off for you.'" Accompanying this gift was a direct appeal. ". . . For the sake of all truth," she begged, "and love," he must not give up "the one true Good—containing all others. . . ." No doubt the letters of which Mrs. La Touche had shown her daughter fragments were concerned with the revolutionary opinions of the Bishop of Natal, John William Colenso, whose seven treatises on *The Pentateuch and the Book of Joshua critically Examined* (which he had been moved to write by the extreme difficulty of explaining Bible history to his puzzled Zulu converts) began to appear in 1862. Ruskin sided with the Bishop; for Colenso's bold stand did much to relieve the burden of his own perplexities. But the La Touche family, as believers in the literal accuracy of both Testaments, were much aggrieved and scandalised; and Mrs. La Touche's distress over her friend's plight very soon infected Rosie, adding to her confusion of mind and deepening her sense of conflict.

From the resultant strain she continued to suffer, physically as well as spiritually. In 1863 she again fell sick; and, writing to Norton in the March of that year, Ruskin speaks of "some over-excitement of the brain" which caused "occasional loss of consciousness," so that "now she often seems only half herself, as if partly dreaming." Yet, groping through the veils of illusion, Rose still made repeated and pathetic attempts to cure him of his disbelief. "How could one love you" (she would demand) "if you were a Pagan?"

That he was a pagan he could no longer deny—at least from the point of view of Harristown or Denmark Hill; but firmly, almost angrily, he rebutted his father's suggestion that, as a result of his loss of faith, his character had suffered. "My mother and you" (he wrote) "have such pain at present in thinking my character is deteriorating? . . . I could easily prove to you, if I chose, but take it on my word, and do not force me to humiliate you by doing so—that I am an incomparably nobler and worthier person, now, when you disapprove of nearly all I say and do, than I was when I was everything you and my mother desired me." In spite of these strenuous efforts at self-justification, the two old people continued to mourn over their apostate offspring, and the atmosphere of their house, whenever he revisited it, seemed equally oppressive. Desperately he longed for a home of his own. The La Touches had at one moment suggested that he should take a cottage beside the river just beyond their park-wall; but the plan, in circumstances which remain mysterious, but which Ruskin described to Lady Trevelyan as "unspeakable" and "somewhat sorrowful," eventually miscarried. It also occurred to him that he might rent a room in Rossetti's house in Chelsea—that curious bohemian establishment, peopled by exotic animals, where Meredith once watched the painter, round about noon, devour with ogreish enthusiasm an enormous breakfast of cold poached eggs which appeared to have slowly bled to death on many slices of thick bacon. It was not a lodging that would have suited the fastidious critic. He did not pursue the project, and at last decided that he would give up any thought of living in England and build an Alpine eyrie. It was to be near Bonneville, a place he especially loved; and there, in spite of his father's intense disapproval, he wished to purchase an entire mountain-top. Since it was waterless, he intended to construct a dam which would catch the water from the snow-fields: a châlet was to be raised, and Edward Burne-Jones must, of course, consent to decorate it. Only the demands of the grasping peasantry, who were convinced that the mad Englishman, with his geologist's hammer, had discovered a vein of gold or stumbled on a coal-deposit, caused his Alpine plans to go the way of all the projects that had preceded them.

James Ruskin was patient but apprehensive. "It is the Building Plan near Bonneville" (he observed to Mrs. Burne-Jones) "that I shall rejoice to see resigned." Meanwhile he would "endeavour to hope that John's Engagements abroad may in future be confined to a Tour with a friend, and that Home Influences may in the end prevail. . . ." But they showed no signs of prevailing when John returned to England in November, 1863. He was as restless as ever, apparently as unwilling or as unable to settle down beneath his parents' supervision; and during the December of that year he wrote from the North of England the letter that contained the fullest, most unsparing condemnation of the "terrific mistakes" which his mother and father had committed in the management of his early life. Spring arrived, and he was again at Denmark Hill. There, late one Saturday night, as he came in from a dinner-party, Ruskin found that the old man had chosen to sit up for him. He was anxious to show John two business letters "on a difficult subject" which he had just completed. He was very proud of them, his son remarked: "so he read them both to me (boring me mightily, for I was dog-tired) . . . I listened to and praised the first: the second . . . I got thinking of something else in the midst of, which he seeing rose and bade me good-night." The next morning it was clear that he was ill, and later that day he experienced a seizure. The following Thursday, March 3rd, 1864,

James died, in the arms of the son whom he had loved and helped to mould and (as John assured him) ruined. He was buried in a churchyard near Croydon, under a brief inscription of Ruskin's own composing. " He was " (his son informed posterity) " an entirely honest merchant. . . ."

VII

SNOW had fallen at the beginning of March; and, if it held till the day of his father's interment, Ruskin hoped that it might muffle the wheels of the funeral carriages as they rolled away from Denmark Hill. All that she could be spared, he wished to spare his mother; but no doubt he had under-estimated Margaret Ruskin's fortitude; in spite of her age and infirmity—she was now eighty-three, very lame and rapidly becoming blind—she emerged from her ordeal extremely "calm and self-possessed," even proposing that John should leave her and go north on a holiday. John refused; for, besides the protection that he felt he owed his mother, he had been involved by his father's death in much tedious financial business. James Ruskin's property was large[1]: to his wife he left £37,000 and the enjoyment for her lifetime of the house at Denmark Hill: to John, £120,000, a collection of pictures worth £10,000, and other solid assets. Some of his inheritance Ruskin decided to reinvest, a plan which he afterwards put into execution, not always very luckily; while £17,000 was distributed to various relations and dependants, members of his family whom he personally liked and whom James Ruskin, in his exclusive devotion to his wife and son, had not chosen to remember. At last he was completely independent. The long period of tutelage, during which he had been his father's pensioner, the recipient of an annual allowance of £1000 or £1500, over and above the sums he received for his books and lectures, was drawing to its natural close.

[1]By the end of his life, Ruskin had almost divested himself of his inherited wealth, and depended for his income on his literary earnings.

Yet the burden of the past could not be sloughed off; and certain tactless friends, in the consolatory letters they wrote, helped greatly to increase it. Acland, for instance; who chose this moment—" a curious time," as Ruskin pointed out—to hazard a guess that his friend might occasionally have spoken in such a way as to cause the old man sorrow. He was quite wrong, Ruskin assured him, though he admitted that, while " I held my father in my arms during the last day and night of delirium . . . I *was* surprised to feel how much light was thrown on the occasions, and they were numberless, on which I might have given my father pleasure by the mere expression of my love for him, and never did." Later, he summed up the situation, once again for Acland's benefit—that of " a father who would have sacrificed his life for his son, and yet forced his son to sacrifice his life to him, and sacrifice it in vain. It is " (he concluded) " an exquisite piece of tragedy altogether—very much like Lear, in a ludicrous commercial way—Cordelia remaining unchanged and her friends writing to her afterwards—wasn't she sorry for the pain she had given her father by not speaking when she should? " The tragedy depressed, but did not crush him. In the face of death, he showed—as he had shown before, and was subsequently to show during a far more cruel loss—an unexpected strength of mind. He declined to adopt the Victorian trappings of grief,[1] refused to dirty his fingertips by writing to his friends on the customary black-edged paper, and persuaded Mrs. Ruskin that she need not wear a widow's cap. Instead she assumed, as Georgiana Burne-Jones noted, " a soft, closely-fitting cap of another shape, with delicate net quiltings round the face and narrow white satin strings," secured, in order to please John, by the decorative addition of " a fine diamond and emerald brooch."

Thus equipped, sternly resigned to Providence, inflexibly devoted to her son, but still keenly and audibly

[1] " I am naturally of a sad disposition and I simply *cannot* go to funerals, I was not at *Turner's*. I differ from every one nearly in my dealings with the living and dead." Ruskin to the daughter of William Hunt the water-colourist 14th February, 1864, on her father's death.

critical both of the heterodox opinions he held and the outlandish friends he introduced, Margaret Ruskin passed her remaining years, and to the end ruled her household as she had always ruled them. They were presently joined by a new and soothing inmate. Joan Agnew, afterwards Joan Severn, the grand-daughter of James Ruskin's mother, was a sensible and warm-hearted girl, and, having arrived on a brief visit, she soon made her home with the Ruskin family, whose contrasted characters and demands she displayed unusual skill in managing. She was Mrs. Ruskin's companion, Ruskin's friend and confidante. He declared that he regarded her as a gift from heaven; and, thanks to her youth and cheerfulness, Denmark Hill, where he was now obliged to spend much of the time he would otherwise have spent in Switzerland or Italy, seemed, if not the dwelling he would have chosen, at least a tolerable place of refuge. His visitors observed the exemplary patience with which he continued to humour his mother's smallest wishes. " John, John Ruskin, what was that you said? " her sharply commanding voice still reverberated down the dinner table; still, when her bell rang, he would leave the friends he was entertaining and hurry off towards her sitting-room; and as of old he endeavoured to keep the peace between Mrs. Ruskin and Anne, the elderly and ill-tempered Scottish retainer who had nursed him in his childhood. Anne, cried his mother, was possessed by the Devil. But then, her own brand of Christianity had a somewhat fierce and gloomy colouring; and the gentle Georgiana Burne-Jones was once prostrated by shyness on being suddenly and peremptorily confronted with the question, fired off in Mrs. Ruskin's usual imperative fashion: " Do you love God? " Mrs. Burne-Jones timidly agreed that she did. " I don't! " retorted the older woman and, while Georgiana shrank within herself, " discoursed to me upon the arrogance of any creature daring to say such a thing about the Creator, so great and so far above us all."

His father's extinction brought Ruskin back to Denmark Hill, to duties and associations that, only a few years earlier, he seemed definitely to be abandoning; but it did

M

not bring him back in his emotional entirety—as once before he had returned when the ungracious Effie disappeared. Many experiences had intervened, and to-day his heart was elsewhere; for, although Denmark Hill and the obligations it imposed might monopolise him physically, in heart he was always with Rose La Touche, a victim of the persistent waking dream, the rapturous hallucination, that had mastered him since 1858. His activities were not thereby lessened—Ruskin published a number of important and characteristic works between 1864 and 1870, and lectured at the Working Men's College and at Manchester and Cambridge; but every activity, he afterwards informed a friend, had been coloured by the idea of Rose; he had had no thought "but was in some part of it hers"; to her he had dedicated every intellectual effort. Thus the history of the next six years is primarily the history of Ruskin's thwarted passion—thwarted by differences of age and outlook, thwarted, too, by something in Ruskin's temperament that caused him to lean always towards the remote and unattainable. Rose's remoteness did not decrease. Her mother spoke of her as still a child, while her devotee was determined to credit his idol with more than adult subtlety; and Rose herself (he gradually became aware) was apt to take refuge in her youth from the difficulties of a position she could not wholly understand. Across the decades that divided them, an emotionally retarded man made desperate, appealing gestures to a precocious adolescent. But Rose's precocity was relative; and it has been asserted by one of Ruskin's closest friends that, from the sexual point of view, she never reached maturity, with consequent grave disturbances both on the physical and on the spiritual plane. Nor did her feelings, we may surmise, ever mature beyond a certain stage. They had developed early, and with promising exuberance; she had revealed an instinctive appreciation of the devotion that she called forth, had humoured and teased and beguiled her admirer, until he assured himself that, notwithstanding all Mrs. La Touche's declarations to the contrary, Rose not only liked and respected, but loved and understood, him. A moment arrived when he demanded definite proof, and at that moment the quality he had prized most—Rose's delicate elusiveness—was an enraging, maddening obstacle. She had gone so far; she would advance no farther. As his signals to her grew more passionate, more despairing, she appeared insensibly to shrink away.

The crisis of their strange relationship, involving a clash of emotions that convulsed his whole existence, finally materialised in 1866, when Rose La Touche was seventeen. During the years that preceded the crisis, he had written to her constantly and had met her as often as his circumstances allowed or her family permitted. But that permission was given by Mr. and Mrs. La Touche with more and more reluctance. Ruskin's plan of settling down at Harristown, in a cottage beyond the La Touches' park-wall, had definitely been put aside. Rose, however, was occasionally in London, and, among her other engagements, could sometimes come to Denmark Hill. Then there were " paradisiacal " walks in his garden, " under the peach-blossom branches by the little glittering stream which I had paved with crystal . . ." This rivulet—by Rosie and Joan Agnew unkindly called " The Gutter "—was fed from a reservoir which Ruskin had built behind a bank of laurel; and on sunny days he would release a " rippling film of water " down the serpentine channel he had paved for it, over miniature rapids and through lilliputian pools and lakes. Rosie might laugh at " The Gutter," but she loved his peach-tree avenue. How often she returned to Denmark Hill, admired the garden and the pictures indoors, or listened to the unseen corncrake, whose mysterious voice sounded all summer long from an adjacent hayfield, there is no means of determining exactly in Ruskin's correspondence. Presumably her visits were few; certainly he remembered them, and hoarded up and brooded over the memory, with undiminished gratitude; but such paradisiacal visitations had, nevertheless, a slowly darkening background. Time passed; and the need that he felt for Rosie's presence grew more acutely painful, more difficult to explain away as the affection of a middle-aged teacher for a beguiling, gifted child-friend, whose youth might excuse her in any deeper sense from sharing it. He had supported the deception with patience and humour and skill, had nourished the legend of Rosie-Posie with a weekly or daily tribute of myths and fantasies and nicknames. Now the amorist, who in previous relationships had seemed to fly reality, grew tired of the vision and grasped distractedly at real love.

The transformation of his feelings was not, of course, immediate. So oddly constituted was Ruskin the lover, that he would appear to have succumbed to the belief that he was "in love" with Rose almost as soon as they first came face to face in her mother's Green Street drawing-room. As early as 1860, when Rose was eleven, he had confessed that he could love no one "except my Mouse-pet in Ireland who nibbles me to the very sick-death with weariness to see her." But he had restrained the impatience of his feelings, and, making use of all kinds of ingeniously playful devices, had done his best to disguise or sublimate their quality. Could her parents reasonably object to the interest he took in their daughter's education? Could they look askance at the nursery-jingles he sent from Switzerland to Harristown?

Rosie, pet, and Rosie, puss,
See, the moonlight's on the Reuss:
O'er the Alps the clouds lie loose,
Tossed about in silver tangles,
In and out through all the angles,
Some obtuse and some acute;
Lakelet waves, though crisped, are mute,
Only seen by moving spangles. . . .

What could be prettier, or more transparently blameless? Whimsical sentimentality was within the compass of most Victorian great men; and, as we know from the biography of the Reverend Charles Lutwidge Dodgson, exceedingly circumspect Victorian parents saw nothing amiss in the behaviour of a distinguished middle-aged man who admitted to an inordinate preference for the companionship of little girls. Ruskin's first visit to Harristown, at least until he broached the subject of his religious backslidings, had been harmonious and enjoyable; true, Rosie had had "queer little fits . . . like patience on a monument" and had "walked like a little white statue through the twilight woods, talking solemnly"; but Lacerta had encouraged St. Crumpet to believe that she still esteemed and trusted him, and he had returned to England full of hopes that his adoration was not wasted. According to an unpublished letter, it was during the following year, in the April of 1862, that the first fatal change occurred; "they took the child away from me—practically." What was said or done we can no longer ascertain; but this separation, Ruskin latterly convinced himself, had been the source of deep unhappiness. Henceforward hope was mingled with suspicion, and passion with anxiety.

If Ruskin's distress is comprehensible, so is the hesitation displayed by Rose's troubled parents. Apart from their objection to Ruskin's religious views, the problem of their daughter's health must constantly be considered. She was not a normal child. At some moments impetuous and high-spirited, racing across the park on her cream-coloured pony, darting to and fro among the peasants' cottages like the wild heroine of a romantic novel about the Irish countryside, at others she seemed to fall into a deep mysterious melancholy, when her ideas became confused and she drifted out of touch with everyday existence. She had been ill in 1863; she was "ill all through '64," according to Ruskin's later and, it may be, partial statement. Himself he imputed her state of mind to the deleterious effects of the stern evangelical creed on which she had been nourished. ". . . I had a little pet of a girl" (he wrote to his friend Vernon Lushington in 1865) ". . . and she went half-mad with religion and nearly died—and now she can't write—or think—consecutively, so that it's just as if she were dead." Under the influence of his passion for Rose, Ruskin's attitude towards evangelical Christianity grew more and more resentful, till, during the course of a lecture given in Dublin,[1] he finally delivered himself of all his pent-up anger, speaking of "the morbid corruption and waste of vital power in religious sentiment, by which the pure strength of that which should be the guiding soul of every nation, the splendour of its youthful manhood, and spotless light of its maidenhood is averted or cast away." It was of Rose La Touche the lecturer thought, Rose whose clear poetic intelligence, which had burned with such enchanting clarity in the earliest letters that she sent him, now flickered unsteady and indistinct, sometimes manifesting a gleam of the ancient promise, only to subside after a few months into obscurity and languor. Ruskin did not despair of his pupil; he believed she might yet recover; the alternative, at least, was too appalling to be contemplated. But in 1864, Rose's parents took fresh alarm, and renewed their previous opposition to this perplexing courtship. Their attempts at discouragement he repulsed with fury. Mrs. La Touche's motives, he began to conclude, were deeply, darkly suspect.

She had "got jealous" of her daughter—that was the sole explanation he could find of Lacerta's fiendish conduct. It is possible he was not entirely misguided; for Mrs. La Touche was an attractive woman, fond of the converse of distinguished men and versed in the pleasing, if unprofitable, intricacies of an intellectual love-affair. She was not in love with St. Crumpet; but perhaps she thought she loved him. Ruskin undoubtedly believed that he had been loved, and afterwards protested that he had done his utmost, "in pure truth to her as wife and mother," to repay Lacerta's feeling. Yes, he had loved her "sacredly and devotedly"; and, conscious of the value of the genuine love he gave, he was astonished that she should have attacked the "deeper love"—his inextinguishable passion for Rose—which she saw had come between them. At the time there was nothing he could do: until Rose had reached her twenty-first birthday, her parents' opposition and her own scrupulous

[1] "The Mystery of Life and its Arts," delivered in Dublin on May 13th, 1868.

hesitations were almost impossible to overcome. Meanwhile he must continue to wait; but he no longer waited patiently; and, as the tension of his feelings became more oppressive, so did the outbursts with which he occasionally relieved them become increasingly embittered. His predicament had a considerable effect on his work. There were moments after his father's death when it seemed to him that he was incapable of any sustained intellectual effort, and when he described himself to a friend as "maundering about" among his fruit-trees, "investigating the subject of currant blossoms . . . as vast a subject as I am fit for yet." But the habit of working presently returned: the only change was in the literary method that Ruskin now adopted. That change was curious and disconcerting. Between the energy, the vivacity and gaiety even, of the lectures delivered from 1857 to 1859 and afterwards published as *The Two Paths*, and such volumes as *Sesame and Lilies* and *Ethics of the Dust*, published in 1864 and 1865 respectively, there is a contrast all the more obvious because the beliefs expressed are similar. Ruskin was inevitably a discursive theorist; but his earlier lectures combine a trick of conversational discursiveness with a general sense of direction that seldom wholly fails him. In *The Two Paths*, for example, his expression of his theories—on the application of design to modern manufacture, and of imagination to the art of architecture—is usually direct and forceful, and very often witty. The result is exceedingly personal; but Ruskin can still stand aside and take an objective view of the subject that he undertakes. In his later books, on the other hand, every subject is apt to be viewed either through a prism of tears or through a mist of anger. The outlines of his subject are blurred or distorted: Ruskin is content to think aloud, without submitting his thoughts to the preliminary æsthetic discipline that might transform them into literature. Few private divagations will bear exact transcription: and the state of Ruskin's mind at this period did not conduce to harmony.

Yet it would be wrong to assume that he was invariably downcast. Human companionship, when it was of the right sort, had still the power of cheering him; and with Carlyle and "some ladies, and a few favourite children" (as Norton had already remarked) his spirits were "exuberant." The choice of companions is revealing; and Carlyle's place in his affections deserves especial notice. Here Ruskin's attitude was that of a devoted son; he addressed the older man as his "Dearest Papa"—a degree of familiarity that the prophet would no doubt have rebuffed in a less attractive correspondent; and William Allingham, during a visit to Cheyne Row, was once surprised to behold Ruskin come suddenly into the room, rush over to Carlyle, who was lying in deep dejection on a sofa, seize his hands and kiss them. His love, in fact, looked upwards or downwards; and, just as it suited him to look up to Carlyle—a majestic parental figure, not unlike those august figures who had loomed above his boyhood—so he was naturally inclined to moods of tender patronage. Among children and women he found the friends he preferred; and, if the children were nascent women, the interest they aroused had a proportionately vivid colouring. Besides, he adored the idea of youth, regretting the waste of his own youth, in which so many generous impulses, so many opportunities of simple, sanguine enjoyment, had needlessly been stifled, and hankering after the promise of renewed youth that Rose appeared to hold out. Rose's promise had not yet materialised; and meantime, during the wearisome years of hope and disappointment, Ruskin would seem to have found a vicarious satisfaction in the frequent visits he paid to Winnington Hall, Cheshire, a large and old-fashioned house, where his friend and disciple Miss Bell had instituted a girls' school on advanced modern principles.[1] Ruskin approved of the principles, admired the situation, and was charmed by his first glimpse of pretty well-groomed children seated on the floor around a huge baronial fireplace. Before long he had adopted Winnington Hall; a room had been allotted to him, and improved by the addition of spacious casements which commanded three views of the river; and

[1]Winnington was among the first schools at which girls were encouraged to play cricket.

he had begun to lend his financial support, as often as Miss Bell's altruistic but too-ambitious schemes involved her in embarrassment. Once again he was the practical philanthropist, and could combine his thirst for usefulness with the consuming love of beauty. . . .

Winnington, then, had a double appeal; but no doubt it was on the artist and lover, rather than on the philanthropist, that the associations of the old house were apt to work most strongly. The sight of the girls at dinner—"the long tables with the bright faces above them"—reminded him of a splendid composition by Paolo Veronese: "the mere picturesqueness of the thing" (he had told his father) "is worth a great deal." In the contemplation of these candid faces, these inexperienced and graceful bodies, he found an image of Rose La Touche many times repeated: in their company, a substitute for the daily and hourly contact with Rose which as yet he could not hope for. Miss Bell's curriculum laid especial emphasis on music. After dinner there would be dancing; and Edward and Georgiana Burne-Jones, whom he brought with him to Winnington during the August of 1863, watched the famous critic in an unaccustomed rôle, surrounded by white-frocked girls and gravely stepping out, now and then, into a country dance or quadrille, looking "very thin" (Georgiana noted) "scarcely more than a black line, as he moved about amongst the white girls in his evening dress." There were also concerts; and musical visitors as distinguished as Mr. Charles Hallé were sometimes coaxed to the piano-stool. One evening (Ruskin recorded) he "actually sat down and played quadrilles for us to dance to. . . . But afterwards he played 'Home, Sweet Home,' with three variations—*quite* the most wonderful thing I have ever heard in music." Mr. Hallé, as it subsequently appeared, had hoped to play some Beethoven; but Ruskin politely dissuaded him, confessing that he did not understand Beethoven and feared he never should have time to do so: at which the pianist had condescended to a less unfamiliar melody, with results equally agreeable to the critic and his young friends; for, while Ruskin admired the almost invisible movement with which Mr. Hallé's expert fingers flew across the keyboard, and the beauty of the variations, "like the murmur of a light fountain, far away," he was aware, simultaneously and no less pleasurably, of the emotional effect upon the hearers. "It was beautiful" (he declared) "to see the girls face round, the eyes all wet with feeling, and the little coral mouths fixed into little half-open gaps with utter intensity of astonishment."

This appreciative virginal audience was to be observed on other evenings grouped at Ruskin's footstool. He lectured to them, as he had lectured to the Working Men's College, without any particular respect for age, tastes, prejudices or powers of understanding, but with that discursive poetic enthusiasm of which he held the secret. *Ethics of the Dust* is staged at Winnington: the "Old Lecturer (of incalculable age)" is, of course, the writer: and, if we are to credit the statement printed in his foreword, that "the following lectures were really given, in substance, at a girls' school . . . which I visited frequently enough to enable the children to regard me as a friend," little coral mouths again must often have fallen ajar with utter intensity of astonishment, and, it may be, an occasional convulsive yawn have needed prompt suppression. For between the pages of this extraordinary volume—a characteristic product of the literary period Ruskin was now entering—playfulness and pedantry make extremely awkward bedfellows. *Ethics of the Dust* did not find favour with the general reading public; but one authoritative critic thought it wholly irresistible. Otherwise so contemptuous of sentimentality and loose thinking, Carlyle announced that it was "a most shining Performance," that he had devoured it "without pause," and that not for a long time had he "read anything a tenth part so radiant with talent, ingenuity, lambent fire. . . . In power of *expression*, I pronounce it to be supreme. . . . The bits of Egyptian Mythology . . . apart from their *elucidative* quality, which is exquisite, have in them a poetry that might fill any Tennyson with despair." To-day it is difficult, either from the didactic or from the literary point of view, to recapture the spirit of Carlyle's fervid eulogies. The book purports to be an introduction to the luminous world of crystals; but Ruskin's capacity for discovering sermons in stones leads him to strew the path of the aspiring crystallographer with sharp-edged moral homilies, which crop up to bruise the reader's heel just when we suppose we are on the track of some important scientific truth. Far from lighting our way through a complex subject, the lecturer seems to be playing at hide-and-seek with us in the avenues of a decorative labyrinth that he has himself created.

He is perverse, whimsical, deliberately eccentric. It is, indeed, as a sketch for a self-portrait, rather than as a popular exposition of scientific theories, that *Ethics of the Dust* still retains its value. Now he is the poet: now the pedant: now a cultured middle-aged man, somewhat feminine and finical, prone to interrupt his interlocutors with a reproving "*Pardon me, puss*," yet agreeably stimulated by the presence of so much youth and innocent freshness disposed around his arm-chair. His playful asides are a trifle embarrassing; but from time to time he seems to forget his audience, whom at more relaxed moments he flirts with, spoils and patronises, and launches into a passionate Ruskinian flight, reminiscent of *Modern Painters* or the boldest paragraphs of *The Stones of Venice*. Here the poet and the scientist—even though his scientific knowledge was, no doubt, superficial—achieve a close alliance; but, after a dozen lines, the bond is usually loosened, and Ruskin begins to moralise or drifts into comparing the fate of "poor little crystals" to the transitory existence of the little girls about him:

"Those gases themselves" (he writes in his ninth lecture, entitled *Crystal Sorrows*) "may be supplied in all variation of volume and power from below . . . and, at changing temperatures, must exert relatively changing forces of decomposition and combination on the walls of the veins they fill; while water, at every degree of heat and pressure (from beds of everlasting ice, alternate with cliffs of native rock, to volumes of red-hot, or white-hot, steam) congeals, and drips, and throbs, and thrills, from crag to crag; and breathes from pulse to pulse of foaming or fiery arteries, whose beating is felt through chains of the great islands of the Indian seas, as your own pulses lift your bracelets, and makes whole kingdoms of the world quiver in deadly earthquake, as if they were as light as aspen leaves. And, remember, the poor little crystals have to live their lives, and mind their own affairs, in the midst of all this, as best they may. They are wonderfully like human creatures . . . spiteful or loving, and indolent or painstaking, and orderly or licentious, with no thought whatever of the lava or the flood which may break over them any day; and evaporate them into air-bubbles, or wash them into a solution of salts."

Thus the lecturer pursues his mazy path; till presently we are reading of " little child-crystals put to school like school-girls ": " unhappy little child-crystals left to lie about in the dirt, and pick up their living, and learn manners where they can ": " fat crystals eating up thin ones, like great capitalists and little labourers ": " politico-economic crystals teaching the stupid ones how to eat each other, and cheat each other ": " impatient crystals," " vampire crystals," " parasite crystals " and " courtier crystals . . . and all these, besides the two great companies of war and peace, who ally themselves, resolutely to attack, or resolutely to defend. And for the close " (continues the merciless Lecturer) " you see the broad shadow and deadly force of inevitable fate, above all this: you see the multitudes of crystals whose time has come; not a set time, as with us, but yet a time, sooner or later, when they all must give up their crystal ghosts: when the strength by which they grew, and the breath given them to breathe, pass away from them; and they fail, and are consumed, and vanish away; and another generation is brought to life, framed out of their ashes."

" It is very terrible," concludes one of his listeners, a slightly aggressive girl named Mary, " of whom everybody, including the Old Lecturer, is in great awe." But, apart from the perplexing or disturbing effect that Ruskin's fantasy about *Crystal Sorrows* may have had upon his audience, it serves to illustrate the increasingly capricious latitude that, as a result both of private distress and of public disappointment, he was now prepared to permit his own creative impulses. He had begun to despair of being loved, just as he despaired of being understood. And, since those he loved would not love him, and those he sermonised would not hearken to him—or at least refused to fall in with his wishes on the terms that he had laid down—he adopted a defiantly sibylline style, and, giving free rein to his teeming fancies, developed a strain of prophetic extravagance not easily to be distinguished from literary self-indulgence. His method, if it can be called a method, was to allow one image, one set of associations, to merge into another; and successive ideas appeared so thick and fast, and in the process of appearing and proliferating became so strangely intertwined, that he was often obliged to confide to his readers (with whom, in book after book, his relationship was destined to grow more oddly confidential) that the task of disentangling them was really quite beyond him. Thus, in *The Cestus of Aglaia*, sub-titled *Nine Papers on the Laws of Art*, contributed to the *Art Journal* in 1865, having embarked on the art of engraving and compared the patience it demands of the artist to that displayed, according to legend, by the exemplary Griselda, he confesses that " I cannot get to my work in this paper, somehow; the web of these old enigmas entangles me again and again "; for the " rough syllable " with which Griselda's name begins, " Gries," " the stone," suggests the " long fall of the Toccia," and, that in its turn, brings " thoughts of the great Alpine patience; mute snow wreathed by grey rock, till avalanche time comes—patience of mute tormented races till the time of the Grey league came; at last impatient. (Not that hitherto it has hewn its way to much: the Rhine foam of the Via Mala seeming to have done its work better.) But it is a noble colour that Grison grey—dawn colour—graceful for a faded silk to ride in, and wonderful, in paper, for getting a glow upon, if you begin wisely."

Of these sentences, Ruskin's most devoted commentator

has remarked, not without good reason, that he imagines that they will be " largely unintelligible to many readers," who may not at once perceive how, by a series of poetic association, Griselda suggests a waterfall beneath the Gries glacier: how Alpine scenery brings him to Swiss history: and how, at last, the sequence of ideas suddenly turning back upon itself, the colour *grey* evokes a memory of Tennyson[1] and reminds him of the grey paper which his ever-admired Turner had employed for water-colour sketches. Such is now and then the method of poetry—used with brilliant success by a Gérard de Nerval or a Rimbaud; but it is not a method that the writer of prose, particularly if his aim is often didactic rather than suggestive, can generally handle to very great advantage. Ruskin's didacticism had not diminished. Desperately anxious to instruct and enlighten, still driven by a passionate desire to establish some genuine communion with his fellow human beings, he attempted nevertheless to satisfy his own tastes, " writing . . . all that comes into my head for my own pleasure,"[2] becoming gradually more diffuse and involved, till even the titles that headed his books and lectures were as far-fetched and enigmatic as an ingenious brain could make them. Another and smaller artist might at this stage of his progress have withdrawn from life completely and shrunk into emotional isolation and intellectual solitude. But Ruskin's behaviour in any predicament was almost always unexpected. The prophet was still a man of affairs; and, while, on the one hand, we observe the deepening obscurity in which he wrapped his prose-style—a reflection of the confusion and uncertainty that now beset his inner life—we also observe his efforts, strenuous and unselfish as before, to deal with concrete problems. His sense of duty was in no way impaired. There were still letters to be written to the press, on half a dozen controversial issues, from the condition of English domestic servants to the state of European politics; and

[1]" . . . Entreat her by my love . . .
That she ride with me in her faded silk."—*Enid.*

[2]*The Queen of The Air.*

when the case of Governor Eyre, who during the autumn of 1865 had suppressed a negro revolt in Jamaica with energetic ruthlessness, led to the organisation of a "Jamaica Committee," headed by John Stuart Mill, Herbert Spencer and Huxley, with the express intention of bringing Eyre to trial for murder, Ruskin joined Carlyle, Tennyson, Kingsley and Dickens in the "Eyre Defence Committee," and himself contributed £100 towards the Governor's Defence Fund. As a determined Illiberal, it was his proper position; and, although committee meetings scarcely suited his genius, he took the opportunity of delivering some violent attacks on liberal-commercial cant and humanitarian humbug, immensely to the delight of Carlyle, who announced that, "while all the world stands tremulous, shilly-shallying from the gutter, impetuous Ruskin plunges his rapier up to the very hilt in the abominable belly" of universal blockheadism. Yet the monster did not succumb to its injuries: Eyre, who had been recalled in disgrace, escaped criminal prosecution but was never reinstated.[1]

Ruskin had joined the Committee at Carlyle's behest, and continued to serve there, as Carlyle's deputy, after his friend had withdrawn to the South of France under the guardianship of Lady Ashburton. The bond that united the two men was especially close in the year 1866. Judging by his subsequent reference to Froude's biography, Ruskin had been informed of, or had divined, the secret of the tormented Carlyle household;[2] he had liked and respected Jane Carlyle who, at least to his face, seems to have spared him her more biting conversational pleasantries; and he had often visited her at Cheyne Row, in her small sitting-room where even the wallpaper she chose reflects the sober hue of disillusionment, but where her restless wit still flashed and sparkled with almost eighteenth-century gusto. She, too, was susceptible to flattery and affection, and appreciated the delicate skill Ruskin displayed in his

[1]He was permitted, on the other hand, to draw the pension of a retired Colonial Governor.

[2]*See footnote* page 112.

friendly management of "Mr. C."[1] Then, on April 23rd, 1866, when he was about to go abroad with the Trevelyans, he called to say good-bye to her. On his arms were flowers from Denmark Hill; but on the doorstep he was met by a weeping maid-servant who told him that that same day, only a few hours earlier, Mrs. Carlyle's life had ended. Her death had been quiet and quick. Driving through the Park in her newly-acquired brougham—a vehicle which she could at last afford, after a lifetime of exhausting journeys by hackney-cab and omnibus—she had put down her little dog, Nero's successor, to take its daily exercise. It had received a glancing blow from the wheels of a carriage, had rolled over, and had protested loudly. Mrs. Carlyle had dismounted, picked it up, discovered it was unhurt and continued on her expedition. As he looked down, her coachman could see only a pair of hands lying smoothly, calmly folded. They did not move, and he became alarmed. Worn thin by suffering and self-pity, by the gnawing consciousness of wasted talent and the sense of deep emotional frustration that her married life engendered, her resistance had given way beneath a sudden heart attack. She had been killed by the hysterical outcry of a badly frightened lap-dog.

To Ruskin's letter of condolence, Carlyle replied on May 10th. "Your kind words from Dijon" (he wrote) "were welcome to me: thanks. I did not doubt your sympathy in what has come: but it is better that I see it laid before me. You are yourself very unhappy, as I too well discern—heavy-laden, obstructed and dispirited . . ." Ruskin's unhappiness, however, had a very different quality; for whereas Carlyle mourned an irrevocable loss (which had left him exposed to unending regrets, "the light of his life as if gone out") suspense, uncertainty and some glimmerings of hope added to the painfulness of Ruskin's plight. The development of the drama is by no means clear; but we learn that, early in 1866, when Rose La Touche had reached her seventeenth birthday, her lover

[1]No one, declared Mrs. Carlyle, managed her husband as well as Ruskin: "it was quite beautiful to see him."

Rose La Touche from a Drawing by Ruskin, 1874

made a definite proposal and received from the beloved's lips an inconclusive answer. Rose's birthday fell on February 3rd: it was on Lady Day, March 25th, that he had his reply—just such a reply as, had he profited by his study of Rose's character, he might have very well have expected. He must wait three years, till she had come of age. Thus the feast of the Annunciation brought with it no felicitous tidings, no promises of assured love, but merely a prolongation of the suspense that had already sapped his peace of mind. For the moment, they continued to meet and talk. During April, Rose came to Denmark Hill on another "paradisiacal" visit, leaving behind her an aura of remembered bliss which, with his usual anxiety to share his keenest pleasures, Ruskin hastened to communicate in a letter to Edward Burne-Jones. "Did you" (he asked) "see the gleam of sunshine yesterday afternoon? If you had only seen her in it, bareheaded, between my laurels and my primrose bank!" But, though her rare visits had a consolatory charm, they were accompanied by no genuine growth of confidence, no real increase of intimacy. Rose's physical condition was as precarious as ever; and in a desperate attempt to escape from the thraldom of oppressive adult feelings, she would appear to have pleaded the state of her health if Ruskin's adoration seemed to be closing round too greedily. She would not, or could not, explain and argue. She appreciated her position as the mystic Rose; but "she is still suffering" (he informed his old Venetian acquaintance, Rawdon Brown) "from the effects of long illness, and does not like to talk seriously of anything, least of all anything likely to give pain either to her parents or to me, and she knows she can't please both. So she stays my child pet, and puts her finger up if ever I look grave." Alas, the time had long since gone by when Ruskin could still be content with his ethereal vision of a child-friend. Rosie was nearly an adult woman. A more important consideration—he himself was forty-seven.

At this moment, however, he gained the support of an engaging, brilliant confidante. Ruskin's passion for Rose had always been undisguised: he had written and spoken of it with considerable frankness and had repeated her name so frequently and so tenderly, both in and out of season, that a casual fellow-traveller was once moved to demand " Who *is* Rosie-Posie? " But, although his friends might sympathise, they could be of very little real help. Mrs. Cowper Temple, on the other hand, knew the La Touche family; and, while that alone would have made her friendship valuable, she had in her own right an especial claim to Ruskin's love and gratitude. In questions of sentiment exceedingly superstitious, he had never forgotten the beautiful English girl—" statuesque severity with womanly sweetness joined "—whom more than twenty years earlier, at a time when he had not yet recovered from his frustrated cult of Adèle, he had looked for eagerly over the heads of crowded Roman church-goers. She had marked a stage of his emotional convalescence: Santa Maria in Ara Coeli—the same church where Edward Gibbon, musing sedately upon the ruins of Rome, felt the idea of depicting its decline and fall first steal across his spirit—had been a resting-place in the history of Ruskin's heart, not perhaps among the most important, but remembered with romantic regret during his arduous course through middle age. Now the angelic stranger had reappeared: in Mrs. Cowper Temple (later Lady Mount Temple), a cultivated woman of the world with intellectual leanings, he had rediscovered the beautiful Miss Tollemache whose far-seen profile, floating like a mirage over the dark alien crowd, had strengthened and uplifted him. A patroness of Pre-Raphaelite painters, Mrs. Cowper Temple was also versed in spiritualism. During the spring of 1864, soon after his father's death, Ruskin at her invitation had attended several séances. If James Ruskin returned from the dead, he did not expect, he warned his friend, to hear " anything very happy. . . ." There had been no manifestations of his father's presence; and the behaviour of the " spirits " evoked had perplexed and disappointed him; for, whereas he had wished to be put into communication with Paolo Veronese, they had continued to prattle away with the inconsequence peculiar to disembodied voices. Still, he had been interested, if not completely converted—Ruskin's mind made a large allowance for the dark and inexplicable; but just now his aspirations had a less incorporeal tendency. He "wanted happiness in this world"; and Mrs. Cowper Temple, with her fund of worldly wisdom and her knowledge of the La Touche parents, had been introduced under such favourable omens that she might somehow help him find it.

Undoubtedly she did her best. For the next two or three years Ruskin and his delightful friend corresponded frequently; and from the letters in which he sought her help—passionate outpourings of injured love, bursts of furious indignation and long, sometimes incoherent attempts at justificatory self-analysis—we gain an impression of his inward disarray so vivid and so explicit as often to be hardly bearable. For Ruskin was not one of those lovers whose mind remains relatively independent of the storms that overtake the heart, and who preserve a certain detachment, the gift of observation and comparison, through the worst emotional hurricanes. His unhappiness struck at a vital centre; and the correspondence with Mrs. Cowper Temple shows not only the immediate agony that his frustrated passion caused him, but the damage done by those sufferings to his whole intellectual fabric. Besides a heart ravaged, we see a mind beleaguered. It is a spectacle that the biographer who has a regard for his subject approaches with some diffidence. Yet, if the subject is to be explored as its merits require, the tragedy of Ruskin's greatest love (on which his elder disciples are inclined to express the hope that any new study of his character may not lean too heavily) cannot be disassociated from the evolution of his life's work. The failure of the one is inextricably bound up with the curtailment of the other; for Rose La Touche, the creature of flesh and blood, under whose unconsciously potent influence the baffled impulses of half a lifetime were now demanding outlet, had also a symbolic importance, and represented, little as she suspected it, a deeper, older problem. His inability to solve that problem had ultimately a crippling effect upon the growth of Ruskin's genius, at a moment when full intellectual maturity might have enabled him to crown the work he had begun with *Modern Painters*, and the rich results of nearly thirty years' imaginative exploration were waiting to be gathered in. The harvest was immense; but Ruskin, though his nervous energy was undiminished, had no longer sufficient sense of proportion, or the requisite degree of application, to make economical employment of the wealth that lay beneath his hand. He used it carelessly and extravagantly, with a capricious disregard for stylistic rule and measure. He impaired his resources by reckless diffusion; much of his talent (we are bound to conclude) was irremediably wasted.

The origin of the problem that defeated Ruskin, like the origin of so many problems, is to be discovered in his childhood; and at the end of his life when he was writing *Praeterita*, and the huge landscape of his past existence lay stretched out far behind him, progressively more distinct as the stages were more distant, he enumerated four " calamities " which, in the considered judgement of an elderly man, had left indelible scars upon his adult character. At this point only the first concerns us: " . . . I had nothing to love " . . . " The evil consequence . . . was not, however, what might perhaps have been expected, that I grew up selfish or unaffectionate; but that, when affection did come, it came with violence utterly rampant and unmanageable, at least by me, who never before had anything to manage." He had loved his parents, of course, but, during the formative period of his childhood, always at a distance; and the love they gave in return, with its sober emphasis on duty, did not encourage the gift he might otherwise have developed of independent feeling. Yet his capacity for feeling was never stifled; and again and again he had broken away in some emotional escapade. The harm caused was of a very different kind: his education had not extinguished his native power of loving, but it had cut him off from the knowledge of *how* to love, and denied him any chance of ever loving happily, because, among its other evil effects, it had deprived him of any real understanding of his fellow human creatures. He could not love upon equal terms. Thus his passions were usually nympholeptic, wild delusive infatuations for some fleeting nymph or fairy; and his many tender attachments, in which attraction played a secondary part, had either a filial or a vague paternal colouring. Similarly, in the realm of friendship, he displayed a curious inability to treat his associates as equals. He must for ever be making conditions (as he had done, without marked success, to Dante Gabriel Rossetti), explaining his own emotional needs or rearranging the relation to suit his own convenience. He had little elasticity, and none of the worldly good humour which accepts friendship warmly and uncritically, just as it accepts and welcomes other mundane blessings: with the result that, although he had numerous intellectual contacts, where love or attraction was not concerned, he enjoyed few rewarding personal intimacies —few intimacies, that is to say, in which he received as much as he gave, or came into stimulating collision with an alien mind or temperament. His sense of isolation was still invincible, his inner loneliness impenetrable. He was an egoist with a passionate desire to love: a spiritual recluse, perpetually struggling and perpetually failing to build some line of communication between himself, secluded in his mental fastness, and the unfriendly world around him.

Here, surely, was the essence of Ruskin's dilemma—on the plane of the emotions, how to love worthily, with definite hope of return: on the plane of the intellect, how to establish a real link with the men and women of his generation, exchanging the invidious rôle of honoured and disregarded prophet for that of friendly assistant and confidential mentor. On both planes he failed to achieve a solution. Of Ruskin, Benjamin Jowett, who had at first objected to the prophet's methods but was eventually won over to sympathetic admiration, later observed that he was "the gentlest and most innocent of mankind, of great genius but inconsecutive," his chief weakness being that he had " never rubbed his mind against others." To the absence of this salutary friction may be attributed the majority of Ruskin's intellectual shortcomings, and not a few of his misfortunes in the sphere of love and friendship. He had no instinctive grasp of human psychology—a form of knowledge that does not always depend upon practical experience—and had seldom been close enough to another man or woman to acquire an empirical understanding of the springs of human conduct. Thus he bestowed confidence and affection with an enthusiasm that was usually generous but often highly injudicious; and it is significant that when, in 1865, he wished to choose a secretary, also intended to act as private almoner, his choice fell, not on some grave elderly personage or earnest youthful devotee, but on that flighty adventurer, Charles Augustus Howell, a modern Münchausen whom Rossetti described as a " Gil-Blas-Robinson-Crusoe hero out of his proper time," but Swinburne called a " pole-cat," and whom even his admiring friends agreed to be one of the boldest, readiest and most imaginative liars that had ever turned to art-dealing. Ruskin may have appreciated Howell's " magnificent Animality," his dashing effrontery and cheerful unselfconscious swagger; but their association was productive in the end only of further disillusionment.

If he wanted judgement in ordinary social relations, and was constantly and acutely distressed by his failure to make himself understood as he wished to be understood, or to persuade his contemporaries to accept him at his real value and act on his prophetic message instead of idly listening, he was yet more unfortunate in his approach to the problem of love and in his vigorous but unworldly attempts to capture worldly happiness. Once again he experienced complete frustration; and this disappointment, which after some bitter months a less sensitive and less romantic nature might at length have lived down, for Ruskin, who was neither cynical nor detached, comprehended all the others. His failure in love summed up his failure in life: Rose's refusal of the devotion he offered was symptomatic of the rejections and refusals that at every turn awaited him, of his general inability to come to terms with mankind. But courage and energy he had never wanted; and, having heard his sentence from Rose's lips—that he must be patient for a further three years, with some vague assurance that at the end of that time she would reconsider her position and give an independent answer—he refused angrily to accept defeat, and embarked on a determined struggle against the La Touche parents. Mrs. Cowper Temple was his ally and counsellor. She at least did not dismiss his love as a wild romantic fantasy, and was prepared to believe that a marriage was still possible. And why not? There was (he told his friend in February 1866) a " quiet trust " between Rosie and himself, which could not be broken " except by her bidding." He was confident that she would not enter into any other engagement until she had first consulted him: that she really valued his regard and sympathy, and that she was learning to value it more and more now that her mother's hold was weakened. For Mrs. La Touche, though her daughter was seventeen, continued to treat her as a mere child; and Rosie, so he liked to imagine, had come to rely upon the moral support that only he could give her. She knew that he was hers to dispose of: that he confided in her implicitly, and that she could command him absolutely.

Should she bid him go, he would leave her without a word of protest. But *she* must give him his dismissal; he would accept it from no one else, and certainly he was not to be deterred by her scheming and misguided parents. Towards Mr. and Mrs. La Touche his attitude during the next twelve months oscillated wildly. Now Mrs. La Touche was the villain of the drama, and he blamed all his sufferings upon her cruel opposition, whereas her husband was guilty of nothing worse than a failure to understand him. Now the father was the principal culprit, inconsiderate to his wife and guilty of " doing terrible things to me without saying why. . . ." But during the spring at least, Ruskin still had their " reluctant permission " to keep up some semblance of his former intercourse with

Rose; and Mrs. Cowper Temple was able to arrange occasional meetings—by inviting them, for example, to the same dinner-party at her house in Curzon Street, a party to which Ruskin implored her not to ask Rossetti, lest the gathering should grow too numerous and Rosie's attention be distracted. On March 20th we learn that she has promised him " a little while "; and there followed that visit to Denmark Hill, when he enjoyed the exquisite felicity of seeing his beloved, haloed in a gleam of pallid early sunshine, standing bareheaded between his laurels and his primrose-bank. At the end of April, he went abroad with his friends the Trevelyans; but the expedition was overclouded by Lady Trevelyan's sudden death, and Ruskin found himself alone and disconsolate at the Hotel of the Giesbach, with Joan Agnew, who had accompanied him, and the Trevelyans' youthful niece, brooding unhappily over the transitoriness of earthly hopes. The sight of the Alps refreshed him; but many of the Swiss towns he had once loved were nowadays, like Interlaken, " all dust, misery, and casino "; while the populace, he lamented, showed " every year, steadier march to decline . . . the youth of the towns, cigar in mouth and haggard-faced, and sullen-mouthed and evil-eyed, frightful to think of and anticipate the future of." Once again rumours of war were surging across Europe; but, so preoccupied was he with the problem of his own fate, that these apprehensions for the moment did not stir him deeply. " The prospect of war " (he wrote to Mrs. Cowper Temple) " is of course painful to me—but chiefly in the intense amazement and sense of solitude with which I see my fellow creatures go mad in heaps, and drift into deepest guilt and misery as helplessly as dead leaves."

During his absence from England, Mr. and Mrs. La Touche took their daughter back to Harristown; and, for the reluctant permission they had given Ruskin to continue on his earlier footing, they now substituted a definite ban on any further intimacy. Meetings and letters were both prohibited. They believed that they were acting for the best—a suggestion that enraged their victim as much as it distressed him. What did they know of their daughter's heart? What could they guess of her real needs, or of the true nature of her lover's emotions and the pangs they made him undergo? No one, he felt, could judge or understand his passion: it was a religion to him (he told his friend in Curzon Street), wasting and parching him "like the old enthusiasm of the wild anchorites"; and he did not know how long he could bear it without dying; for he was "not sure even how far in its conceivable happiness it might be endurable by me—it might kill me soon if the least pang of doubt or regret for her mingled with it." And just as no one could judge the strength of his love, so no one could estimate the extent of the sacrifices to which it might inspire him, assuming that they were commanded by Rose herself, not dictated by a third person. If, at this instant, she were to announce that she loved another man whom she could not see unless her rejected lover helped her, he would do all that he could to bring about her wishes, endure the pain of watching them every day, "be their footman and walk behind them—nay—be their servant after they were married. . . ." Yet the sacrifices that love offers are, however sincere, however perfervid, another form of egotism; and Ruskin's devotion was too exclusive, too unbalanced, to be anything but self-centred. Indeed it could hardly have been otherwise, given the circumstances in which that devotion had developed, and the extraordinarily elusive personage round whom his cult had grown up. To adore Rose was to adore a phantom—often separated from him by many hundred miles: when physically she was closest, still a partial stranger. The wraith materialised, but again dissolved. Rose seemed affectionate and trustful; and then he was content to ask no questions, to respond to the appeal of her mutely-lifted forefinger, happy in the half-promises that from time to time she threw out; but when she had left him her accent changed, and he heard an echo of that grim evangelical faith he so much feared and hated. She had returned to a world of dark religious abstractions; and, although her pious fancies were "earnest and lovely," they were also, he feared, "conditions of exaltation connected . . . with her past illness." He recognised resentfully the influence of her mother and father, and caught a note of ecstatic renunciation that foretold her final goodbye.

Rose La Touche eluded Ruskin's grasp; but no less bewilderingly has she eluded his biographers and readers. For us, too, she is a fugitive apparition, difficult to sum up as an individual character, hard to visualise as a corporeal entity, "the fair well-bred Irish girl" known to the inmates of Denmark Hill, Mrs. Cowper Temple and the tenantry at Harristown, whose hair curled prettily above her forehead and whose blue eyes, as she grew older, had grown a little paler. She might be a figment of Ruskin's imagination, so accurately does she follow the pattern of previous loves and longings, the nymph destined to lead him astray on his last prolonged emotional escapade. Yet she existed. The letters that she wrote to Mrs. Cowper Temple—with their big, loose, cursive, somewhat undistinguished but not undecided handwriting—are there to be handled and read; and two likenesses, a drawing by her admirer, executed in 1874 when she was twenty-five, and a small *carte de visite* photograph, taken, evidently, at Harristown, help to crystallise the impressions derived from Ruskin's prose-portrait. Rose has just returned from a ride or is just prepared to set forth; for she stands on the cobblestones of a stable yard, a white-washed wall behind her, and Bruno, her immense dog, squats back upon its haunches with both its massive paws raised, one paw in its mistress's right hand, while in her left she holds a lump of sugar. Her tall slender body is sheathed in a dark habit; under her arm is a riding-whip; on her head a straw hat, high-crowned and rather unbecoming, her hair—again not very becomingly—being pushed away beneath it. Of the features themselves all that we can see is a small and misty triangle, inexpressive, minutely mysterious, which even under the magnifying glass still defeats our scrutiny. Yes, the nose is beautifully straight; but the ear, viewed in profile, is perhaps too large at its lower edge to be really very well-formed. The chin is small in relation to the rest of the face; and the short sensitive upper lip projects above the lower, which has a suggestion of the pensive droop that goes with discontent and melancholy. In spite of the concision of the classic upper lines, it is a vulnerable personality these features seem to hint at—a puzzling combination of firmness and weakness, of spiritual obstinacy and personal indecision.

Such a reading of Rose's physiognomy is confirmed by Ruskin's pencil-sketch. The effect it produces is naturally more romantic; but indications of inward vulnerability accompany the same air of almost classic gravity. Again the lower lip droops; but the line of the nose and forehead is pure and calm and sculptural. Rose's appearance, we remember, was afterwards described by Ruskin as having been " too severe to be entirely delightful to all people." She was also said to have resembled " a young sister of Christ "—one of those Leonardesque Christs, no doubt, whose chiselled distinction betrays their antique ancestry. It was in this mood that Ruskin portrayed her, head sunk, eyelids lowered, a wreath of Pre-Raphaelite bell-flowers around her tight-bound tresses. So she remains at the centre of Ruskin's legend; and so the student of his life, putting away the magnifying-glass, is bound at length to leave her—a creature never wholly explicable, because she did not understand herself, and because Ruskin's attempts to understand and explain her were seldom very penetrating. What she needed was possibly a commonplace love—some affection that made no demands, admiration realistic and warmly matter-of-fact rather than romantic. The impact of Ruskin's character was exciting yet disquieting; and, though she respected and was accustomed to him and could not bear to give him up—St. Crumpet had been a flattering conquest, a queer but entertaining play-fellow—she shrank from the experiences in which he seemed to wish to plunge her, and adopted the easiest, safest course, that of submission to her parents' will.

It was her duty; and in the word " duty," strongly supported by her evangelical creed, she found a precious safeguard. For Ruskin, too, the word was intensely significant; it had dominated him during his childhood, inspired and encouraged him throughout his early manhood; and not until he had arrived at middle-age had he begun to examine the influence it exerted, and, finding that the harm done probably exceeded the good, had approached the conception of duty from a very different standpoint. Then, his earlier notions, imbibed at Denmark Hill, had been discarded, together with the type of religious faith represented by the " little squeaking idiot " whose platitudinous sermon had exasperated him in Turin. The duty he envisaged was now towards himself; for only if he were himself happy, and at peace within his own nature, could he hope to realise his opportunities of further social usefulness. He was a pagan, he had admitted wryly; and, though Ruskin's loss of faith recalls not so much a revolution as a change of parliamentary governments, it had involved the disappearance of many inherited standards and the temporary eclipse of some stringent moral taboos. His sexual puritanism, later markedly aggressive, ceased to affect his opinions in the realm of art and literature. He appreciated Rossetti's *Jenny*, expressing his regret, however, that he could not submit it to Thackeray for inclusion in the *Cornhill*—he did not mean, he explained, " that an entirely right-minded man never keeps a mistress," but that the character of the speaker, with its mixture of brutality and sentimental scrupulosity, struck him as unnatural; and, when the *Rubáiyát of Omar Kháyyám* appeared in 1859, he fastened with delight on " such a jolly stanza:"

> *Then to the rolling Heav'n itself I cried,*
> *Asking " What Lamp had Destiny to guide*
> *Her little Children stumbling in the Dark?"*
> *And " A blind understanding," Heav'n replied.*

Charmed by the poem's pessimism, he did not demur at the incitements to hedonism with which it was embroidered.

Even more surprising was Ruskin's generous championship of Algernon Charles Swinburne. With his aureole of flaming red hair, his feverishly dancing limbs and perpetually fluttering hands, that prodigious youth had burst through the enchanted forest, the Tennysonian Broceliande, of late-Romantic poetry, to the shrilling of bacchic flutes and the crash of corybantic cymbals. Often his verses had a Pre-Raphaelite colouring—*Poems and Ballads*, indeed, was dedicated to his admired friend, the blameless Edward Burne-Jones; but the extravagance of his poetic invention, the wild impetuosity of his bounding measures, and the violently sensual turn he chose to give his imagery, made him a strange visitor to the shadowed and sheltered universe which the Pre-Raphaelites inhabited, where Burne-Jones' solemn virgins drooped in a perpetual pensive stupor, and even Rossetti's Renaissance courtesans appeared to be absorbed in an endless narcissistic trance. Nor did those extraordinary productions bear much resemblance to the rich medieval fantasies spun by William Morris. Both in the sphere of art and in the sphere of life, Swinburne seemed concerned to exploit his native talents with self-destructive energy, driving them as far as they would go, superbly regardless of the consequences. *Poems and Ballads*, when they were published by Moxon in 1866, appalled a large section of the British reading public; their inspiration was denounced as " swinish "; and some of his acquaintances suggested to Ruskin that, in his rôle of censor and guardian of British taste, it might very well become him to deal a striking counter-blow. But the censor refused. *Atalanta*, he wrote to Norton, was " the grandest thing ever yet done by a youth—though he is a Demoniac youth. Whether ever he will be clothed and in his right mind, heaven only knows. His foam at the mouth is fine, meantime." And during the autumn of the same year, to another correspondent: " As for Swinburne not being my superior, he is simply one of the mightiest scholars of the age in Europe . . . And in power of imagination and understanding simply sweeps me away before him as a torrent does a pebble. I'm *righter* than he is—so are the lambs and the swallows, but they're not his match."

Here we return to one of the main themes of speculation that had concerned and troubled Ruskin since 1858. Purity was not always powerful: goodness (in spite of the comforting message of his earlier books) did not always conduce to true æsthetic excellence: artists twittered and bleated with the lambs and swallows, yet never achieved the leonine splendour of a Paolo Veronese. He had reached this conviction through patient research; but there is no doubt that the example of his own life and the pressure of his emotions helped to underline and strengthen it. He was deeply, passionately in love; and the love that he experienced was now physical as well as spiritual. An aspect of his nature, long suppressed but essential to his future growth, was waiting for fulfilment; and he had finally become aware of the need at a time when every hope of fulfilment seemed on the point of vanishing. Hence the agony of mind into which he was thrown by Rose's elusiveness. During the earlier part of 1866, his letters to Mrs. Cowper Temple, even when they betray most clearly the agitation of his heart, suggest a mind not yet incapable of calm, considered judgment. His tone changes during the summer and autumn. Rose's enforced silence had begun to try him cruelly; and though he protested that, if the ban were removed and they were once again allowed to correspond, he would play her parents " wholly fair, and treat her simply (as she herself told me she wished to be still treated) as my child friend. . . ." it is evident that that phase of their relationship was already far behind them, and that nothing could now satisfy him but to be accepted as her adult lover. Meanwhile he begged his confidante to glance through a collection of Rose's treasured letters, " that you may see a little what the child has been to me for so long, and how cruel it is of them to take her from me so utterly and in an instant—how cruel, and vain. . . ." Mrs. Cowper Temple agreed; but her reply, after she had performed the task, puzzled and disturbed him. Rose certainly loved him, she wrote; but " it may have been *then* with a child's love." Did she mean by this that the devotion had failed to mature: that he must never hope for any equality either of feeling or of understanding?

Having done so much, would his trusted adviser not plead his case at Harristown? He implored repeatedly that she would make a special visit, and was aggrieved and bitterly disappointed when she informed him in a brief note that she could not, at that moment, cross the Irish Channel. But he revived the proposal again and again. To a woman of the world like herself, he admitted in a contrite letter, "this poor little story of mine," the story of his "foolish too-late love," might, no doubt, seem somewhat trifling; but to him it was a question of life and death, and she *must* consent to go to Ireland; for she alone could find out for him "whether Rosie is acting only in childish love and pity, or whether there is indeed any feeling on her side, deep enough for me to trust to. . . ." It was not that he feared rejection: let his friend discourage him "thoughtfully and sternly" if the situation warranted it, and he would endeavour to get back to his work and to a steady existence of unaspiring, unloved usefulness; but while the uncertainty remained, he dared not cast away his last hope. . . . Mrs. Cowper Temple delayed or demurred; and, during the autumn of 1866, Ruskin continued to importune her in long and feverish missives. Anxiety is usually repetitious: the opinions and resolutions of an unhappy and anxious mind are almost always contradictory; and Ruskin clung to the subject that obsessed him with painful perseverance, reviewing and reconsidering it from a dozen different points of view. He was sure of Rosie: and yet he was not sure. She had promised: and she had not promised. Should she reject him, he would continue his work: and yet he was persuaded that he could not work without her, and that his power of working had been already, by their separation, irremediably damaged. The La Touches should reflect on that—"all my work has been wrecked—all my usefulness taken from me." Those who needed his help he could no longer assist: even among his workpeople there were hundreds, "literally hundreds . . . more or less paralysed and broken " because he, their leader, had not the strength to lead them. Into his grief crept a strain of defiance, a touch of moral arrogance. He had a little good in him, he believed, which might have been a great good. No man lived, he declared, " of honester or simpler purpose "; no man was more just and merciful, and none of kinder heart: " I am pure-hearted—pure-bodied. . . ." Yet every gift that he could claim was being spoiled and laid waste—not by Rose (for she was entirely blameless) but by two misguided or malevolent persons, one of them " religious," the other a former friend who still professed to love him, but whose jealousy, the " unavoidable womanly pain of dethroned, or abdicating beauty," had in recent years come to prevail against her better judgement. Such were the unworthy enemies to whom he owed his shipwreck.

Though self-pity, accompanied now and then by flashes of angry self-love, was as characteristic of Ruskin in acute distress as of most tormented spirits, he did not exaggerate the seriousness of the catastrophe or over-estimate its consequences. More was involved than the immediate frustration. This was his " *last* hope," he declared; and on the word ' last ' he was beginning to dwell with apprehensive vehemence. Finally, towards the end of September, Mrs. Cowper Temple, who, so far as we can judge from Ruskin's letter, had not yet gone to Harristown, made him " very happy " by agreeing that Rosie really cared for him. Her incredulity had pained him much—" you seemed to think it so fearfully improbable " (he wrote) " that she *could* care for me "—and his emotion overflowed into a long excited outburst. At heart he had never distrusted Rose: what he had suspected, and still at times suspected, was that, blinded by pitying affection, she did not know her own mind. He was prepared, nevertheless, to wait, as patiently and faithfully as Rachel's suitor waited: he would submit to the same degrading conditions, and, if Mr. La Touche cared to engage him as a farm hand, he would be content with a shed to sleep in and the husks that the swine did eat. . . . Even now, he exclaimed, he was so distraught

William Bell Scott, Ruskin and Rossetti
in 1863

with longing that, were it not for fear of troubling Rose, he would go at once to Ireland "and lie down at their gate, and let them do what they chose with me, but I would see her." No one, not Rose herself, understood the exquisite agony that separation caused him. It may be she pitied: perhaps she loved: but had she not said to Joan Agnew, in her perverse and puzzling Irish way, that "now I had waited so long, it couldn't much matter to wait that little bit longer!" Time might run fast at Harristown; but for him it did not slip by easily. Already he was reckoning the days, marking off the period he had lived through, calculating the endless stages that he must yet accomplish. It was now September 28th 1866; and eight hundred and twenty-eight days, each twenty-four hours long, somehow to be endured before Rose came of age and he could expect to hear her answer. Morally excruciating, the strain imposed on his fortitude was also physically exhausting. By mid-October he felt "strangely weak and ill," and looked, he told Mrs. Cowper Temple, "horrid and old and pale." The old year died; and early in 1867 "the first warning mischief to my health showed itself. . . ." January had started smoothly, and he had forgotten some of his unhappiness in the meticulous representation of various shells and birds; but his painting was brought to an end by several threatening symptoms. He was giddy: his sight grew misty: "floating sparks" drifted before his eyes, and he lost the power of concentration. By day he was irritable and morose. From the underworld, beyond the gates of horn, vivid and fantastic dreams appeared at night to trouble him.

VIII

THERE were also waking dreams: it was not only while Ruskin slept that the dislocation of his inward life revealed itself in the emergence of dark disturbing fantasies. The frontier that divides sanity from insanity is evidently somewhat nebulous; and no literary biographer should rush in with a measuring-rod where the professional psychologist often seems to hesitate. But this much at least is clear—that at a certain stage of mental disturbance the connection between cause and effect tends gradually to melt away. Up to a point Ruskin's complaints against society, though expressed in unmeasured terms, had a strictly rational basis. It was true, his eyes assured him, that the English landscape he had so much loved, that he had learned to know so well as a child from his post of observation in Mr. Telford's travelling chariot, was being ruthlessly devirginated by nineteenth-century opportunism: till even the streams he had known in his youth, for instance, the little Wandle, running swift and bright across the Surrey meadows, had been choked "by the free public with old shoes, obscene crockery, and ashes." It was true that the cathedrals of France, if not so completely ruined as he at times imagined, had been scraped and disfigured by insensitive restorers: that the urban population of Europe did not present, on the whole, a very edifying spectacle: and that the mountains and valleys of Switzerland resounded to the chatter of vulgar Cockney tourists, "red with cutaneous eruption of conceit; and voluble with convulsive hiccough of self-satisfaction." But each phenomenon had a social cause; and, so long as the cause was kept firmly in mind, for each might at length be discovered some fitting social remedy. The plight of the world was grave: it was not entirely hopeless. But now that he was beginning to despair of his own existence, Ruskin's attitude towards the surrounding universe became slowly more irrational. He was inclined to dissociate the effect from the cause, and to find new and fantastic causes both for the phenomena that he deplored and for the *malaise* that pursued him; a nightmarish quality suffused his view of real life.

Thus a moment would soon arrive when he had convinced himself that the partial desecration of his beloved Alpine solitudes was due, not exclusively, nor even primarily, to the encroachment of railways, the invasion of tourist hordes, or the misguided commercial enterprise of greedy local businessmen, but to some subtler, yet more destructive agency, some immense mysterious climatic change, which had dimmed the lustre of the sky, sapped the strength of the glaciers and polluted the purity of the deepest and broadest lakes. During his lifetime, he announced in *The Queen of the Air*, he had seen " strange evil brought upon every scene I best loved, or tried to make beloved by others. The light which once flushed those pale summits with its rose at dawn, and its purple at sunset, is now umbered and faint . . . their very glacier waves are ebbing, and their snows fading, as if Hell had breathed on them; the waters that once sank at their feet into crystalline rest, are now dimmed and foul. . . . These are no careless words—they are accurately—horribly—true. . . . This morning, on the Lake of Geneva, at half a mile from the beach, I could not see my oar-blade a fathom deep." Air, light, water, all had been defiled. *The Queen of the Air* was not published till May, 1869; but far earlier his sense of a maleficent force abroad throughout creation was rising to the surface of Ruskin's mind, from recesses where for many years—perhaps since his childhood at Perth, or, less indefinitely, since he had been struck by the diabolical aspect of the country behind Naples—it had slumbered and stirred in insecure captivity. And if the natural world appeared terrible, so, as his age increased, did the countenance of mankind. "The English nation" (he wrote in 1867) "is fast, and with furious acceleration, becoming a mob to whom it will be impossible to talk about *any*thing"—a mob not merely of middle-class idiots but of proletarian yahoos; and during the late spring of the same year, Carlyle, as he turned over the pages of *Time and Tide*, a political and economic treatise in the form of a series of letters exchanged by the author of *Unto This Last* and Thomas Dixon of Sunderland, the philosophic cork-cutter, was bewildered to see attributed to him a highly provocative and grossly garbled statement. Carlyle, according to Ruskin, had alleged that "in the streets of Chelsea, and of the whole district of London round it (some twelve or fifteen miles of disorganised, foul, sinful, and most wretched life)" he could no longer walk abroad without receiving insults, "chiefly because he is a grey, old man; and also because he is cleanly dressed"—two conditions immediately resented by the brutish London populace, who recognised in them claims to "some kind of reverence . . . to be instantly crushed and jeered out of their way." Carlyle was never apt to spare his fellow human beings, to condone their enormities or seek to shield their follies. But this was altogether too much! As a respected citizen of Chelsea, who wandered at large unmolested through the length and breadth of the metropolis, saluted by omnibus-drivers, amiably acknowledged by staid suburban shopkeepers, in his voluminous cloak and his sweeping broad-brimmed hat, he felt that such an assertion (which the newspapers eagerly took up) must not go unchallenged. He protested forcibly, on behalf of a "whole vast multitude of harmless neighbours . . . who all behave . . . in an obliging, peaceable, and perfectly human manner to each other. . . ." The paragraph in question, he roundly stated, was "altogether erroneous, misfounded, superfluous, and even absurd." Ruskin, however, did not take correction mildly; and it was characteristic of his present mood that, rather than dispute the facts involved, he should have made a personal issue of his old friend's public counterblast. He complained that

Carlyle had given the lie direct "in the most insulting terms . . . to the man who probably of all men living most honoured you." He demanded an immediate retraction; and some angry correspondence ensued before the offended pessimist and his *protégé*, the aggrieved misanthrope, could at length be reconciled.

In *Time and Tide* Ruskin had informed his readers that he meant to "close his political work for many a day"; his "right work," he explained, was "to be out among the budding banks and hedges, outlining sprays of hawthorn and clusters of primrose." During May 1867 he delivered the Rede Lecture at Cambridge, choosing as his subject *The Relation of National Ethics to National Arts*, and received an honorary degree from the grateful University; but that summer he devoted to rest—as much rest as could be achieved by a man who (he wrote to his mother) had "the secret of extracting sadness from all things, instead of joy" —and spent July and August rambling round the Lakeland. He was accompanied both by his valet, who was put to work carrying and packing the mineral specimens he collected, and by the gardener at Denmark Hill whom he had brought to "hunt up ferns"; for his mother had expressed an anxious hope that he would "always have someone with him on his mountain rambles," and from his youth he had been accustomed to travelling with a devoted menial escort. He enjoyed snatches, nevertheless, of high romantic solitude, perched near the summit of Skiddaw, gazing out over the distant clear-seen hills of Cumberland —"great masses 2000 feet high looking like little green bosses under one's hand"—while white clouds gathered below and foamed majestically towards him, and "answering white fleeces started into being on Scawfell and Helvellyn. . . ." In such surroundings he often knelt and prayed: "even at my naughtiest times," he admitted in a letter to Joan Agnew, he had had a way of praying on hill summits. Although Ruskin's religious faith had been severely damaged, he still clung to Christian observances; and during 1867, whether in hope or despair, we learn that he had reverted to his study of the Bible, attempting to take omens from the text at which he opened it. These Biblical omens were now and then consolatory. In May and again in August they promised spiritual rewards—"the crown of life" and "the oil of gladness"—as recompense for the temptations he had subdued and the sufferings he had undergone.

Neither prayers nor omens were of any avail in the distracting year that followed. No letters dated 1867 were preserved among her archives by Mrs. Cowper Temple. But in 1868 their correspondence about Rose was resumed with double urgency; and Mrs. Cowper Temple's powers of sympathising and understanding were once more exposed to a severe and lengthy test. Though the outlines of the situation remain unaltered—Ruskin desperate and imperative: his mistress still irresolute: her parents still determined that the lovers should not meet or correspond—the details of its development are often somewhat puzzling. Ruskin's probationary period had yet a year to run—Rose had undertaken to give him an answer at the beginning of 1869; but it would seem that she promised to write to him at Christmas. This promise she had failed to keep; and Ruskin, exalted by expectation, when no letter arrived at Denmark Hill, had been cast down into an abyss of jealous and resentful misery. All Christmas Day, 1867, and all the next day he had roamed abroad, "so giddy and wild" with despair that, as he looked back on his state of spirit, he felt that he could understand "the worst things that men ever do. . . ." Here the small, neat, slightly cramped handwriting grows feverish and dishevelled; and as his pen races nervously ahead, the succession of his ideas loses all coherence. Rose, he declares, has no cause for regret. He does not blame her because she has denied him the complete unqualified love that now alone could bring him happiness: she had imagined that he wished to live with her on terms of pure and unimpassioned friendship, as, she believed, he had once lived with his first wife, and when he demanded more, had refused him fearlessly and honestly. . . . But he has other causes for complaint; and the recollection of those grievances whipped him into sudden anger. He could not forgive her for submitting to her parents' will, or for the religious protestations that her conduct turned to blasphemies. He could not forget that she had "ruined a great Life"—a life that had been wholly trusted to her: that she had destroyed his faith in womanhood, and become "the patient murderess . . . of the creature who . . . loved her more than all creatures living." Christmas Day henceforward would remain an accursed festival, a yearly reminder of her broken faith and cruelty.

Further to aggravate Ruskin's feelings, his cousin Joan would seem at this period to have slipped into some kind of engagement with Rose's brother, Percy, and to have been unkindly treated by her fickle suitor, who broke off the relationship. But "my poor little lamb of a cousin" provides a secondary theme in Ruskin's correspondence, which continues to revolve around his own predicament and around the bewildering elusiveness of Rose's personal character. Now exasperation and, at times, something like hatred begins to mingle with professions of unaltered faith and loyalty. But in the confusion of his sentiments certain thoughts were uppermost. If she insisted, he would accept Rose on any terms that pleased her. He would never aspire to be more than a friend; yet, although he could resign himself to any degree of self-abnegation if he were sure that she desired it, he was often uneasily mindful of the disaster of his first marriage. Then he had been "hissed and screamed at" because he had failed to understand the needs and moods of woman. And what might not the world say should he on a second occasion agree to a marriage that was a marriage in name only? He was also troubled by the manifestations of Rose's deep religious strain. At moments he was touched and charmed; but her calm assumption of infallibility—her "insolent habit . . . of constituting herself judge of all things and all men"—was none the less infuriating, a form of spiritual conceit productive in the end of a dozen evil consequences. So the struggle raged miserably on, reaching a fortissimo during the black and bitter March days. That month was exceptionally cheerless; and its frosts and storms were coloured for Ruskin by a gleam of supernatural horror. "It is very frightful and wonderful," he wrote. "The sense of demons in the dark air, and in the cold" harmonised strangely with the feeling of utter desolation that overwhelmed his consciousness. He had recourse as of old to his Prayer Book; but "the terrible Passion Week services" were not entirely comforting.

In March, so far as we can judge, some explosive letters passed between Harristown and Denmark Hill, and Ruskin behaved with even less reserve and discretion than might have been expected. It had occurred to him that Rose, when she insisted that their relations must remain those of Teacher and Child, might have some ulterior motive. By putting himself for the second time into such a false position, he would injure his personal credit beyond all prospects of recovery, and "my power of doing good by any teaching may be lost—and lost for ever." Was Rose physically abnormal? Beneath the weight of this "fearful question," his tact completely broke down; and he wrote to Ireland, either to Mrs. La Touche or to a Lady Higginson, one of Rose's confidantes, imploring or demanding that he should be informed—and without more ado, by telegraph—whether in Rose's case there was indeed, as he suspected, "incapacity of marriage." It is perhaps not altogether surprising that the La Touches were offended: that Mr. La Touche should, about this time, have sent him a letter which he described to Mrs. Cowper Temple as "insolent in the last degree": and that for some days his last hope should seem to have been extinguished. But the rupture was not definitive. The end of March brought some amelioration, and assurances from Rosie that she would "always love me—with her child-love"; while for the opening of May was reserved a brilliant burst of sunshine. Rose was his, he joyously informed Mrs. Cowper Temple: no power on earth could any longer separate them, unless the adult love of which she as yet knew nothing should at length surprise her: and then he would give her up, feeling that he obeyed God's will, with sadness but with perfect peace of heart. The demons of March had dissolved in storm: Rose had resumed a pre-eminence which, except at her own volition, she need never to forgo.

Once doubt and antagonism have crept into a love-affair, they can very seldom be so thoroughly exorcised as to leave behind no traces. Rose, in the summer of 1868, was not the unquestioned divinity she had been a few months earlier. Ruskin's passion was still acute, but his critical faculties had been awakened; and resentment against the cool, unapproachable, high-minded young woman who had caused him so much suffering now co-existed with his perfervid devotion to all she represented. The object of a fanatical cult, she was simultaneously a misguided, perverse, and, it might be, even somewhat silly girl. He had not ceased to love, yet—perhaps rather to his astonishment—he found that he could smile at her. Such self-confidence in matters of religion could not but astonish him. He had been, he admitted, " more and more amused —more and more saddened—more and more puzzled," as he read through Rose's last letter: its assurance was " so royally calm and divine," its presumption was so exquisite, that together they made her " the most glorious little angel, and the most impertinent little monkey " ever created to torment " true lover's or foolish old friend's heart." He could no more talk to her than he could to a fawn or a peewit; but, alas, the limitation of her understanding did not make her less adorable; and " the white Doe of Rylstone or the Dove of the Ark couldn't be more divine messengers, or more to be revered in their narrow natures." What should he do with her? He couldn't reason with her, or she would have a headache. He couldn't tell her that she was a little goose, for she would not understand him. Yet her habit of preaching and persistent assumption of an air of angelic superiority were becoming almost unendurable.

No doubt he hoped for better things if he could contrive at length to see her; and an invitation to lecture in Dublin provided him during the spring of 1868 with the pretext that he needed. But Rose's parents were on the alert; and a brief note, enclosing two rose leaves, was presently delivered at his address in Merrion Square: "I am forbidden" (she explained) "by my father and mother to write to you, or receive a letter." That was all. At first Ruskin had contemplated throwing up his lecture. Then he rallied and fulfilled his commission, though there were moments as he spoke when his voice grew faint and indistinct. Having made an end, he was handed "a rather large white paper parcel," which he took ungraciously and carried carelessly home, only to discover, upon opening it, that it contained another message. Forbidden to write, Rose had resorted to flowers. Here was a large sheaf of *Erba della Madonna*, which had always been considered Ruskin's plant at Harristown, with two vine leaves and, among the more exuberant blossoms, two small symbolic bouquets: a rose half-open with lilies-of-the-valley and a scented geranium leaf of white and green. The message of the first bouquet he appears to have understood, but the second slightly puzzled him; and by some means he endeavoured to write back, once again assuring his mistress that he would accept her and continue to love her on any terms she laid down. Meanwhile, to lessen their separation, he began to look around for an Irish country house, and travelled by jaunting car with a party of friends, who included several attractive young women, about the neighbouring districts, "through wildernesses of hawthorn" and over gorse-illumined hillsides. No house was found that suited his tastes: in this, as in more important respects, his visit proved abortive. All that remained was a sheaf of flowers, too substantial to press and enshrine in his herbarium, and destined to wither at last "into dark clusters of frankincense." But it was during this visit to Dublin that he flung out one of his most emphatic protests against the La Touche family, against the principles that stiffened and hardened them, and the faith that made them pitiless, castigating "the morbid corruption" of their religious sentiment and the waste of hope and youth and vitality in which such a creed resulted.

Soon afterwards he returned to London; and during July, 1868, when a special congress of the Social Science Association met to discuss Trade Unionism and the relations of Labour and Capital, we hear of Ruskin on the platform under the chairmanship of his old acquaintance William Ewart Gladstone. But though these activities might have a palliative effect, the relief they brought was temporary, and the same summer saw a disastrous intensification of his tormenting private problems. So far Mr. and Mrs. La Touche had based their objections to Ruskin as a son-in-law partly on the difference in age—and twenty or thirty years between bridegroom and bride were not always considered prohibitive by mid-Victorian parents—partly on the condition of Rose's health, and lastly, and perhaps more decisively, on that catastrophic loss of faith which he had himself acknowledged. But they had other and vaguer fears. The scandals which followed his first marriage had never quite been lived down; and rumours of "decadence" and "immorality," dimly existent since 1854, sprang up with renewed zest as soon as the report was circulated that he had the intention of re-marrying. To her previous arguments with Rose, from whom during the last few years she had suffered some estrangement, Lacerta would seem to have added the suggestion that St. Crumpet was an immoral man, or, at least, that there was that in his past life which a perfectly pure-minded young girl would not wish to scrutinise. The terrible mysteries of sex were in some way darkly hinted at; and Rose, already alarmed by her lover's fierce insistence, frightened by the pressure of feelings which she neither shared nor understood, appears to have recoiled from the revelation as her mother had intended. She communicated her distress to Ruskin, presumably with the help of Mrs. Cowper Temple; and Ruskin's dismay was profound; for he knew that these ignoble phantoms had still the power to harm him. His only recourse was to confront them boldly. A defence, drawn up with painstaking candour for Mrs. Cowper Temple's benefit, was composed at Denmark Hill on June 2nd, 1868.

How far does his defence, which is also a confession,

affect the modern reader? To what extent should our study of a writer's works, and of the personal temperament that underlay and coloured them, develop into an examination of minor private vagaries? It may be desirable to "draw a line." But is it possible to determine exactly where the line should fall? In considering Ruskin, this proves doubly difficult, so strange was the character of his achievement, so close the connection between his works and personality. His achievement, indeed, often reminds us of the baroque *Annunciation* by Tintoretto commemorated in *The Stones of Venice*. While the angel of inspiration descends from on high, startling us with the rush of "horizontal and rattling wings," the creative spirit sits tense and expectant; but all around are the massive ruins of monumental edifices, and over the whole scene broods an atmosphere of romantic incompleteness. Romantic, yet tragic too. Where we look for conformity and symmetry, for the classical harmony of pillar, arch and sculptured frieze, we find the magnificent confusion left behind by some intellectual earthquake. To appreciate Ruskin's genius then, we must seek to understand the nature of the convulsion that tore his plans asunder, and reduced huge sections of his later work to piles of splendid fragments. The disaster had a complex origin; but not a few of the forces that caused it were predominantly personal, and derived from his failure to reach an emotional balance, his inability to reconcile the conflicting claims of the body and the intellect, or to satisfy his appetite for beauty yet escape from the conviction of sin which had always dogged his footsteps. That sense of sin was a persistent visitor. We remember, for example, the mood of agonised despondency that had overtaken him in 1847 when he revisited the scenes of his beloved Scottish childhood, and how, in 1845, fresh from the religious revelation that had suddenly occurred after an attack of "nervous fever," he had been conscious, as soon as he returned to England, of sinking back once again "into the faintness and darkness of the underworld." Spiritual arrogance, of which it must be admitted that Ruskin had his full share, could not hold at bay a recurrent recognition of his own extreme unworthiness; and, because he appeared to himself unworthy, he continued to distrust those simple sensuous pleasures—the unfettered freedom of sensation and experience—for which another side of his temperament still obstinately clamoured.

A conviction of sinfulness, imbibed in youth and childhood, not infrequently survives the religious beliefs that first of all impressed it. Margaret Ruskin's creed was of the sternest sort; the God she worshipped was to be feared, not loved; and it was natural enough that the effects of his early training should have left a mark upon Ruskin's mind that even his own loss of faith and many years of adventurous speculation could not wholly charm away. In childhood occasions of sin had been few: misdemeanours, once detected, had been promptly, sharply chastised. But adolescence introduced a wider range of problems; and during adolescence, and the period that immediately followed, Ruskin's hyper-sensitive conscience sustained grave and lasting injury. A lonely and imaginative child, he became a solitary, self-centred, deeply passionate adult. That his passions were unusually strong has been demonstrated both by the letters he wrote to Effie Gray and by the account that he gives us of his unhappy early love-affairs; but, owing to the circumstances in which his parents reared him, these impulses were denied any hope of normal overflow. He was forced back into the life of the imagination; and the imaginative life, from the standpoint of the Victorian moralist, was beset with numerous pitfalls. To-day our standards are perhaps more lenient; for, if modern psychology has done nothing else, it has at least produced a more understanding attitude towards the various sexual phases through which every childhood passes; and so-called "solitary vice" is no longer supposed to fill our asylums and our graveyards. According to the testimony of Ruskin's letter, in his unfriended and self-centred existence the auto-erotic practices of youth had continued into manhood, accompanied, emphasised and, no doubt, extended by an abiding sense of guilt. Had he not often told her (he wrote to Mrs. Cowper Temple) that he was "another Rousseau"? This was true, but with an important difference—that the end of his life would be the best; since "the evil that was its death" had been definitely extirpated long before he came to know Rose. She would save him from sorrow: from sin he was saved already. The offences of his early life were "past as the night." His devotion was completely pure: should she accept his hand now, she would find him as spotless as she had ever thought him. . . .

So commonplace is the source to which it seems that we may trace the original derivation of much of Ruskin's *malaise*. But for the offspring of an evangelical household, whose comminations against "impurity" were backed by the terrifying voices of embattled Jewish lawgivers, the offence was not insignificant: with every relapse and every repetition, the gates of the underworld appeared to yawn in front of him. Sin and Death crouch on the threshold of Milton's spacious Hades; but the modern Inferno is kept by Guilt and Anxiety; and both demons discover an easy prey among susceptible and intelligent beings of Rousseau's or of Ruskin's cast. To their influence may be attributed the collapse of Ruskin's marriage—he connected pleasure with guilt, and therefore could not associate it with the consummation of romantic love; while his desperate attempts somehow to break the spell, to circumvent the psychological barrier that shut him off from happiness, disturbed and at length disgusted his wholly inexperienced bedfellow. The law judged him "incurably impotent." In fact, his impotence might well have been cured, since it was less an infirmity of the flesh than an affliction of the spirit. Latterly he admitted that he had never once possessed a woman; and his loss, he understood, was not only in physical pleasure (of which, we may conclude, he was not entirely unappreciative), but in the spiritual enlargement such a connection might have brought him. It was a deprivation, he said, that he regretted deeply—never to have been chastened by a woman's affection or strengthened by her fortitude. In Carlyle we seem to detect a genuine sexual coldness: he was a man from whose constitution had been omitted certain vital elements: Ruskin, on the other hand, was passionately aware of what his fate denied him. Carlyle existed in a world of monochrome: the charm of his portraits is their sharp uncoloured outline: whereas its sensuous warmth and liveliness is a distinguishing feature of Ruskin's imagination. He adored the beauty of the physical universe, to which Carlyle, whose days were passed among words and ideas, remained gloomily indifferent; and from the rocky structure of the earth to the conformation of the clouds, through the immense fascinating labyrinth of flower- and tree- and animal-life, his love extended, misanthropy notwithstanding, to the contemplation of the human species, who perpetually dazzled and attracted, however frequently and bitterly they were apt to disappoint him. "A girl's hair and lips" (he had written) "are lovelier than all clouds"; and this delighted preoccupation with the world of the flesh, tempering the sternness of his intellectual puritanism, gave his prose its peculiar light and shade—an imaginative quality within the reach of few contemporary English essayists. It was the product of a mind at once subtle and adventurous. But Ruskin lacked the gift of co-ordination; and his failure to combine and control was exaggerated, almost from the beginning, by unhappy private circumstances. . . .

When he announced to Mrs. Cowper Temple that Rose's doubts and delays, and the stupidity and obstinacy displayed by both her parents, must eventually ruin all his hopes of usefulness, he came nearer to the truth than his friend perhaps suspected. Some types of activity might still be possible—he could still recapitulate his message to those who cared to hear it, advise and admonish his protégés, draw, copy and arrange in the seclusion of his work-room; but work of a more ambitious kind, which demanded self-possession and vigorous concentration, nowadays presented almost overwhelming difficulties. Rose alone, he was convinced, could help him by her surrender to become the man he wished to be; and only if he achieved inward harmony could he do the work he wished to do. It was with this conviction that he insisted, so repeatedly and strongly, at times so ill-advisedly, on Rose's obligations towards himself, and spoke with such bitter contempt of the conflicting duty that she thought she owed her parents. He could not believe, he exclaimed, that "the powers of giving happiness, and of insight into natural and beautiful things" had been entrusted to him by Providence merely to be wasted and extinguished. The last protest was wrung from him after yet another setback. His letter of June 2nd, declaring his present blamelessness but admitting past offences, evidently failed to disperse the suspicions that Lacerta had created; and the atmosphere of mistrust, temporarily lightened, soon grew even heavier. Once again the outlines of the story become a trifle puzzling. It has been generally assumed that Ruskin, at Rose La Touche's request, waited patiently for three years, and that, at the end of that time, she was obliged to confess that she still found herself unable to give a definite answer. In fact, as we have seen, Ruskin during the years of probation was not altogether patient, and a breach with Rose had occurred before the close of 1868. Letters he omitted to date, but which were presumably written in that decisive period, show him attempting to come to terms with an accomplished tragedy. Henceforward, he had decided, he would never pass through Curzon Street: too painful was the mere sight of Mrs. Cowper Temple's doorstep, though a year earlier, to see Rose pass, he would have lingered on the pavement among the crowd of night-beggars. Mrs. La Touche had begged Mrs. Cowper Temple to "help him to forget us." That he counted an unforgivable sin; and, as he considered it, his condemnation of his former friend achieved new heights of violence. Lacerta, the subtle and charming serpent, was now a demoniac reptile, a very "horror of iniquity"; she recalled to his mind a Lamia, "only with a strange Irish ghastliness of grotesque mistake mixed with the wickedness." She was part of an immense conspiracy against his work and health and peace of spirit.

Yet life meant work; and he could not desist either from living or from working. In 1869 he produced *The*

Queen of the Air, a small volume made up of three lectures on Greek myths delivered at University College, London, of which he afterwards observed that it was the best he had ever written, " the last which I took thorough loving pains with, and the first which I did with full knowledge of sorrow." Carlyle, now reconciled, was once more enthusiastic, and, in a hyperbolical congratulatory letter, assured Ruskin that " many, many are the Phoebus Apollo celestial arrows you have still to shoot into the foul Pythons and poisonous abominable Megatheriums and Plesiosaurians that go staggering about, large as cathedrals," through the darkness of the nineteenth century. Certainly his prose echoes with the twang of Ruskin's bow-string. But at what are his arrows aimed? For though some of his targets may be solid enough, his shafts are often directed at phantoms, wraiths and nightmares, which loom up and stagger away and hugely, ominously re-emerge, as the wild hunter, impelled by prophetic fury, ranges to and fro among them. Ruskin's ostensible subject was classical mythology, its symbolic basis in the beliefs of the past, its moral application to the problems of the present day; but he digresses on botany, touches here and there both on physics and on metaphysics, and wanders at length in the wildwood of his own economic doctrines. Even more definitely than *Ethics of the Dust*, *The Queen of the Air* is chiefly interesting as a self-portrait. He could not, nor did he attempt to, exclude reminiscences of the emotional crisis through which he had been passing. Thus the Harpies are taken to represent " the gusts of vexatious, fretful, lawless passion "; and, when he describes their symbolic import, he appeals to the experience of " any who have ever known the weariness of vain desires; the pitiful, unconquerable, coiling and recoiling and self-involved returns of some sickening famine and thirst of heart. . . . You will know what was in the sound of the Harpy Celaeno's shriek from her rock; and why, in the seventh circle of the ' Inferno,' the Harpies make their nests in the warped branches of the trees that are the souls of suicides." Equally characteristic, for those who know his story, is the elaborate play he makes with certain private references. The idea of Lacerta, and of her religious beliefs, constantly intrudes and never fails to madden him. He returns again and again to the theme of the snake, and enlarges on the serpentine strain in human life and conduct. ". . . Truly, it seems to me" (he writes) "as I gather in my mind the evidences of insane religion, degraded art, merciless war, sullen toil, detestable pleasure, and vain or vile hope, in which the nations of the world have lived since first they could bear record of themselves—it seems to me, I say, as if the race itself were still half-serpent . . . a lacertine breed of bitterness. . . ." Elsewhere the repulsion that he feels is not unmixed with fascination; and in a passage of typically poetic daring—oddly reminiscent, by the way, of a far more recent prophet[1]—he discusses the snake as first a hieratic symbol, then a natural mystery:

> "The serpent crest of the king's crown, or of the god's, on the pillars of Egypt, is a mystery; but the serpent itself, gliding past the pillar's foot, is it less a mystery? Is there, indeed, no tongue, except the mute forked flash from its lips, in that running brook of horror on the ground?"

Was the snake a symbol of "permitted evil"? But not content to feed his imagination upon its beauty and its strangeness—"that rivulet of smooth silver. . . . It literally rows on the earth, with every scale for an oar. . . . A wave, but without wind! a current, but with no fall! all the body moving at the same instant . . . one soundless, causeless march of sequent rings, and spectral procession of spotted dust, with dissolution in its fangs, discoloration in its coils"—he allows the image of the ancient reptile to introduce a succession of very different images, derived from his observation of evil all around him:

> "Why that horror? (he now demands of his audience). We all feel it, yet how imaginative it is, how dispro-

[1]Both in their poetic brilliance and their illogicality, Ruskin and the author of *Sons and Lovers* often reveal an unexpected kinship.

portioned to the real strength of the creature! There is more poison in an ill-kept drain—in a pool of dish-washings at a cottage-door, than in the deadliest asp of Nile. Every back-yard which you look down into from the railway, as it carries you out by Vauxhall or Deptford, holds its coiled serpent: all the walls of those ghastly suburbs are enclosures of tank temples for serpent-worship; yet you feel no horror in looking down into them, as you would if you saw the livid scales, and lifted head. There is more venom, mortal, inevitable, in a single word, sometimes, or in the gliding entrance of a wordless thought, than ever '*vanti Libia con sua rena*.'"

Thus, within the compass of a few pages, Ruskin's imagination has whirled him to and fro among the centuries, from the temples of Egypt to the slums of Deptford, through varying phases of horror and admiration, each productive of some poetic flash which breaks dazzlingly across his prose-style and then as swiftly dies out. The subjects attacked are multitudinous, but, except by the loosest of connections, largely unrelated. We read of reptiles and birds and flowers: of Grecian and Egyptian cults and their divinities and demons: of the relation of faith to art—which produces the somewhat surprising pronouncement that "the religious passion is nearly always vividest when the art is weakest; and the technical skill only reaches its deliberate splendour when the ecstasy which gave it birth has passed away for ever": of the achievement of individual artists and the genius of Luini, "a man ten times greater than Leonardo; a mighty colourist, while Leonardo was only a fine draughtsman . . .": of the author himself, his virtues as a man and his qualifications as a teacher: and of the courage and spirit of republican independence displayed by common house-flies. The fly is awarded an eloquent paragraph; for he is the type of personal liberty and complete political irre-sponsibility—"a black incarnation of caprice—wandering, investigating, flitting, flirting, feasting at his will, with rich variety of choice in feast, from the heaped sweets in the grocer's window to those of the butcher's back-yard, and from the galled place on your cab-horse's back, to the brown spot in the road, from which, as the hoof disturbs him, he rises with angry republican buzz—what freedom is like his?"

The word "freedom" has a subtly disturbing sound. Freedom for what? Ruskin inquires. How conferred, by whom, and with what moral object? He has scarcely patience to hold his pen, "as I remember . . . the infinite follies of modern thought . . . centred in the notion that liberty is good for a man, irrespective of the use he is likely to make of it. Folly unfathomable! unspeakable! unendurable to look in the full face of, as the laugh of a cretin." Such were the passages that, scattered among mythological and botanical disquisitions, claimed Carlyle's special sympathy. But neither from the didactic nor from the æsthetic standpoint can the design of *The Queen of the Air* be said to be harmonious. It shows no failure of energy; but the power that it reveals is tragically disorganised; the habit of divagation has become a literary disease, and the writer is swept along from paragraph to paragraph by a torrent of ideas that he neither will nor can control. His new book had been finished before the spring was over: whereupon, in accordance with his usual custom, he at once said goodbye to Denmark Hill, following one of those lines of pilgrimage—journeys of the spirit as well as odysseys through space and time—that he had been tracing and retracing ever since his boyhood. But he remained abroad somewhat longer than usual; and on this occasion even his mother's importunities could not make him change his plans. She seemed to think, he protested, that "I do not like coming home while you are alone; but you never were more mistaken." If his future prospects were unlimited, he would have come home instantly. "But I am fifty, and my sight *may* fail soon of its present power—and I am quite certain that my duty is just as much here, and not at Denmark Hill, as if I were a rector ordered to a foreign church, or a colonel sent abroad on active service." This comparison may have comforted his mother, and was perhaps a trifle less disingenuous than it would appear at first sight. By remaining abroad he certainly pleased himself; but his pleasure and his duty were for once identical.

As usual, the joy was mixed with pain. Immense was the satisfaction of revisiting Verona, of looking from his hotel window "at the morning light on the tomb of the Count Castelbarco (my favourite old red one)," of drawing and measuring the buildings he loved, and, when his day's work had been put aside, of walking through the illumination of a rich Italian sunset. Moreover, he had some pleasant acquaintances; and one morning, as he sat drawing in the main square of Verona, "there came up the poet Longfellow with his little daughter, a girl of twelve or thirteen, with *springy*-curled flaxen hair—curls, or waves, that wouldn't come out in the damp, I mean. They stayed talking beside me some time"; and it occurred to Ruskin —"I don't think it was a very vain thought"—that, could a photograph have been taken "of the beautiful square . . . in that soft light, with Longfellow and his daughter talking to me," some people, both English and American, might have wished to have a copy. But, if he was often pleasantly occupied, and sometimes, no doubt, far happier than he ever admitted to his correspondents, there were still shadows perpetually threatening his peace—visitants from the depths of memory and intolerable sights and sounds that daily crowded in upon him. "The horror of living among these foul Italian wretches" (he told Norton) "and seeing them behave exactly like dogs and flies among the tombs and churches of their fathers," was more than he could endure "with any power of rational speech left. . . ." The faces of "the younger men and boys" were "dreadful in utter insolence and cruelty"; while as for the very young, his enjoyment of the cathedral of Verona was disturbed by "the vilest wretches of ape-faced children" clustered around the porch and "riding on my griffins." Some of the buildings he loved were ruinous and neglected: others had been restored, or were soon to be restored, beyond all recognition. The remains of Theodoric's palace had been pulled down by the city-fathers, and from its site a gigantic and hideous barracks now dominated the ancient town.

Yet abhorrence did not breed cynicism, nor disgust result in lassitude; and it was at this period that he began to outline one of his most ambitious projects—a plan for harnessing the waters of the Upper Rhone, catching the rainfall as it descended the hillsides and, by means of a series of dams and artificial reservoirs constructed at his own expense, transforming the malarial country beneath into safe and prosperous farmland. He intended to begin with a single hillside. Such a plan might be expensive, but it would set an example, he believed, that the grateful inhabitants of the whole valley were bound in time to follow, and provide a fascinating personal employment that would absorb him till his old age. How and where to make a definite start as always was the main problem; and meanwhile he continued to wander to and fro among the cities of Northern Italy, between the tombs of Verona and the pictures and palaces of Venice, a solitary abstracted, carefully-dressed figure, in no respect bohemian, usually accompanied by an attentive body-servant. Such was the appearance he presented to Holman Hunt when, during the summer of 1869, after a lengthy separation they once again came face to face. Both of them were middle-aged men; the ardours of Pre-Raphaelitism had long ago evaporated; Millais, that angelic youth, was now the father of a growing family and a highly successful academic painter; Holman Hunt had experienced a tragic bereavement, had been derided and applauded, and underpaid and overworked, and at the moment was about to embark upon a second eastern journey. On his first expedition, in 1856, he had already given lurid form to his vision of *The Scapegoat*—a gaunt glassy-eyed animal, its horns correctly encircled with the traditional scarlet fillet, against a background of vitreous salt-lake and incandescent mountain-line. Every pictorial subject that he adopted—Biblical scapegoat, Arcadian hireling shepherd or contemporary "fallen woman," the last being a subject that took the virtuous but highly conscientious artist to certain suspect establishments in the region of St. John's Wood—Hunt handled with the same thoroughness, the same literary enthusiasm, the same extraordinary innocence of any true æsthetic feeling. His life had been a protracted struggle; and it was as a visitor from another plane, a world of wealth and leisure and security, that he beheld Ruskin stepping towards him across the pavement of St. Mark's Square. He at once expressed his surprise and delight; the critic accepted his tribute "in silence," concluding, however, "that he should enjoy my company at all places where the precious pictures by Bellini, Carpaccio,[1] Titian, Giorgione, Tintoretto and Veronese were collected." A visit to San Rocco was then proposed, and they made for Ruskin's gondola.

Eagerly Holman Hunt studied his companion. Ruskin, he noted, was at this stage of his career "a man of nearly six feet in height" but exceedingly thin, even emaciated, with rusty hair, bluish-grey eyes and a fresh transparent skin, though his complexion had been marred by the sun and violet-hued veins appeared around his eye-sockets. He was "faultlessly groomed", and, in spite of his soft felt hat, looked not at all the art-specialist: "no passers-by stared at him": he moved unnoticed through the crowd which accepted him as they would have accepted any other well-to-do *forestiere*. His treatment of Hunt was benign and yet authoritative. Entering the Scuola di San Rocco, the two Englishmen came to a halt beneath Tintoretto's strange *Annunciation*, centre of the famous and dramatic passage which Hunt, who had never outgrown his love of Ruskin's prose, still remembered with respect and awe. But as often happens, his recollection, now twenty years old, proved very different from the picture. Far more haunting was the air of dilapidation; the Virgin was represented in a setting of "ugly broken-down bricks, crumbled stones, and unseemly mortar"; "delectability" (he considered) "should certainly be a preponderating element in every work of art"; and the impression made

[1]It was during this visit that Ruskin first fell in love with the paintings of Carpaccio.

by this canvas was neither delectable nor tranquil. Ruskin's interpretation of the underlying symbolism suggested further difficulties. Was it perhaps unduly far-fetched? But the critic himself presently proceeded to set his reader's mind at rest; and, beckoning to his valet who hovered nearby, he took from him a volume of *Modern Painters* and read aloud the paragraph. When he had finished, he handed back the book, remarking that, contrary to his expectation, the effect was not exaggerated. "I am well content," he decided; and, from time to time, as they continued their examination of the gallery, he would again call for *Modern Painters* and again read out a few lines. "Yes, I approve," was the judgement he passed on each successive prose-flight.

As a critic he might be unshaken: in other fields of activity Ruskin during the last twenty years had suffered many changes. The "intensity" of his religious convictions, which once delighted and encouraged Millais, had shown a steady falling-off; and to Hunt, for whom his feelings while they roamed around the Scuola di San Rocco had evidently been growing warmer, he now admitted how completely and, as he feared, irrevocably his early faith had left him. This revelation occurred over a Venetian dinner-table. Ruskin had inquired whether, when he spoke to him that morning, he had had any serious purpose, observing that although Hunt's studio in Camberwell was not very far from Denmark Hill, he had allowed years to go by without a sign of friendship; to which Hunt frankly replied that certain circumstances, unnecessary to particularise, had at one time stood between them, but that more recently he had held aloof because he could not approve of some of the "men you had about you"—an oblique reference, no doubt, to the nefarious Charles Augustus Howell. Ruskin had not dissented; he had never, he agreed, been a good judge of character, and some "most objectionable people" had entered his entourage. Having cleared the air, Hunt immediately set out in search of fresh enlightenment. He had noticed, he said, that, when considering pictures, Ruskin now dwelt almost exclusively on their æsthetic merits. What of their symbolism? What of their moral value? Ruskin's response, as reported by Holman Hunt, has something of the heaviness and dullness of the reporter's individual prose-style; but Hunt was by disposition equally painstaking and serious-minded; and it seems unlikely that he would have exaggerated or distorted so deliberate and so grave a statement, upon a subject, moreover, that had always touched him closely. He had come, Ruskin now declared, "to regard the whole story of divine revelation as a mere wilderness of poetic dreaming. . . . Since it is proved to be so, it is time that all men of any influence should denounce the superstition which tends to destroy the exercise of reason. Amongst the chaotic mass there are exquisite thoughts, elevating aspirations, and poetic mental nourishment, and it would be a pity that these riches should be lost to the world." Here, then, was the plan he proposed: "I want you, who have done a deal of harm by your works in sanctifying blind beliefs, to join with me and others to save these beautiful fragments, lest the vulgar, when indignant at the discovery of the superstition, should in their mad fury destroy what is eternally true in the beautiful thoughts with what is false." Finally he delivered his summing-up: "The conviction I have arrived at leads me to the conviction that there is no Eternal Father . . . that man has no helper but himself. I confess this conclusion brings with it great unhappiness. . . ." Hunt would admit that he was a kind-hearted man; and, since he was of a friendly and benevolent nature, his sense of personal solitude proved doubly grievous. He, who comforted his fellow men, must go through life uncomforted. . . .

Such was the declaration that, in the dining-room of Danieli's Hotel, Ruskin boldly poured forth. Earlier he had suggested that a photograph of himself with Longfellow would have made a useful record; but his interview with Holman Hunt is a scene that the modern reader might prefer to have immortalised. Hunt himself is not difficult to evoke; for we possess a pen-drawing by his own hand which depicts him, during the spring of 1869, finishing a lonely dinner in some small Italian *pension*—solid and compact and serious-visaged, with his abrupt nose, abundant square-ended beard and heavy waving brushed-back hair. Ruskin is more elusive; but many portraits show us the blue eyes, whose expression of strained intentness is reflected by the surrounding features; and we have numerous contemporary accounts of the prophet's gestures and intonations when his eloquence was given free rein, and the mournful music of his voice swept, rising and falling, insinuating, soothing, stirring, across the imagination of his listeners. From the problem of faith, he soon turned back again to the question of æsthetics. There had been a stage in his critical career when he had asserted that ages of faith were ages of creation, and that periods haunted by disbelief were inevitably periods of decadence. Latterly, in *The Queen of the Air*, he had not hesitated to put forward a contradictory point of view; and, Hunt having inquired whether he really supposed that "Tintoretto's convictions are of no value to us," he retorted that "Tintoretto did not believe any more than I do the fables he was treating," and that "no artist in illustrating fairy stories troubles himself about the substantiality of the fiction." But it was clear that the poetic quality of the myth could still command his reverence; for next day they visited the Salute, and Ruskin, who had climbed the steps of a side-altar, anxious to draw Hunt's attention to the shell-fossils in a marble shaft—"evidence of the much greater antiquity of the earth than the bible records state"—was bidden to descend by an indignant sacristan; at which he promptly congratulated the man both on his piety and on his sense of duty, explaining that "it is now over twenty years since I was in Venice, and your words to us are the first signs I have found in this day of due veneration for the claims of unseen authority. I do not pretend to be a Christian, I speak to you simply as a philosopher. . . ." The sacristan "looked bewildered," and did not cease to display his astonishment, till the eccentric foreigner, after a brief discourse on the desecration of Venice, the pollution of its canals and the destruction of its ancient buildings, with renewed congratulations on his piety bade him a ceremonious farewell.

Hunt's destination was Jaffa, and thither he soon departed by way of Rome and Alexandria. Ruskin delayed in Northern Italy throughout July and the opening days of August; but mid-August saw him once again in Switzerland, whence, towards the end of the month, he set his course for Denmark Hill. In Switzerland he had found an important letter. Since 1854 efforts had been made by his friend Henry Acland and other well-intentioned persons to arrange for the establishment at Oxford of a Professorship of Fine Art. As Professor, Ruskin was the obvious choice; but year after year the plan had always miscarried. At last, in 1868, a wealthy collector named Felix Slade bequeathed to the nation the sum of £35,000, to be employed in the endowment of the Slade Professorships of Fine Art in the Universities of Oxford and Cambridge and in University College, London. Ruskin's Oxford friends immediately rallied, and he was elected Slade Professor by unanimous vote during the summer of 1869. A decade earlier, the effect upon his emotions might have been electric; but although he was certainly pleased and flattered, his reaction, when the news reached him at his hotel beside the Lac de Brientz, would appear to suggest that he was no more than duly grateful. Still, he promised Acland that he would try his hardest, and, with a touching sympathy for the qualms that his academic supporters might perhaps experience, he also promised that they would be " greatly surprised . . . at the caution with which I shall avoid saying anything . . . which may be either questionable by, or offensive to, even persons who know little of my subject, and at the generally quiet tone to which I shall reduce myself in all public duty." Liddell at Christ Church received similar assurances; Ruskin undertook to " avoid the expression of any of my own peculiar opinions when I speak by permission of the University," adding that " my own impression is that I must work for very slow results, trying to lose no ground once gained." In fact, his hopes were decidedly moderate. But then, hope was a pleasure with which he no longer much indulged himself. Looking forward, he felt he must work, because intellectual labour was an exercise to which he had grown accustomed; looking back, he considered that the past was " more like a strange dream of things that I once cared for, than a reality." As he reviewed the ten years that had just elapsed, he could not decide whether they were " Divine or Diabolical." Those who wished him well had often done him harm, and usually most harm when their intentions were most kindly. " My Father—my Mother—and R." had each contributed to damage him; but they had been of even greater help; " and they all three did the best for me they knew how to do." His father was dead: his mother, an old and exacting woman with whom he must be patient. Rose remained an insoluble enigma; and towards this problem, though it still distressed him, the attitude he had begun to adopt was one of hopeless acquiescence. Words, omens, promises and prayers, he wrote to Mrs. Cowper Temple (whom he now addressed as *Philé* or Isola, the affectionate nicknames her Irish friends had given) had failed him too often to leave him any care for them. He was beyond either helping or hurting. " I can never be to her, what I was to her once —nor she what she was to me. . . ."

IX

RUSKIN delivered his inaugural lecture as Slade Professor of Fine Art on February 8th, 1870, his fifty-first birthday. So large was the original gathering that Acland suggested to the audience that they should adjourn from the lecture-room in the Museum to the Sheldonian Theatre, and the entire assembly left the Museum, with Ruskin at their head. Such scenes of enthusiasm had not been witnessed in the placid Oxford world since 1841, when Dr. Arnold had lectured for the first time as Professor of Modern History; and certainly no more remarkable or more magnetic personage had appeared within recent memory on any academic platform. Combined with his other unusual attributes, the new Professor revealed an outstanding gift of showmanship. His lecture was a studied performance; and to the effect he produced voice, gestures, even the clothes he wore, each contributed some distinctive detail. His appearance alone would have set him apart; for with the velvet cap of the Gentleman Commoner and a voluminous gown—frequently stripped off and tossed aside when it wrapped itself in inextricably perplexed folds around his sweeping gestures—he wore an old-fashioned frock-coat and double-breasted waistcoat of a light-hued homespun tweed, and the ample blue tie which was his only concession to æstheticism or bohemianism. Otherwise, we are told, he somewhat suggested an antique country gentleman; but his mobile hands were "peculiarly delicate," his fingers expressive and tapering; and in a face that was furrowed and sad, beneath the ragged projection of his thick and bushy eyebrows, were set bright blue eyes that glittered out at the audience with an extraordinary brightness and intentness. As he developed his discourse, a winning and gentle smile would break across his features. His changes of mood were rapid and unconcealed; while he spoke (noted a listener) " one saw the same strange afflatus coming and going " in his eyes, his voice, his movements. But it was his voice that stirred his audience most profoundly, held them most compulsively —a voice not very strong, with an old-fashioned pronunciation, an odd roll of the r's and unmistakable trace of an earlier Scottish accent, yet always clear and penetrating, which achieved effects of solemn magnificence as often as he read aloud. The voice of a prophet and visionary, of a poetic sage crying in the wilderness, full of mysterious echoes and romantic reverberations which accompanied and transcended the message it delivered. ". . . That singular voice of his " (wrote an Oxford disciple, the author of *The New Republic*) ". . . haunts me still sometimes. There was something strange and aerial in its exquisite modulations, that seemed as if it came from a disconsolate spirit, hovering over the walls of Babylon, and remembering Sion." His introductory words were apt to be quiet and staid. Poised behind his desk, he would concentrate on the manuscript notes that lay spread out before him, and, consulting some relevant classic, would read aloud a page or two. Then gradually the afflatus descended. His encumbering gown was discarded and thrown away: desk and manuscript notes soon had ceased to hold him; and he was striding excitedly to and fro, up and down the platform, pouring out " a rhapsody of exalted thought " cast in musical and rhythmic language. That it was impossible to transcribe even his disciples admitted; but, so long as the voice continued, a mood of reverential enthusiasm possessed the whole theatre.

Should a disciple, on the other hand, be tempted to ask himself in what the spell consisted, and seek to translate into cold prose the critical content of these astounding dithyrambs, he became aware that the impression he had received was predominantly emotional rather than intellectual. A succession of ideas had dazzled him; but the ideas Ruskin threw out were almost always half-formed. He had been stimulated by a profusion of images; but the lecturer's images, however suggestive, however beautifully phrased, were seldom sharply focused. "Ruskin's Oxford lectures" (to quote an admirable pamphlet by the present Slade Professor[1]), "although they contain some of his happiest inspirations, are not his best work." They include little that is new, much exhausting repetition of what he had already said. In his inaugural address he was at considerable pains both to regulate his prophetic extravagance and to curb his natural ardour. He was determined to keep his promise to Acland; and Acland, he told his mother, had literally wept with relief when the inaugural lecture was concluded. It was not that he had betrayed his faith; but he had expressed his views on society with unusual moderation. He also sought to give them a positive and optimistic colouring; for though his examination of the present state of English art includes many weighty criticisms, and though he announces that the English mind —owing, among other characteristics, to "a delight in the forms of burlesque which are connected in some degree with the foulness of evil," witness the improprieties of Chaucer and of Shakespeare—was never likely to produce masterpieces of ideal or theological painting, he concludes on a note of hope, sketching the magnificent future that, if they exerted themselves worthily, was promised to the English race. Ruskin the Imperialist (whose lectures enchanted the youthful Cecil Rhodes) has received relatively little attention from modern readers and admirers, who have preferred to discuss his individual brand of Socialism. Yet, as a supporter of authoritarian rule, he proclaimed his belief in the virtues of colonial expansion as resolutely and unashamedly as any late-Victorian empire-builder. England, he declared, "must found colonies as fast and far as she is able . . . seizing every piece of fruitful waste ground she can set her foot on, and there teaching these her colonists that their chief virtue is to be fidelity to their country, and that their first aim is to be to advance the power of England

[1]See *Ruskin at Oxford.* An Inaugural Lecture by Sir Kenneth Clark, 1947.

by land and sea. . . . These colonies must be fastened fleets; and every man of them must be under authority of captains and officers, whose better command is to be over fields and streets instead of ships of the line; and England, in these her motionless navies (or, in the true and mightiest sense, motionless *churches*, ruled by pilots on the Galilean lake of all the world), is to 'expect every man to do his duty.' . . ." As if to soften the effect of this slightly demagogic passage, the lecturer then slips into a strain of pure Ruskinian eloquence, reminding his listeners that before she attempts to assume dominion over lesser breeds, England must have the courage to put her house in order; since "the England who is to be mistress of half the earth, cannot remain herself a heap of cinders, trampled by contending and miserable crowds; she must yet again become the England she was once. . . . And under the green avenues of her enchanted garden, a sacred Circe, true Daughter of the Sun, she must guide the human arts, and gather the divine knowledge of distant nations, transformed from savageness to manhood, and redeemed from despairing into peace."

Judging by Acland's approval, Ruskin in his inaugural lecture adhered closely to the outlines of his argument as they were laid down in his written text. In his subsequent discourses, however, he usually strayed far afield. His notes were merely a leaping-off ground, from which he plunged into the labyrinth of theory, prejudice and fancy; and by 1873, and probably much earlier, he was allowing himself as fantastic a latitude as in any published volume. From the Lion of St. Mark's he sprang to Gothic history: from Gothic history to Theseus: from Theseus to Edward III: and so on, by way of the college boat and Goldsmith's *Deserted Village*, to sunset clouds, Sir Walter Scott, Victor Hugo and John Stuart Mill. Among undergraduates, Ruskin's lectures, which combined the excitement of a revivalist meeting with the interest of watching a practised stage performer, provided naturally a very welcome diversion from the ordinary round of academic studies. The atmosphere was electric: the nature of the entertainment always unconventional. Even the specimens and diagrams with which he enlivened his talk were a subject of fascinating speculation from the moment when his valet arranged them on the platform. This shrouded rectangle might be a Turner sketch: but it might equally well be a caricature, illustrative of the extreme depravity and repulsive deformity of the modern "self-made" man. Such specimens he used in his own way. Pouncing on Turner's presentation of the ancient bridge at Leicester, he would splash with his paint-brush across the glass that covered it his version of the "improvements" that the present age demanded—an iron bridge and factory chimneys, an asylum and a prison building. Then he would seize a sponge and, with a single dramatic sweep of the hand, obliterate these hideous proofs of nineteenth-century vileness.

Very different were the methods employed by the average Oxford lecturer. Inevitably his university associates were not altogether well pleased; and, while some rejoiced at the discomfiture of their less intelligent contemporaries, faced with the provocative statement that "a chalk stream does more for education than 100 National schools 'with all their doctrines of Baptismal Regeneration into the bargain,'"[1] others, though they denied that they were shocked, deplored the intemperance of Ruskin's delivery, his lack of the delicate circumspection so justly esteemed in academic circles. Dr. Jowett spoke for a large group; and readers of Mallock's *New Republic* will not have forgotten how, after "Mr. Herbert," an obvious portrait of Ruskin, had brought his lecture to an eloquent close, "a still small voice" became audible from the obscurity of a side box, murmuring: "*Very poor taste—very poor taste.*" The voice was attributed to "Dr. Jenkinson"; and, whether or no the words ever really proceeded from the trim pursed mouth of Dr. Jowett, they represented his point of view, and that of a large number of Oxford intellectuals. But Oxford society, in spite of its conservatism, is also strangely tolerant. Oddity lets oddity live; and Ruskin lived un-

[1] J. R. Green, the historian, to E. A. Freeman, 1870.

disturbed as Slade Professor of Fine Art from 1870 to 1878. True, his outbursts were sometimes alarming, his paradoxes disconcerting. At table, hearing Doré praised, he would put down his knife and fork, with the miserable ejaculation: "You have spoiled my dinner"; and, when an unlucky don admitted that "Inductive Psychology" was the subject of his latest course of lectures, a shout of "Oh, the Devil!" followed by the noise of rapidly retreating footsteps and a sonorous crash as his outer door was slammed shut, testified to a listening college that the Slade Professor had a vehement detestation of abstract modern theories.

His preferences in matters of entertainment were also voted awkward; for he reproved the opulence and ostentation of University dinner-parties, and did his best to set an example of frugality and low living. Here he had little success. *Mouton aux navets* might be endured for a single meal; but even at Balliol, recorded the Dean of Durham, "champagne and truffles were always lurking behind the door ready to rush in on a hint." Still, the Professor's sherry was good; and his conversation, had he not been unduly roused, revealed a peculiarly winning charm, compact of gentleness and shrewdness. On occasions he was an excellent listener, "diffident as a young girl" (noted Max Müller) "full of questions and grateful for any information." When he spoke, his language was "simply perfect. He was one of the few Englishmen" (Müller continued) ". . . who, instead of tumbling out their sentences like so many portmanteaux, bags, rugs and hat-boxes from an open railway van, seemed to take a real delight in building up their sentences, even in familiar conversation, so as to make each deliverance a work of art." About the social demeanour of Ruskin during middle age there was, indeed, a suspicion, if not of artificiality, at least of conscious artifice. As he grew older he grew more feminine; and the thunderous critic, the impassioned prophet, could at times be as beguiling and disarming as any female luminary. Feminine, too, was the slightly malicious skill with which, now and then, he would attract attention and yet appear to shun it. Jowett, who was "suspicious of æstheticism," was equally perturbed by Ruskin's "enthusiastic manner," of which, one evening in his own drawing-room, he became the helpless victim. The Master, who stood with another group, "suddenly broke into a hearty ringing laugh"—a laugh which no doubt conveyed some hint of lusty moral self-assurance. Leaving the companion with whom he was seated, the Professor sprang up and straightway rushed across to him. "Master," he exclaimed, seizing both reluctant hands, "how delighted I am to hear you. I wish *I* could laugh like that!" At which "all the room laughed—except Jowett," whose magisterial self-importance was for a while completely snuffed out.

That Ruskin was not unhappy at Oxford, that he enjoyed both the duties and the privileges he found there, and that he appreciated the opportunity of shocking some dons and, with elaborate, romantic, old-fashioned courtesy, mystifying others, is sufficiently proved by his private correspondence. Acland had originally housed him; but during the spring of 1871 he received an honorary fellowship of Corpus, and moved into comfortable rooms which overlooked the meadows. The ceremony of admission he made an excuse for some characteristic feats of charm, puzzling the aged President by his fanciful allusions and at luncheon delivering a pretty speech in which he compared himself and his Oxford colleagues to little birds who built their nests beside the mighty waters of Niagara, "while the great torrent of humanity rushes by us to its doom." In the same discourse, we are told, he likened trees to cities, "with their countless multitudes, not merely of sentient buildings, but also of restless, wind-stirred leaves. . . ." "*So busy, so busy!*" he murmured, gazing out perhaps over the heads of embarrassed fellows into the vernal college garden. Altogether, remembered a sympathetic celebrant, the "impression left of the day's proceedings was medieval, romantic, idyllic." At home in his rooms on Staircase Number Two, the atmosphere Ruskin created was as romantic and as other-worldly.

Many precious items from his collection were soon installed around him; four wax candles in silver candlesticks illuminated his Titian portrait and Turner's *Bolton Abbey*; his portfolios were stocked with prints and sketches; and twin cabinets, once the gift of his father, enshrined his mineral specimens. He had peace, leisure and security, and, should he choose to descend his staircase, such diversions as he needed: he could hear music in a cathedral-stall, receive the flattering attention of a cultivated Royal Prince, the wise and virtuous Leopold, or play with the juvenile daughters of his kindly friend, Dean Liddell, Alice and her delightful sisters, who looked forward to the Professor's amusing visits almost as eagerly as they looked forward to the calls of Dr. Dodgson. He grumbled, of course: that was a condition of life. But, as he admitted in a letter to his cousin Joan, his academic retreat did much to soothe and satisfy.

Yet at heart he remained unsatisfied: in spirit he was unappeased. The main problem continued to defy solution; for Rose, though again and again he informed his friends that he had abandoned every hope of winning her, still represented the only possible escape from the conflicts of his inward life. But Rose's character had not changed. The religious mood was as dominant as ever; and in 1870 she published a slender volume of frail devotional musings, verse and prose mixed, under the pensive title *Clouds and Light*. Some lines seem to deserve quotation, so pallid is their eloquence, so transparent their despondency, so dramatic the contrast they suggest between Ruskin's urgent demands for love and the state of melancholy abstraction, dignified as religious resignation, into which Rose had slowly drifted:

I would look back upon my life to-night,
Whose years have scarcely numbered twenty-two;
I would recall the darkness and the light,
The hours of pain God's angels led me through;
Out of His love He orders all things right,
I, slow of heart, would feel that this is true.

I, in those years, have learnt that life is sad,
Sad to heart-breaking did we walk alone.
I, who have lost much which I never had,
Yet which in ignorance I held mine own,
Would leave that clouded past, its good and bad,
Within His hands to whom all things are known.

Yet St. Crumpet was not completely forgotten; and, although it is possible to exaggerate the strength of her attachment to him, and although the quality of that attachment certainly fell far short of Ruskin's desires and expectations, he was, nevertheless, together with her parents and God, one of the central realities of Rose's small existence. She regarded him as her earthly master. . . . " Mr. Ruskin's teaching when I was about twelve " (she confided to her diary) ". . . made me first take to looking after the poor." And again: " The letters Mr. Ruskin wrote me only helped me, and did me no harm. . . ." For " Mr. Ruskin taught me that which was good "—good at least in this world. Throughout the earlier storms of their relationship her trust remained unbroken; and she could not understand why her anxious lover should so often, and at times so painfully, seek to probe her feelings. She felt all that she could feel " with my child-heart, or woman-heart, whatever some might call it "; but she must not only think of her own emotions, and she dreaded giving St. Crumpet hopes which might later bring him misery. Yet " care for him " she undoubtedly did. Why must he refuse to accept the position, and to recognise the limitations that a peculiar fate imposed upon her? Had Rose been a mature and normal girl, she might at length have escaped from the dilemma, and found some means of reconciling or rearranging her divided loyalties. But to a spirit that was over-scrupulous she added a body that would appear to have lacked the ordinary human zest for life. Instinct might have helped her to win the day; but instinctively she was as torpid and immature as, intellectually and spiritually, her mind was over-active. And then, Ruskin was an inexperienced lover: he was neither equipped to kindle the spark of passion, nor to encourage its genial development once a spark had been elicited.

Far from weakening Rose's opposition, his importunities exaggerated her fears and strengthened her resistance. A further grave misunderstanding overshadowed the winter of 1869 and the spring of 1870; and, while he was still at work on his opening Oxford lecture, an entry of tragic significance was committed to his private journal: "Last Friday" (he noted) "about 12 o'clock at noon my mistress passed me and would not speak." Mrs. Cowper Temple again received his confidences. For the moment, he declared, he was not to be beaten; but, "if she really does not care for me any more at all," he did not know how long the struggle could be kept up: he could not go on—"the whole thing will have been so horrible that every word I tried to say about God or right would choke me." Had his friend ever experienced "that feeling of breathlessness" which often overcame him? It was not induced by ordinary human grief so much as by a "sense of frightfulness and bitterness." Yet in present bitterness the beauty of the past was not entirely lost to view; and the same letter describes a radiant evening when he had travelled by railway from Milan to Como; and every omen had appeared to hint that he might one day be happy. It was behind *Monte Rosa* that the sun had descended, "drowning the whole mountain in light"; and, as the sun's disc touched the edge of the crags, they had drawn up at a station and the traveller had read the name—"*Stazione di Desio*," the station of desire and longing! Such omens seemed futile to-day. There were times when he felt that every effort towards happiness and harmony had better be abandoned. He was by no means sure, he added, that to *resist* the devil was, in all circumstances, the most effective method of prevailing. Should one not yield? Suppose, for instance, he were to produce what his well-wishers "would call good and victory" out of the misery and confusion which at the present day involved him, the world would delightedly acclaim the result, and "saintly pink personages" would inflict identical torments on other likely sufferers; whereas if, after delivering a few preliminary phrases to indicate the direction of his original hopes and plans, he were to explain to his Oxford audience that he had no longer the energy or inclination to execute his projects and, throwing up his professorship, retreated into solitude, "*then* people would understand that wrong *was* wrong": the devil would be vanquished, and he would have the consolation of following his natural bent, instead of struggling, obstinately and wearily, in the contrary direction.

That he was confused, he admitted freely: his mind was "getting so mixed up," darkened by the "desire for revenge" and the "kind of hatred love is changing into," and a "shame and anger at myself, increasing day by day," that his whole existence, he feared, was becoming radically distorted. Yet, as we know, the Oxford lectures reached completion; and, in February, the inaugural lecture was triumphantly delivered. It was, he commented to Mrs. Cowper Temple, "not nearly what it should have been": fog and east wind had kept him indoors, and his happiest inspirations always descended when he was walking in the open air. But most of the responsibility lay with "that unlucky child" whose "ineffably stupid and—everything that's bad—letter" had left him so numb with pain that the labours of three weeks had proved very largely useless. She had made him deeply unhappy; she had also made him angry; and his anger had even extended to his well-meaning little cousin; for Joan had had "actual hold of the creature" and had let her go again "without telling her a word of truth about her selfishness and cruelty." Epistolatory chastisement was inflicted on Rose herself; and during the latter part of the month of February, she replied from Harristown in a note to Mrs. Cowper Temple, enclosing a letter addressed to Ruskin which "dearest *Philé*" at her discretion was to forward or to hold back. Since this missive remained among Mrs. Cowper Temple's papers, we must assume that, as a guardian of Ruskin's peace, she decided to withhold it. Though scarcely cruel, its tone is cold and aggrieved. Rose complains that she has been bitterly misjudged, protests that she does not believe that she has communion with angels or cherish an arrogant belief in her own unfailing rectitude. She, too, had been deeply perturbed—" utterly wearied and perplexed," with no single guide to help her, conscious that she was losing her parents' love, " the only love that is a real possession to me now," and aware that by an idolatrous lover she was neither understood nor trusted.

Yet under the resentment lingers a strain of regret. She *had* loved as far as she could love; and, though she bids good-bye to him for ever, it is not without a benediction. She could not accept the responsibility for his happiness which he had tried to thrust upon her: she could not promise him that she would " rule " his life. " And yet——

> ' *This is my prayer, if Thou dost send*
> *Blessing or pain to him or me,*
> *Give me the pain—but bless my friend*
> *Whom I have loved eternally.*' "

Had this scrap of doggerel been Rose's parting message, had she thereupon retired into profound seclusion, and had Ruskin abandoned his last hopes and Mrs. Cowper Temple her final attempts at diplomatic advocacy, the long confused unfortunate story might have had a less disastrous ending. But *Philé*, who still possessed considerable influence at Harristown, did not cease to plead St. Crumpet's case and endeavour to dissipate some of the suspicions that hung about his good name. During the autumn of 1870 she revived her attack upon Rose's tender conscience, begging that Ruskin should be allowed to renew his suit and thus reap the reward of many years of faithful service, and insisting that his past career, whatever scandal-mongers might suggest, had been entirely blameless. Reverting to the subject of his marriage, she rehearsed the account that he himself had given her: he had married to please his mother and father, and, though he was not and had never been impotent, he had respected his wife too sincerely to wish to consummate a loveless union: their tastes had been incompatible, yet he had done his best to make her happy. . . . But if *Philé* was a persuasive advocate, in Lacerta Ruskin had now a determined and resourceful adversary. The steps she took were extremely practical; and it is known, for example, that she had already consulted a solicitor as to Rose's position were she to marry Ruskin, receiving a remarkably discouraging reply with which she proceeded to enlighten Ruskin's much too sanguine confidante.[1] The new attack upon Rose's emotions demanded yet more stringent counter-measures. Rose, it would seem, was prepared to succumb, or at least there appeared to be some possibility that she might slip back into a hapless irresolute condition from which her parents had just rescued her; whereat Mrs. La Touche decided on a move that she may have long been meditating. It was equally painful, effective and indelicate: she wrote direct to Effie Millais.

More than sixteen years had elapsed since Effie Ruskin and Mrs. Gray had bidden good-bye for the last time to Effie's unsuspecting husband. She had divorced him: she had happily re-married: a bevy of handsome children were growing up around her. But although her personality had developed, it had not grown more mellow. The young girl revealed in her early letters might very well have been transferred from a novel by Jane Austen, with her gaiety, her juvenile frivolity and the touches of worldly wisdom which overlaid, but did not disguise, her fundamental innocence. That young girl was irretrievably lost. Gone was the Effie who loved pink bonnets, sailed delightedly through London ballrooms, and observed John's distinguished acquaintances with a candid yet critical eye. She was becoming a disciplinarian, a stern Victorian matron. Perhaps the damage done in the years of her first marriage

[1] Mrs. La Touche had been advised in Dec. 1868 that, if it were to be discovered that a man divorced on the plea of impotency was not really impotent, the divorce would be *ipso facto* annulled: a second marriage would be nullified, and any children rendered illegitimate. This advice, however, would appear to have been wholly unsound. No doubt the legal position was investigated at the time by Ruskin or his advisers.

had penetrated to a deeper level than she herself imagined; certainly it had helped to harden her character, to make her moral judgements merciless; and, when Mrs. La Touche, asserting a mother's privilege, laid Rose's case before her, she emerged from the past like an avenging spirit, nothing forgotten and nothing forgiven, convinced that by annihilating Ruskin's hopes she merely did her duty. Another young woman, she no doubt reflected, was treading the same path that she had trodden, attracted by the same intellectual lures, towards the same frustration. Self-analysis she had seldom indulged in: and it seems improbable that at this moment she scanned her motives carefully. She would have denied that she was avenging a private hurt; and yet a tone of intense personal bitterness rings through every paragraph. Some parts of Ruskin's statement, as Mrs. Cowper Temple had repeated it, were disposed of without difficulty. "Our marriage was *never arranged*," she assured Mrs. La Touche, and had been preceded by "professions of the most devoted kind." It was a "perfect falsehood to say that I did not agree with his pursuits"; for they had read and studied together, and she was always fond of history. No, their marriage had failed for other reasons, very different, much less obvious, very much less creditable. They were to be hinted at, rather than expressly divulged; but the avenging spirit's hints had the explosive force of accusations.

"From his peculiar nature," she declared, Ruskin was utterly incapable of making any woman happy. "He is quite unnatural and in that one thing all the rest is embraced." And elsewhere: "His conduct to me was impure in the highest degree, discreditable, and so dishonourable that I submitted to it for years not knowing what else to do. . . ." She could easily understand, she remarked in another passage, the hold Ruskin had gained and the "peculiar influence" he exerted; but she prophesied that, if Rose succumbed to his spell, she would be subjected to the same treatment and that her health in time would break down. . . . Such was Effie's final appearance on the stage of Ruskin's history, such the repayment she exacted for the lingering misery of her married life. That her motives were conscientious, or at least, since she was neither an intellectual nor an introspective woman, that she was convinced she performed a duty, seems now beyond all question; and, although her accusations and insinuations, taken at their face value, were evidently exaggerated, it is not difficult, granted our knowledge of Ruskin's sexual difficulties, and the attempts we may assume he made at circumventing or concealing them, to divine the nature of the experiences that had disturbed her thus profoundly. But Mrs. La Touche was in no mood, indeed in no position, to adopt an indulgent or sympathetic standpoint. Effie's letter confirmed her worst fears; and from this moment it became unthinkable that she should agree to any compromise. Ruskin's fate had been decided; and in a grateful letter of reply, Mrs. La Touche announced that Rose, she felt sure, at last was out of danger. She had promised her father that she would snap the remaining link; and her family had promised that in her hearing the name of her unworthy lover should not again be mentioned.

Once more, in the study of Ruskin's life, we notice how private misfortune spurred him to a fresh outburst of philanthropic energy. His work at Oxford he regarded as by no means the most important part of the tasks that lay ahead of him; for although the young gentlemen assembled there certainly needed his instructions, and demonstrably benefited by being obliged to distinguish between good and bad art, they were, alas, but a small minority; and around them and beyond them, in the slums of Vauxhall and Deptford, in the hideous shabby-genteel suburbs that now encircled him at Denmark Hill, in the industrial towns of the North where modern enterprise was reproducing some of the worst features of the ancient London rookeries, another nation demanded his help, the workmen and artisans of modern industrial England, some of whose representatives he had already met at Golden Square. They, too, had a claim on his loyalty. Notwithstanding his private distress, never had Ruskin's sense of public obligation appeared more fierce and urgent; and during the spring of 1870, in his preface to a catalogue planned for an exhibition of sound contemporary handicraft, he made a declaration of faith surely among the most moving he had ever uttered.[1] It is exceedingly personal, like most of his finest writing; but here the personal element achieves a harmonious fusion with the prophetic message. He begins quietly, simply, lucidly, describing how "at half-past six on the morning of April 21, 1870," he had been walking beneath the fruit trees of his Denmark Hill garden: "The air was perfectly calm, the sunlight pure, and falling on the grass through thickets of the standard peach . . . and of plum and pear trees, in their first showers of fresh silver, looking more like much-broken and far-tossed spray of fountains than trees." But this curiously Proustian passage serves merely to let through a graver, deeper undertone; for "meantime, in the still air, the roar of the railroads from Clapham Junction, New Cross and Crystal Palace . . . sounded constantly and heavily, like the surf of a strong sea three or four miles distant; and the whistles of the trains passing nearer mixed with the nightingale's notes." The moral conclusion was inescapable: to-day even the enjoyment of the nightingale's song was an economic luxury: "That I could hear her at all, or see the blossoms, or the grass, in the best time of spring, depended on my having been long able to spend a large sum annually in self-indulgence, and in keeping my fellow-creatures out of my way. Of those who were causing all that murmur . . . and of the myriads imprisoned by the English Minotaur of lust for wealth, and condemned to live, if it is to be called life, in the labyrinth of black walls, and loathsome passages between them, which now fills the valley of the Thames . . . not one could hear, that day, any happy bird sing, or look upon any quiet space of the pure grass that is good for seed." Thence he rises to a prophetic vision: "But they might have the blessing of these things for all, if they chose, and that vast space of

[1]For drawing my attention to this passage, lost in the dense thicket of Ruskin's collected works, I am indebted to Sir Kenneth Clark's lecture, *Ruskin at Oxford*.

London might be full of gardens, and terraced round with hawthorn walks. . . . And now, gentlemen, I beg you once for all to understand that unless you are minded to bring yourselves, and all whom you can help, out of this curse of darkness that has fallen on our hearts and thoughts you need not try to do any art-work—it is the vainest of affectations to try to put beauty into shadows, while the real things that cast them are left in deformity and pain."

It was in this mood, with a determination that such light as he could yet diffuse should not be confined to a sheltered Oxford lecture-room, that on January 1st, 1871, Ruskin began his succession of open letters "to the workmen and labourers of Great Britain," collected under the enigmatic title *Fors Clavigera*. A noble project; but the choice of a title alone—*Fors* being variously interpreted as *Force*, *Fortitude* and *Fortune*, bearing, in accordance with her requirements, the *Club*, the *Key*, the *Nail*—seems by its eccentricity to hint at Ruskin's weakness. The introduction to the catalogue is, above all things, nobly straightforward; but although his letters, in sudden bursts, are often simple and direct enough, no continuous design unites them: there is no progression that can be immediately followed from one sibylline page to the epistle that succeeds it. Again the author is deliberately wayward; and as we contrast the simplicity of his plan with the intricacy of its execution, his professed desire to meet his proletarian readers on a man-to-man footing with the maze of irrelevancies through which he allowed his mind to wander, we recognise, not for the first time, how deeply and fatally his nature was divided. His intention is to be direct and forceful. Misery, he says, is omnipresent; he is no Evangelical, and not even by temperament an unusually unselfish person: "I have no particular pleasure in doing good. . . . But I simply cannot paint, nor read, nor look at minerals . . . because of the misery that I know of, and see signs of, where I know it not. . . . Therefore, as I have said, I will endure it no longer quietly. . . ." He wishes to help so far as he can, and he wishes to explain to the workmen of England the manifold methods by which, having cleared their heads of cant and superstition, they might profitably help themselves. Yet no sooner has the declaration been made, than a second, more ambiguous personality takes charge of Ruskin's prose style. For a moment he is the practical teacher, anxious to find his place among his fellows in the common struggle for a better life: then a fundamental sense of solitude once more overwhelms him: he falls back into the old reveries, into the dream-world of prejudices and fancies from which there was no issue.

Of *Fors Clavigera*, Manning, who wished to praise the letters, remarked that they were like "the beating of one's heart in a nightmare." Nor was the comparison inexact; for just as in a nightmare we have the impression of being helplessly cut off from everyday existence, towards which with repeated efforts we try in vain to reascend, so as we read Ruskin's effusions, though the subject is usually topical and the literary tone colloquial, we seem to be imprisoned in a lonely universe visited by phantoms of real life, shapes distorted or terribly magnified, but seldom by realities. This is true, not of Ruskin's matter, which has almost always some connection, however tenuous and far-fetched, with the problems of the present day, but of the effect produced by his manner and by the imprint of his personality stamped on every paragraph. His audience is supposedly definite: he visualises the immense masses of the half-educated waiting for improvement; yet such was the perversity of his fate that his last desperate attempt to establish some real communion between himself and mankind is of all his works the most self-centred, the most deeply personal and inescapably Ruskinian. *Fors Clavigera* is not a public address: it is a long and passionate soliloquy. To vary the image, reading *Fors* often reminds us of listening to some unknown neighbour, whom we catch talking to himself in an adjacent hotel bedroom. We are aware of the echoing loneliness from which his protestations reach us. He imagines interlocutors, but they do not really exist: solitude gives a hollow ring to every laugh and to every burst of scorn. Yet nowhere had Ruskin striven more honestly or more energetically to break down the barrier that kept him from his fellow men. He will spare them nothing; and he is, in his turn, unsparing of his confidences. He is determined that, before they decide to trust him, they shall learn to know him thoroughly: what was his childhood, what is his income, how much of his fortune he is laying out in public works. He makes them the confidants of his private quarrels; frankly and delightfully he sketches—in his early youth, describes his garden, his dependants and his charming room at Denmark Hill. Yet the more strenuously he endeavours to approach, and to become the familiar friend—albeit a reproving friend—of his errant fellow countrymen, the farther does he appear to recede, the deeper the air of isolation that gradually encompasses him. He is still John Ruskin, a perplexed and solitary being, an artist weighed down by a prophet's robes, a stern critic of society who cannot forget that he is, in spite of all, an artist.

The letters composing *Fors Clavigera*, issued not by an ordinary publishing firm but by his protégé, George Allen, whom at a week's notice he had set up as his publisher in a small Kentish villa-residence, continued to tumble out in monthly instalments from January 1871 till the autumn of 1878, when, owing to the collapse of his health, they were for a while suspended. A man of ordinary vitality might have felt well satisfied with the work that he was accomplishing. But Ruskin's constitution was in every way exceptional: the more he did, the more he seemed impelled to do; and during the comparatively brief period of activity that had begun in 1870 and came to a sudden end in 1878, besides writing his monthly *Fors* and speaking and teaching at Oxford, he published a long series of collected lectures, under titles as variously perplexing as *Aratra Pentelici*, *Ariadne Florentina* and *Love's Meinie*, and three guides to Italian art, *Mornings in Florence*, *St. Mark's Rest* and a *Guide to the Principal Pictures in the Academy of Fine Arts at Venice*, revised and reissued two of his previous books, started a publishing firm, organised a drawing-school and launched a national crusade, established a shop for the sale of tea and coffee, and embarked on such bold experiments in practical philanthropy as street-sweeping and road-building. Yet, although his energy was prodigious, it had a somewhat feverish character. He had not the zest of a happy and healthy man—nothing, say, of the youthful fire that burned in William Morris, who had been heard to observe that if a fellow could not at the same moment compose an epic poem and weave a tapestry on a hand-loom, talking meanwhile with children and friends, he had very little use for him. To Morris work was enjoyment: the path of endeavour was the path of personal happiness. "One can't get much enjoyment out of life at this rate," he had remarked of the type of career to which modern life doomed a vast majority of his fellow human beings; and it was originally during his search for happiness (which, since he was a naturally generous man, included the happiness of others) that he had arrived at the beliefs which supplied his life-long impetus. Morris was pure gold, Ruskin announced; and an impression of singular virtue was registered by every contemporary on whom his friendship lighted. Than dear "Topsy," whose shaggy mane, when he was exasperated, rose horrendous as a "burning crest," whose whiskers and moustaches bristled forth "like pine needles," in the whole assemblage of Pre-Raphaelite artists there was no more endearing, no more powerful, figure. Beneath the subtlety of an artist's temperament, he concealed the strength and the directness of an essentially simple mind.

A comparison of Morris and Ruskin has already been attempted; and at this point of Ruskin's history it may be carried a stage further. The beliefs they held were largely identical. Art (Morris was to tell his students) could not be dissociated from morality, politics and religion: it was a form of personal morality: it was—or it should be—a source of human fellowship: and "fellowship is life, lack of fellowship is death." We return, in fact, to Ruskin's doctrine of art as a universal language; but whereas the fellowship to which Morris aspired was not beyond his personal scope, and he derived a deep satisfaction from the public projects which absorbed his time and energy, the complications of Ruskin's temperament stood always in his own way, and his most strenuous creative efforts were often self-destructive. For the main problem was still within himself, and so long as that problem remained unsettled, his view of external problems was usually vague and not infrequently distorted. Morris, on the other hand, had no tormenting inner difficulties, or, if they had ever threatened to develop, had successfully subordinated them to the fulfilment of his outward purpose. His private life was a secondary concern; and though it is possible that Jane Morris, dark and remote and beautifully sad, the object of Rossetti's poetic and platonic cult, received from the existence they shared a somewhat dusty answer, his household at Kelmscott and in Hammersmith was equally harmonious and active. In these pleasant surroundings the burly hirsute master-craftsman did what he felt he had to do, using the weapons that suited him best, with a superb disregard of methods and opinions that he saw he could not manage. "To speak quite frankly," (he informed a Socialist gathering) "I do not know what Marx's theory of value is, and I'm damned if I want to know." With the same frankness and unabashed directness, he continued throughout his career to thrust turbulently straight ahead.

Neither Ruskin's temperament, nor the circumstances in which it involved him, would permit of such an easy fate. He was already weary when he arrived at Oxford; and during 1871 a succession of misfortunes tried him to the uttermost. His spirits were low when the year began. Month after month he had been following the course of the Franco-Prussian conflict—"this marvellous and ghastly war"—and brooding over the probable fate of French cities, pictures, churches. Yet here again, his attitude was inconsistent. As a disciple of the author of *Frederick*, he was, on the whole, more sympathetically inclined towards the victorious Prussians than towards their vanquished adversaries, since modern France (he declared at the end of August 1870) represented "the purest and intensest republicanism . . . joined to vanity, lust and lying," while in the opposite camp he thought that he recognised "a Personal, Hereditary, Feudal government as stern as Barbarossa's, with a certain measure of modesty, decency, and veracity. . . ." His attitude had changed by the time he wrote the opening letter of *Fors Clavigera*, dated February 1st, 1871, in which he likened the Prussian forces to the band of medieval marauders commanded by Sir John Hawkwood, and concluded that "the actual Prussian expedition into France merely differs from Sir John's in Italy by being more generally savage, much less enjoyable, and by its clumsier devices for taking towns; for Sir John had no occasion to burn libraries." Of the American civil war he had once observed that it was hideous, yet as remote from his comprehension as a war of red and black ants; and similarly, considering events in France—the bombardment of Strasbourg, the siege of Paris and the rise and suppression of the Commune—it was the desperate folly they revealed that he felt most inclined to emphasise. Were they not part of a wider and deeper calamity, a process of moral and physical disintegration that was undermining Europe, that had dimmed the splendour of Alpine snowfields as surely and inescapably as it had overcast his own life?

Every support was crumbling and vanishing. During the early spring died Anne, the aged, cantankerous, devoted servant who was inextricably connected with the memories of his childhood; and soon afterwards he understood that his mother, too, was failing him; her prodigious vitality had begun to ebb away; it seemed quite impossible that she should live to see another New Year. The spring proved gloomy and cold: a "black east wind," of the kind that he most abominated, scoured the English landscape; and more and more he became possessed of the belief that Nature herself concealed an evil principle, and railed at her "barbarity," "clumsiness" and "darkness." Even the sky and the blossoms were "Dead." In the summer he visited Matlock, but there fell ill with a complaint described as inflamation of the bowels, which brought with it strange dreams and left him weak and languid. Ruskin had only recovered (so he told a friend), by disregarding all his doctors. Clearly he was a difficult patient; and on one occasion he insisted that he should be supplied at two o'clock in the morning with " cold roast beef and mustard." Meanwhile the matriarch of Denmark Hill was slipping slowly beyond human help. His father's extinction had been violent but rapid; it was far more painful to watch his indomitable mother receding step by step into the limbo of unconsciousness: " the sinking . . . back into the bleak Mechanism was difficult to bear the sight of ": and to-day his cousin Joan, though she was still an affectionate *aide* and had nursed him faithfully at Matlock, was no longer the inseparable companion she had been since 1864. During the spring she had married Arthur Severn, youngest son of the painter Joseph Severn who, forty years earlier, had sat by Keats' death-bed.

Margaret Ruskin died at Denmark Hill on December 5th, 1871. She was ninety years old——

> " . . . *Nor was dearer earth*
> *Ever returned to earth,*
> *Nor purer life*
> *Recorded in heaven*——"

her son presently declared on the tomb that he erected. Her powerful reign had reached its conclusion; and with her disappearance came the closing-down of Denmark Hill, that monument to commercial prosperity, evangelical piety and stern domestic virtue, where, until the end of her life, on the solemn Sabbath days, dark shades were still drawn over Ruskin's favourite pictures. In death, she looked " very pretty and young "; the hand which lay across her breast was as light and graceful " as if Mino of Fésole had cut it "; her severity had been laid aside; and she expired with the modest and confident hope that although she might not be permitted to join her husband in the next world, she would be allowed, nevertheless, to see him at a distance. Everything she had she bequeathed to her son. He was "more surprised by the sense of loneliness," he wrote to Norton, than he had expected; but he did not desist, even momentarily, from the labours he had set himself; and the same month found him engaged in a somewhat fantastic, yet highly characteristic, project. His plans of reformation had grown increasingly practical. Eloquent pleas, literary invective, had too often failed to make a mark. It was not that they had glanced off a giant's armour, but that they had slid into the vast bulk of British middle-class complacency, which had immediately closed over and tolerantly absorbed them. Ruskin was a "great writer," whose wild expeditions into politics and economics, though commendable as literature, need not be taken very seriously. He was now determined to produce results. Confining his attention to simple immediate problems, he would employ only the simplest, humblest, most straightforward and least intellectual methods.

For instance, he would demonstrate to the population of London how they ought to sweep their pavements. In this task he was inspired by his mother's example; he had "inherited to the full" Margaret Ruskin's "love of cleanliness and tidiness"; and he could never forget that many years earlier, when she had complained that the stone stairs of a Swiss inn had deteriorated since their last visit, and the proprietor and inn-servants had refused to heed his admonitions, he himself had brought buckets of water, had poured them down fifteen or twenty steps—creating thereby an agreeable reproduction of the waterworks at Versailles—and had scrubbed with a long broom till each successive step was damply clean. It was, he recollected, "quite the happiest bit of manual work I ever did. . . ." In December, 1871, he sent a letter to the *Pall Mall Gazette*, informing its readers that, as from January 1st, 1872, he meant to "take three street-sweepers into constant service," concentrate their organised activities upon a single stretch of pavement, and show once and for all that, given hard work and genuine good will, a London thoroughfare might be kept as unsullied as the deck of any battleship. His proposal was duly carried out. But a part of St. Giles's, then one of the filthiest districts of proletarian London, was the area selected; and although Ruskin opened the campaign by handling a sweeper's broom, although his gardener, Downs, was appointed foreman, and the Professor, with parties of friends, frequently appeared in his carriage to watch the work proceeding, his expectations were constantly disappointed, as across the region his sweepers had cleared a fresh wave of mud was trampled by the feet of men and animals. The inhabitants of the district were " passive ": not all the sweepers he had engaged were equally industrious. Summoned away to attend to his new country house on Coniston Water, he found that it was impossible to give them the encouragement they needed.

So the project was temporarily put by—written off as a modern general writes off some unsuccessful " side-show." His main plans of attack were bold and definite. In Letter VIII of *Fors Clavigera*, issued at the beginning of August, 1871, he announced the foundation of St. George's Guild and explained the financial arrangements he was making for its upkeep. He had promised to contribute himself a tenth of his possessions: and the St. George's Fund was launched with a free gift from Ruskin of £7,000, placed in the hands of trustees, William Cowper Temple and Sir Thomas Dyke Acland, to which a recalcitrant public added £236:13:0 during the next three years. But although the dimensions of the fund might be comparatively small, its objects were gigantic; for it aimed at nothing less than the reformation of the entire social system, the destruction of the industrial dragon, and the replacement of industrial society by a hierarchy of masters and servants, of artists, artificers and manual labourers, planned to include all that had been best in the civilisation of the Middle Ages. St. George's Guild, the most grandiose of Ruskin's schemes, the most dramatic of his failures, may profitably be considered from several different aspects. In its inception it was exceedingly practical. Ruskin believed that neither by politicians nor by economists could the world be restored to its earlier grace and sanity. Only men of good will, freely associated in the common interest, could hope to bring about this miracle, and their concern must not be with political forms or economic theories, so much as with the material conditions of life, the actual surface of the globe on which men lived and laboured. Wherever waste land could be reclaimed or natural forces harnessed, wherever beauty could be substituted for squalor and harmony for confusion, even if it were by sweeping an urban pavement or cleansing a country stream that modern enterprise had clogged and fouled, a precious advance had been made and the evil powers that threatened humanity had received a telling set-back. Thus he proposed that the immediate aim of St. George's Guild should be to do for some small plots of English soil what he had endeavoured to do for the pavements of St. Giles's, to encourage agriculture, discourage industry—except where it was the industry of the artist or the craftsman—and ensure to the inhabitants a safe and decent livelihood. He and his friends were to cleanse the Augean stables, but were glad to begin, modestly and quietly, by sweeping out the stable yard.

Such was the immediate plan; but attached to it was a dream, fantastic both in scope and nature. Prolonged study of Plato's *Republic* and *Laws*,[1] working on the conception of society he had inherited from his father's household, where every one had an appointed place—the old servants pottering contentedly about their daily labours,[2] as much as Master John at his writing-desk or his mother in her sitting-room—and the whole system appeared to revolve with almost solar smoothness, had intensified his distrust of egalitarian doctrines. It was no Liberal paradise he planned, but a hierarchical structure, based upon authority. The Guild of St. George was, in fact, a pyramid; at its

[1] "As we read him we begin to feel that 'the strongest poison ever known' came not 'from Caesar's laurel crown' but from the bay-leaves of Academe." *Ruskin at Oxford:* Sir Kenneth Clark.

[2] Once established, the Ruskins' servants were seldom or never dismissed. When asked what was the office of a particularly ancient and apparently unemployed housemaid, Margaret Ruskin replied with some acerbity that *her* function, of course, was to lay out the dessert.

apex was Ruskin, self-elected "Master"; beneath him were to be "Marshals" and "Landlords," who bore the title of "Companions" or "Comites Militantes," agents, farmers, field-labourers, and persons engaged in necessary commercial tasks. The Master had dictatorial powers; but Ruskin apparently imagined that since all the members would have joined of their own free will and have subscribed to the eight articles of St. George's Vow, which began with a declaration of trust in "the Living God, Father Almighty, Maker of Heaven and earth" and ended with a promise of submission to "the laws of the Society called St. George," the authority he wielded would require no enforcement. But it was in his social and sumptuary ordinances that he gave his imagination widest play. Social distinctions were not to be abolished, but emphasised by the style of dress prescribed for separate social classes. The new world was to be as variegated and full of colour as heraldry could make it. Beauty and luxury were to be universal—a luxury purified of any taint of laziness and licence; for all would work according to their special abilities; and, though the landowner did not lose his land or the nobleman his title, he was expected to earn and deserve it, and plough back into the soil a large part of his revenues. The landowner's wife would be beautifully garbed; and, adopting a different fashion, women of a lower class would display their wealth in gold and silver hair-ornaments. Nor were the pleasures of the table neglected; cookery ranked as an important art; and among young girls there was to be keen competition in manufacturing Yorkshire pies. Wine was allowed; but, mindful of the foundation of his father's fortune, Ruskin ordained that no vintage should be drunk that had not matured for ten years. Adulteration in any shape was, of course, anathema. Bad food and bad wine were to be cast on to the bonfire, with ugly clothing and impure books. The coinage in use was to be of gold and silver unalloyed. Jewels might be worn, provided that the innocence of precious stones was not impaired by cutting.

Ruskin's vision of human felicity made, it will be

observed, very few allowances for the freedom of the individual. His subjects might cultivate virtue on the lines that suited them, so long as they ate and drank at the Master's direction, wore the clothes that he designed, admitted to their manor-houses, workshops and cottages the books and pictures he had chosen. "Discipline" was a word that often recurred: "the youth of both sexes," for example, were "to be disciplined daily in the strictest practice of vocal music," taught to "speak truth with rigid care, and to obey orders with the precision of slaves"; and a reader reluctantly arrives at the conclusion that, had Ruskin's Utopia ever materialised in real life, at its best it might have resembled that benevolent and harmonious tyranny which the Jesuit Fathers once imposed upon the Indians of the New World, while at its worst, under the pressure of circumstance, it might have acquired some of the ugly traits of later dictatorial régimes. But the Guild of St. George was never put to proof. Possibly (his admirers considered) Ruskin, with the strange whimsicality—one might add, perversity—that very often characterised him, did not intend that their interpretation of his message should be altogether literal. Up to a point his aims were concrete: beyond that point he was content to please himself, planning for the sake of planning and dreaming for the sake of dreaming. Certainly the results he achieved were meagre: a small cottage museum planted on a hill near Sheffield, some workmen's dwellings in Wales, and a number of unproductive acres in Worcestershire and Yorkshire. Attempts were made to give the Guild of St. George a solid legal basis; but the discussion of legal documents is seldom very stimulating: and, when his subordinates called for the Master he was often unobtainable, wrapped in one of his favourite studies or botanising with a sketch book.

X

MUCH of Ruskin's spare time was now devoted to his newly-purchased country house. During August, 1871 to oblige an impecunious acquaintance, he bought a small property in the Lake District, overlooking Coniston Water. While he was ill and feverish at Matlock, the rippling coolness of that grey northern lake had haunted his imagination; and, as soon as he was offered Brantwood, although he had never seen it, he had decided that it must be his. So the house and the ground were bought—"a bit of steep hillside, facing west, commanding from the brow of it all Coniston lake and the mass of hills of South Cumberland . . . half copse, half moor and rock," with "a pretty field beneath, less steep" and "a white two-storied cottage." At a first glance he liked it well enough: on closer acquaintance he began to love it dearly. By the end of March, 1872, Denmark Hill had been given up; and once the house itself, which he had found "a mere shed of rotting timber and loose stone," had been repaired and newly furnished—an operation that cost him £4,000, as he punctiliously informed the readers of his monthly letters—he settled there with his rich accumulation of pictures, books and specimens. Henceforward it was his home and refuge, and he was never tired of beautifying it, adding terraces and a hill-top orchard and constructing a harbour on the shore of the lake in which to moor his pleasure-craft. There he presently welcomed Joan and Arthur Severn. In London they inhabited the modest house on Herne Hill from which James and Margaret Ruskin had moved to the larger, more impressive Denmark Hill establishment. At Herne Hill, they kept his old nursery always ready in case Ruskin wished to visit them; and at Brantwood Joan, kindly and sympathetic as ever, assumed the rôle of hostess, attending to the comfort of his numerous and often tiresome visitors, watching over her cousin's delicate health, and protecting him, so far as she could, against the shocks and irritations of everyday existence. It was no easy task, but she had her reward. Ruskin's gratitude increased with the years: after a time his relation to his protectress became that of a brother to a devoted elder sister. . . .

In the summer months of 1872, the Severns were his companions on an extended foreign tour. They visited Pisa, where Ruskin watched his beloved Chapel of the Thorn being destroyed by restoration as he stood by furious and helpless, and Lucca, where another favourite building proved to have undergone the same fate. Later they travelled to Rome; and there, in the Sistine Chapel, he made a devout study of the work of Sandro Botticelli, an artist who at that period had just begun to claim his reverence.[1] By June he had reached the destination of almost every pilgrimage. He was in Venice, rapturously enlarging his knowledge of Carpaccio, when a telegram arrived from England which bore the signature of George MacDonald, and contained a suggestion that, a few years earlier, would have raised his spirits to the highest pitch. The Scottish storyteller was a trusted friend; he was also a friend of the La Touches; and in this double capacity he had been elected as one of Rose La Touche's counsellors.[2] During the spring of 1872 she wrote him several letters, long and pathetic effusions in which she struggled to resolve some of the perplexities that gnawed her spirit. For while Ruskin contended with the problems of conscience, and sought, and occasionally achieved, relief in a round of tireless hard work, Rose, idle and alone at Harristown, confronted similar problems, but, except in prayers and melancholy self-abnegation, could find no means of

[1]Ruskin's first reference to Botticelli was in an Oxford lecture of 1871.

[2]For a full account of this relationship, see *Reminiscences of a Specialist* by Greville MacDonald, 1932.

easing them. A deep anxiety possessed her mind. Was it possible, she wondered, that "God ever puts us into positions where we cannot do His will? . . . Does He teach us truths we are powerless to obey? And how are we to keep ourselves from being tortured with disquiet when this is so?" Her temperament might prompt austerity: at home she could not escape from a world of prosperity and luxury. What her parents asked might seem little enough—it was merely that she should be happy, and gratify them with the sight of her contentment like a good Victorian daughter; but the conditions of existence they imposed could not fail to make her miserable. She was too restless, the days were too long. Hour followed unoccupied hour: she drove and walked, visited some of the poor people who depended on her patronage, painted and read and turned her mind to music; yet always when night descended, she felt (she told George MacDonald) "like a child tired out after a long, lonely holiday." Her spiritual needs, which were "enormous," at least had taught her sympathy; but that sympathy was spent in the void, and though she believed that she loved her fellow human beings, she had come to despair of making any real contact. True, she visited the poor and sick; but from the peasants in their cottages beyond her parents' park wall a gigantic gulf divided her. "They lead a life so much more like Christ's than mine"; and, as soon as she had left them and gone "jingling off from their doors in the carriage with my ponies and bells," the old ache settled on her heart, a sense of weariness and deep unworthiness, a spiritual nostalgia that she could neither hope to shake off nor, in the last resort, could ever fully analyse.

"I would die" (she wrote) "for Papa and Mama"; but to live for them, and live with them, proved very much more difficult. Mr. La Touche, who, though one of Spurgeon's converts, was also a successful banker, was fond of suggesting that benevolence should begin at home, and that social evils we could not cure must be endured with Christian fortitude; while his wife, who as long as Rose was sick had tended her devotedly, could not conceal her irritation at such perpetual wool-gathering. Angry discussions were succeeded by sleepless nights. Of St. Crumpet, Rose spoke to her friend in a tone at once regretful and coolly, distantly reproachful. He had brought her "pain and suffering and torture and division": she was sorry, nevertheless, that she had not kept his friendship, and that alien emotions had later overwhelmed them: for "if there had never been anything but friendship between us—how much might have been spared. . . ." About the same time, Rose sent to George MacDonald (who, not without reason, decided to withhold it) a lengthy epistle addressed to Ruskin, in which she deplored his loss of faith, referred vaguely to his own admissions concerning the errors of his past life, and concluded, with more unction than discretion: "How the angels must sorrow over you, and some hearts are sorrowing still." MacDonald was a just and generous man, who knew or suspected the part played by Effie in the annihilation of Ruskin's hopes. Convinced that a great writer, for whom he had deep affection and respect, had been grotesquely misjudged, and that Effie Millais' statement had been vilely misinterpreted, he determined to enter the battle himself; and when Rose, whose doctors had advised a change of air and scene, came unaccompanied to stay with his friends the Cowper Temples, first in London and afterwards in Hampshire, he seized the opportunity of making a last attempt to dispel her doubts and prejudices. His pleas evidently had a certain effect; and, believing that success was near, he telegraphed to Ruskin in Venice and begged that he would return home.

Ruskin refused. He would not move (he telegraphed back) "unless in certainty of seeing her. If you and Mrs. MacDonald can bring her to Italy I will meet you at Geneva." In a letter written the same day—June 30th, 1872—he enlarged on his refusal. Only "absolute certainty" of seeing Rose would persuade him to leave Venice. He would have no discussion, no equivocation; thrice already Rose's behaviour had threatened his existence, and the little life that remained was now dedicated to another cause. It must never again be poisoned with anger. He had trusted Rose with his whole heart; and "she threw it to the dogs to eat. . . ." "I am not a saint" (he observed bitterly). "Rose is—but a cruel one." Then the mood of resentment began to dissolve. He could not forgive the harm she had done; yet, if she genuinely desired to make peace, he must perforce agree to humour her. Soon afterwards he returned to England, and about the 7th or 8th of August met Rose at the MacDonalds' house in Hammersmith. A few sentences tell the rest of the story. Fragmentarily, as if he could scarcely trust himself to examine the full extent of his astounding good fortune, he recorded his impressions of the halcyon days they spent together. No one—least of all Rose's embittered lover—could have expected such an outcome: that the clouds of misunderstanding should have suddenly lifted, and that "with the first full look of her eyes" she should have brought him back into life "and put the past away as if it had not been." She was still happy (he noted) in his company, if she would let herself be happy; "and she can't forbid my loving her, though she fain would." He had ceased to grieve over memories of the past; for "how infinitely better this is for me, than if I had never found the creature!" Better the pain he had endured than to have gone on through life "with nothing to love . . . as I might, twelve years ago." As to the future, he had no illusions. The state in which he discovered Rose did not encourage false hopes.

That it was "very grave," he saw immediately: her disease, besides sapping the body, had undermined the spirit, "her entire soul being paralysed by the poisoned air" she breathed, in fact by the pernicious atmosphere surrounding her at Harristown. The adventurous and carefree child had become an almost spectral young woman —"amazingly thin" remembered Greville MacDonald, with huge eyes and a high colour and lips "exquisitely red" where "the tenderest of smiles" now and then alighted. So weak that she could not sit at table, she took her ascetic meals, consisting one day of three green peas, the next of a single strawberry and half an Osborne biscuit, apart from the family, only waited on by Ruskin. But her stay with the MacDonalds was brief; and from Hammersmith she went to Broadlands, the Cowper Temples' country house. Again Ruskin was at her side, and their reconciliation promised to achieve an even firmer footing. For him it was a period of enchanted calm. Looking out from his bedroom window, he saw the dawn-mist among the trees of the park, its blue folds faintly coloured by the warmth of the advancing day; and " for the first time these ten years " he felt that he was happy. As he dressed he picked up a book, and the sentence " *Grâce à Dieu pour son ineffable don* " captured his attention. Nor was the ineffable gift at once withdrawn. On August 14th, so intense was his bliss that he could not keep his journal; and on Sunday 18th, having meanwhile left Broadlands for Toft Hall, Cheshire, the home of the Cowper Temples' friends, Mr. and Mrs. Ralph Leycester, to his supreme satisfaction he knelt beside her in a village church. Proportionately dreadful was the reaction, and disastrous his fall from Heaven. The same day they were obliged to separate; Ruskin bade Rose good-bye and returned by train to London. That night, before he slept, some brief expressive notes were committed to his diary: " In the morning, in church at Toft, beside R. Now at the corner of a room in the Euston Square hotel, altogether miserable." What could be said to have been achieved? Pathetically little in the last analysis. Rose was still the victim of duty, still her parents' prisoner. True, her feeling for him was more genuine than he at times suspected; and she had written to George MacDonald of the " strongly spiritual love and faith " which Ruskin once inspired in her, and which nothing but his own religious backsliding could have ever swept away; but it was a terrestrial, not a spiritual, response for which her lover hankered; and that response she was still unable to give—grew indeed, more incapable of giving as her hold upon existence became more and more precarious. His protestations might be those of pure unimpassioned friendship; but beneath them she distinguished a very different fervour. " I cannot be to him what he wishes " (she wrote from Broadlands to Mrs. MacDonald), " or return the vehement love which he gave me, which petrified and frightened me. . . ." Thus the reconciliation of the summer months was necessarily incomplete; and when September came and Rose had either already retired, or was about to retire, to her secluded life at Harristown, a sense of peculiar desolation, aggravated by the inescapable sense of sin, was recorded in his diary. " The ending day," he wrote on September 7th. And on September 8th: " Fallen and wicked and lost in all thought. . . ."

" . . . Must recover by work," he added. And he continued to work as obstinately and faithfully as if Rose had never reappeared, and the unforgettable August days had never existed in any real calendar. Ruskin was " good and affectionate," observed Carlyle, but had " fallen into thick quiet despair again on the personal question; and meant all the more to go ahead with fire and sword upon the universal one." This he did in his own peculiar manner, by multiplication of his employments and interests rather than by any attempt to concentrate his energies. Besides lectures on engraving, afterwards published as *Ariadne Florentina*, which gave him the excuse to repeat some provocative criticisms of the art of Michael Angelo, he delivered a discourse on " The Nature and Authority of Miracle," followed by " Three Lectures on English and Greek Birds as the Subjects of Fine Art." During the course of the ornithological series—the basis of *Love's Meinie*—he launched a vigorous attack against the whole " Darwinian system "; for although many of his own pursuits were bound up with modern science, he was profoundly mistrustful of the scientific method. His preparation of his material could not have been more diligent; but nothing could have been less scientific, and at times more poetic, than the latitude he was accustomed to allow himself in subsequent embroidery. Thus his ornithological lectures, which had been preceded by many visits to the British Museum and the Zoological Gardens, and by the production of a large number of realistic drawings, contain, according to a natural historian, "some of the most delightfully wilful thoughts about birds ever yet published."[1] Speaking of the life of the swallow, so romantically-disposed a lecturer could scarcely fail to take wing. How should its volatile beauty be imprisoned in scientific language? No, a swallow is "an owl that has been trained by the Graces. It is a bat that loves the morning light. It is the aerial reflection of a dolphin. It is the tender domestication of a trout." Matter-of-fact ornithologists were inclined to shrug their shoulders; but then for Ruskin, as earlier for William Blake, there was discernible in the creatures he loved and admired "an immense world of delight" not to be measured by the keenest modern instruments. Hence the "interwoven" texture of all his later prose-writing. Imagination accompanies observation, mingling strangely with the pattern he appears at first to sketch out, now and then enriching the original design, often, as he grew older, confusing and obscuring it.

To the end of a working-existence, which stretched altogether over nearly half a century, from the opening volume of *Modern Painters* to the closing passages of *Praeterita*, though in some respects he suffered a steady decline, we see no alteration in his gift of feeling, and little diminution of his power of enjoyment. A brief account of Ruskin's career may well produce an impression of gloom unrelieved and personal failure unqualified. This impression is largely misleading. Ruskin, we must admit, was a man whose passions had been frustrated, whose hopes had been disappointed, and whose dearest schemes had gone awry. But to love the visible world as Ruskin loved it cannot fail to bring rewards. Every year might be accompanied by fresh griefs; yet every season had its pleasures. Old and tired and sick at heart, he was still surprised and fascinated by the ingenuity with which, "under the dextrous hands of a neighbour farmer's son," walls and terraces were added to his demesne at Brantwood, each stone "taking its proper place, and the loose dyke holding itself as firmly upright as if the gripping cement of the Florentine

[1] W. Warde Fowler in *A Year with the Birds*, quoted by E. T. Cook.

DETAIL OF CASTELBÄRCO TOMB, VERONA,
BY RUSKIN, 1869

towers had fastened it . . . Intelligent laying of stones" (he concluded) "is always delightful." Nor did he cease to pore over pebbles, shells and blossoms. Now, amid the sands of the Lido, his eye was caught by a finely spotted snail-shell; now he observes that he has been "much revived and pleased by a crimson convolvulus and three nasturtiums on my white breakfast-table. I never saw before what a wonderful thing a nasturtium was, in the set of it on the stalk. . . ." Above a miraculous earth extended astonishing skies. His head was crowded with a confusion of plans, so that he despaired at length of reducing them to any intelligible order; yet, wandering in his Brantwood garden, he could still enjoy the sunset—"a quite exquisite Italian sky . . . with divinest jewels of white cirri, and a long riband like a Renaissance angel's sash, or Botticelli's Madonna, flying to the zenith." His sensuous appreciation of the splendour of the natural universe constantly fortified him against his inward adversaries.

Thus his imagination preserved its freshness, and his vision as an art critic, even at his most unbalanced, retained its subtlety and gusto. New discoveries were continually made, and new details emerged from some familiar canvas. Very often the details he noted were recommended to his attention by their sensuous human quality. His days were vanishing "like the dust in the wind"; everything that he hoped to grasp seemed to be slipping through his fingers. Then, as he stood in the Sistine Chapel and gazed up at the Biblical frescoes of Sandro Botticelli, the artist spoke to him of another plane of existence, where what was fragile and fugitive on earth reappeared fixed and transfigured by a high creative intellect. How the painter had worshipped life, how shrewdly he had caught its forms! Here, for instance, was Moses, staff in hand, leading his family as they departed from the house of Jethro; "the infinitely wonderful little dog is carried, with the bundle, by the eldest boy; its sharp nose and living paws marvellously foreshortened." Similarly, when he was studying Carpaccio's pictures of St. Ursula, besides the admiration that he felt for their strictly formal merits, he experienced a warmly personal attraction towards the characters they introduced and the domestic scenes they represented. After a while he transferred to the virginal saint something of the passion with which Rose's memory filled him, and devoted several pages of *Fors Clavigera*, between a disquisition on the evils of swearing and a note on transatlantic barbarism, to a delicately voluptuous portrait of his imaginary princess:

"The bed" (he informed his workman-audience) "is a broad four-poster, the posts being beautifully wrought golden or gilded rods, variously wreathed and branched, carrying a canopy of warm red. The princess's shield is at the head of it. . . . Her little blue slippers lie at the side of the bed—her white dog beside them. The coverlid is scarlet, the white sheet folded half-way back . . ; the young girl lies straight, bending neither at waist nor knee, the sheet rising and falling over in a narrow unbroken wave, like the shape of the coverlid of the last sleep, where the turf scarcely rises. She is some seventeen or eighteen years old, her head is turned towards us on the pillow, the cheek resting on her hand as if she were thinking, yet utterly calm in sleep, and almost colourless. Her hair is tied with a narrow riband, and divided into two wreaths, which encircle her head like a double crown. The white nightgown hides the arm raised on the pillow, down to the wrist. . . . So dreams the princess, with blessed eyes, that need no earthly dawn."

In such a passage as this, quite apart from its decorative charm and the painstaking accuracy with which it renders colour, shape and attitude, we observe the mood of troubled tenderness to which Ruskin was aroused by his contemplation of the sleeping girl. She is a blessed creature, ignorant of sin or sorrow; and the writer goes on to compare his ideal maiden with two American girls, encountered in a train, whose thin white frocks came "vaguely open at the back" as they stretched and yawned and wriggled, who had chewed lemons and lumps of sugar and thumbed through dog-eared novelettes, thereby exemplifying modern maidenhood at its commonest and most accursed. But not all his reverence for St. Ursula's sanctity can quite disguise the significant fact that her appeal to his imagination was by no means wholly spiritual. He is aware of the young girl beneath her saintly trappings; and his preoccupation with the beauty of the flesh was, as I have already suggested, from a literary point of view among his major virtues. Indeed, only when we have acknowledged the sensuous aspect of his temperament does much of Ruskin's æsthetic criticism assume a true perspective. He adored life and evidences of organic growth, as they were reproduced, for example, in the arboreal intricacies of early Gothic architecture; and where he thought that he detected an image of death, as in the revived classicism of the great Renaissance builders, or in the work of any artist who seemed to prefer the formal and the geometric to the romantic and the natural, his dismay was immediate and his condemnation violent. Ruskin understood the nature of his own gifts far better than the majority of his contemporary followers. He had no desire to pose as a man of reason; but, since he lived in an age that believed itself to be reasonable and was at all times disputatious, he attempted, seldom with marked success, to give his instinctive apprehensions an intellectual backing. The unfortunate results have been noted elsewhere; and the contradictions in which his divided temperament repeatedly involved him were not limited to the sphere of his æsthetic doctrines. Just as he had long been disposed to acknowledge that æsthetic excellence was not inseparably connected with the strictest moral purity, so now and then he was inclined to doubt whether the finest types of civilisation were necessarily based upon the principles of social justice. The patrician ideal was one that he could never wholly shake off; and while *Fors Clavigera* rings with indignant protests against the modern upper classes, as he observed them circulating in Hyde Park or entertaining in Belgravia, he felt obliged to admit that these products of wealth and privilege had a strongly decorative attraction, which he could no more withstand than he could resist the earthly magnificence of Veronese's pictures. It was an appeal that he found equally impossible either to ignore or justify; and he, too, though the fortune on which he depended had been earned by grinding hard work, shared many of the advantages of the hereditary aristocrat, since the aristocracy of the mind itself battened on other human beings' labour. That he was a gentleman, he must perforce admit; and "we live, we gentlemen, on delicatest prey, after the manner of weasels; that is to say we keep a certain number of clowns digging and ditching, and generally stupefied, in order that we, being fed gratis, may have all the thinking and feeling to ourselves." Yet there was "a great deal to be said for this," he decided half reluctantly; for a "highly-bred and trained English, French, Austrian, or Italian gentleman (much more a lady) is a great production; a better production than most statues; being beautifully coloured as well as shaped . . . a glorious thing to look at, a wonderful thing to talk to; and you cannot have it . . . but by sacrifice of much contributed life." Once again the puritan revolutionary was vanquished by the æsthete—vanquished, but not completely subdued. The visible world might abound in beauty, but the sense of sin was omnipresent.

Abroad, however, it was usually less active than when he lived in England; and year after year with increasing eagerness, Ruskin had hurried away across the English Channel, bound for Switzerland and his favourite Italian cities in which peace and a measure of happiness even now awaited him. During 1873 he was kept at home by Brantwood and his lectures; but in the spring of 1874 he made his usual foreign expedition, travelling south through Naples—"certainly the most disgusting place in Europe" —as far as the Sicilian coast, where he watched the flush of sunrise and sunset descend upon the snows of Etna, and northwards, by way of Rome, to Pisa and Assisi. At Assisi he lived with the friars, whose simple-minded faith impressed him as refreshing and delightful, and paid a rapt court to the masterpieces of Giotto. It was a period of spiritual appeasement. He worked in the cell that had belonged to St. Francis, a saint whose "Catholic wholeness," which had induced him to "call the very flowers sisters, brothers," seemed profoundly sympathetic;

and every day the sacristan of the convent, remarking "*C'è una piccola cosa, ma credo che San Francesco lo farà*," prayed to his patron saint that their amiable English visitor might at length rejoin the true church. Ruskin remained unconverted; but, as he copied Giotto's frescoes, he began to suffer a spiritual change perhaps even more momentous. An old doubt was gradually dispelled: Titian and Veronese, types of the worldly artist, little by little relaxed the disturbing influence which they had exerted on Ruskin's imagination since 1868: and he "discovered the fallacy under which I had been tormented for sixteen years—the fallacy that Religious artists were weaker than Irreligious. I found that all Giotto's 'weaknesses' (so called) were merely absences of material science. He did not know . . . so much of perspective as Titian. . . . But I found that he was in the make of him . . . a very much stronger and greater man . . ; that the Religion in him, instead of weakening, had solemnized and developed every faculty of his heart and hand. . . ." At the same time, his general attitude towards the problems of faith became "more distinctly Christian," while suggestions of a resurgent puritanism crept into his prose style.

When he returned to England, he had his earthly recompense; for that autumn "the loveliest letters" were addressed to him from Harristown; and during October Rose herself, "finding" (as he told a friend) "she can't get on without some of the love she used to have," reappeared in London. Her physical condition had not improved; and Ruskin wrote to inform Carlyle that, although he had hoped to bring "poor Rosie to see you," she was "too ill to bear coming out just now." On this visit she sat for her portrait, and Ruskin executed the delicate pencil-sketch of her declining beauty, as she drooped forward with eyes half closed, like the young priestess of some Lethean religion which condemned its votaries to an early death. He had not entirely abandoned hope—"by peace and time," he liked to imagine, her "state might be redeemable"; but, even though she was not lost to the world, there could at present be little doubt that she was for ever lost to Ruskin. Otherwise this meeting in London —probably their last—has left behind no record. That it was brief, we assume: certainly it was as inconclusive as all their previous interviews: Rosie slipped back to Ireland, and her lover flung himself once again into his busy life at Oxford. In 1874, two schemes, both of them launched during the earlier part of the year, on the eve of his long tour through Sicily and Italy, received some attention, much of it derisive, from the British press and public. He started a tea-shop and endeavoured to build a road. "Mr. Ruskin's Tea Shop," over which presided two old servants trained by Margaret Ruskin, was modestly situated at 29 Paddington Street, a dismal London thoroughfare, and had been designed to "supply the poor in that neighbourhood with pure tea, in packets as small as they chose to buy, without making a profit on the subdivision. . . ." An eminently practical plan; but the most utilitarian institution need not be unbeautiful; the shop window was enlivened by a display of antique china; while about the colour and lettering of the shop-sign Ruskin (as he confessed to readers of *Fors Clavigera*) had hesitated for several months, debating whether it should be "of a Chinese character, black upon gold; or of a Japanese, blue upon white; or of pleasant English rose-colour on green. . . ." But none of these artful additions seemed somehow to catch the fancy of nineteenth-century slum-dwellers, who preferred to buy their tea where it was "brilliantly lighted and eloquently ticketed." Moreover, in their gloomy back streets, a taste for crude spirits was gradually lessening the demand for tea and coffee. Business languished, profits disappeared; and when one of the shopkeepers died, Ruskin's crusade joined the roll of earlier lost causes.

His road-building scheme, on the other hand, though it enjoyed a shorter existence, had a more conspicuous history. Again it was inspired by the spirit of St. George's Guild, and by the Master's firmly-expressed conviction that any practical task was worth attempting if it tended to beautify the surface of the globe and make the conditions of everyday modern existence a little less intolerable. He had failed to cleanse the pavements of London. Very well, he would show what an English country road should be and still might be—dry and firm under the traveller's foot, the green banks between which it ran exquisitely flower-embroidered. At the end of March, 1874, he wrote at length to Acland, begging him to intercede with Mr. Harcourt, of Nuneham and Stanton Harcourt, a sympathetic Oxford landowner, through whose estate meandered a charming lane "along the foot of the hills past Ferry Hinksey." It was a site that cried out for improvement—". . . That country road under the slope of the hill with its irregular line of trees, sheltering yet not darkening it, is capable of being made one of the loveliest things in this English world by only a little tenderness and patience in easy labour." The necessary labour was to be performed with love; he wanted, said the Master, "no rough workmen on the ground," and proposed to redesign this fragment of landscape "with delicatest touching." Mr. Harcourt did not refuse his permission, and Ruskin proceeded to recruit a band of undergraduate road-workers, first of all from Balliol, presently from other colleges, and gave a preliminary breakfast-party at Corpus on March 24th, 1874. Then, as it were with a friendly wave of encouragement, he at once set out for Italy, remaining abroad till the October term had started, while the helpers whom he had enrolled undertook the spade-work. But on his return he gave them particular attention; the breakfast parties were, of course, resumed; and to the beginnings of the Hinksey road he paid many earnest visits. In general charge of the operations he had placed David Downs, his gardener, a devoted and long-suffering *aide*, always ready to obey his employer's urgent summons, whether his duty was to collect ferns, learn how the French grew melons, or superintend the efforts of a gang of urban street-sweepers. "Darling Downs" certainly earned his wages; but then, Ruskin himself, though his mind was perpetually overfull and his attention apt to wander, took an intensive course in the mysteries of stone-breaking, seated on a heap of flints with a professional stone-breaker beside the London main road. It always pleased him to acquire a new art; and he had noticed that his enthusiastic young friends mishandled their tools and very often smashed a hammer-head.

Thus, into the season of autumn rains, the task went slowly forward. In their white shirts and their ribboned boaters, with here and there a steep-crowned bowler hat, enthusiasts for Ruskin's gospel of work discovered the satisfaction of honest muscular toil as he had outlined it at his breakfast-parties. Here were Alfred Milner and Arnold Toynbee, delving, carting, shovelling; here, too, was a large-limbed undergraduate, whose features, in their slightly florid fashion, suggested the coarse but regular good looks of a Hellenistic deity—Oscar Wilde, a talkative Irish youth who boasted that he had frequently been allowed to trundle Professor Ruskin's private barrow. While the diggers were at work below, the banks of the road above were usually peopled with curious Oxford tourists and with a straw-chewing assemblage of delighted local farm-labourers. "The world naturally laughed"; and journalists and cartoonists continued to amuse themselves at the expense of Ruskin's cultured navvies; but such are the mollifying effects of the English temperament that enthusiasm remained within bounds, and the abuse and ridicule provoked never grew outrageous. On neither side was there a hint of violence; for England does not quell her revolutionaries by a display of violent methods, but, wherever it is possible to do so, by gently overwhelming them. No one attempted to impede the diggers: the opposition was tolerant, its laughter mild and good-humoured: and even Ruskin presently agreed that, though his pupils were commendably industrious, road-making, to judge by results, was not a job for unskilled labour. The road they had constructed was remarkably bad—possibly, as he once declared, the most atrocious in the three kingdoms. But professional opinion considered that it might have been worse; and Mr. Harcourt's bailiff, in a mood of Christian charity, observed that the young gentleman had done no harm that could not easily be undone. . . .

Ruskin had, at this time, other examples of the deep-rooted impracticability of his perplexing fellow-countrymen. His Oxford Drawing School had not succeeded; and although at his lectures he could always rely on a large and lively audience who enjoyed his dramatic effects and applauded the comic asides with which he occasionally relieved them, at the Drawing School, planned to assist the comparative study of art and enable undergraduates to acquire the underlying principles of good draughtsmanship by practical experiment, the attendance was exceedingly poor, and usually limited to two or three. Ruskin was surprised and distressed; but during the winter months of 1874 the consummation of a more important reverse tended to overshadow all his minor setbacks. The news from Harristown was growing steadily darker: hopes of Rose's ultimate redemption were now revealed as baseless: and on January 1st, 1875, readers of *Fors Clavigera*, though presumably they were inured to shocks, received a startling revelation of the author's private misery. ". . . The woman I hoped would have been my wife is dying," he wrote in the course of a long self-justificatory letter. Rose's agony continued for several months. Broken in body and broken in mind, she is said—on somewhat doubtful authority—to have refused to allow Ruskin to see her for the last time unless he could promise that his adoration of her was second to his love of God, and, because he declined, to have preferred to die uncomforted. The story may be apocryphal, but it is certainly consistent with our knowledge of her closing phase. Her parents' religion had finally claimed her; and she expired at Harristown, without a farewell to Ruskin, towards the end of May, 1875. Ruskin had been finishing his *Academy Notes* and was setting out for the open fields, "to see buttercup and clover and bean blossom, when the news came" (he told Carlyle) "that the little story of my wild Rose was ended, and the hawthorn blossoms, this year, would fall—over her." Grief at its worst is often strangely passionless; and Ruskin's attitude to his loss was calm and almost stoical. He did not dally with dreams of reunion; for, as he once remarked to an elderly and charming friend, Miss Susan Beever, whose house was near his own at Brantwood, "I wanted my Rosie *here*. In heaven I mean to go and talk to Pythagoras and Socrates and Valerius Publicola. I shan't care a bit for Rosie there, she needn't think it. What will grey eyes and red cheeks be good for *there*?" Cory's lines, "Mimnermus in Church":

You bid me lift my mean desires
From faltering lips and fitful veins
To sexless souls, ideal quires,
Unwearied voices, wordless strains:
My mind with fonder welcome owns
One dear dead friend's remembered tones—

provoked his immediate admiration and moved him to exclaim reflectively: "So true of me also."

It might be possible to bear his loss; for Rose's disappearance was merely the culmination of a long series of losses that he had already lived through; but he was conscious that, with her physical extinction, a new stage had been begun in the history of his heart and mind. He confronted the future despondently, but none the less determinedly. "That death is very bad for me" (he wrote to Dr. John Brown)—"*seal* of a great fountain of sorrow which can never now ebb away; a dark lake in the fields of my life as one looks back—Coruisk, with Sarcophagus Mountains round. Meanwhile I live in the outside of me and can still work." Since the moment when the news arrived, scarcely a day had passed, he assured Carlyle, during which he had not been engaged in some form of active business; casual onlookers saw little change; and in company he liked he was often gay and captivating. Improvements at Brantwood continued busily; and his visitors were charmed and impressed by the patriarchal state he kept, amid his pictures and prints and manuscripts, with the group of devoted attendants whose days revolved around him. Even his parlour-maid studied the Professor's tastes, and, on the occasion of a particularly beautiful sunset would appear respectfully in the drawing-room to suggest that the view across the mountains perhaps deserved his notice; at which he would courteously thank her and seek an upstairs window. Joan and Arthur Severn were now inseparably attached; and in July, 1875, he took them with him on a posting-tour through Derbyshire and Yorkshire, for which he had designed and had built a splendid and elaborate posting-carriage—a reminiscence, no doubt, of Mr. Telford's chariot—with "good strong wheels, a place behind for the luggage, and cunning drawers inside for all kinds of things we might want on the journey." In Sheffield, Ruskin's equipage caused some surprise and amusement among the urban proletariat. The postilion's breeches were remarkably white; and, noticing that the crowd seemed to suspect a wedding, the Professor insisted that the Severns should play the part allotted to them, while he himself occupied the box as they rattled off towards the open country.

Such was the surface of his well-ordered existence; but beneath the surface there was increasing confusion and a gathering sense of darkness. This state of mind Ruskin attributed to causes partly physical. As early as 1871, he had acquainted the readers of *Fors Clavigera* with his belief that the skies above Europe were losing the brilliance and purity he remembered from his childhood. It was not rain-cloud that covered them, "but a dry black veil, which no ray of sunshine can pierce. . . . And everywhere the leaves of the trees are shaking fitfully, as they do before a thunderstorm; only not violently, but enough to show the passing to and fro of a strange, bitter, blighting wind." The storm-wind had returned with double force; a malevolent spirit was at work in the physical world; and, simultaneously, his conviction of moral evil received a disconcerting impetus. Ruskin who, during the 'sixties, had championed Swinburne, admired FitzGerald, and had remarked to Rossetti that he did not mean to imply "that an entirely right-minded man never keeps a mistress," was reverting to the sexual puritanism associated with his parents' creed. He became obsessed by images of sin;

and the crocodile[1] (which, during the construction of the Oxford Museum, he had recommended for an honoured place in sculptured "flower and beast borders") was relegated with the frog, the serpent and the eel to the category of accursed animals, representing lust and its accompanying degradation. Thus *St. Mark's Rest*, a guide-book to Venice, published in 1877, contains an alarming and striking passage, through which, as the critic discourses of sensual love, and of the symbolic connection between the idea of lust and the noxious and loathsome creatures his fancy brings before him, runs the complaint of a modern St. Anthony, surrounded by all the phantasmagoria of the Middle-Eastern wilderness. Nor was it on the more repulsive modes of desire that his imagination concentrated; in Botticelli's "Mars and Venus" the face of the sleeping, satisfied god suggested the features of a dead man: "such brutish paralysis" (he observes, lest the inference should escape us) "is with scientific accuracy made especial to the male," whereas the female gazes out of the canvas with an air of proud complacency. Botticelli's visions of Venus Anadyomene were also found disturbing. The foam-goddess reveals her reptilian lineage; for, although "both pictures are most subtly beautiful, yet in the former the lizard likeness shows itself distinctly in the face, and a lizard's tail appears in manifest form as pendulous crest of the chariot, while in the latter not only contours of profile and back, but the selected attitude of the goddess . . . irresistibly recall a frog."

Yet, as his fear of the flesh developed, there was a corresponding development of romantic and sentimental impulses. Rose achieved canonisation; and for the various relics she had left he devised appropriate reliquaries. The letters they had exchanged were committed to a rose-wood box which he took with him when travelling; and Detmar Blow, a young disciple, once privileged to support it on his knees, felt that he had received a con-

[1] ". . . The crocodile . . . couchant on his slime, born of it, mistakeable for it—his grey length of unintelligible scales, fissured and wrinkled like dry clay . . . as it were a shelf or shoal of coagulated, malignant earth." *St. Mark's Rest.*

spicuous mark of the Professor's approbation. Plates of beaten gold protected the single letter that he carried in his breast-pocket. Rose's memory perpetually accompanied him, and there were times when from the battlements of another world he thought she might watch over him; for, soon after her death, he had again sought the dubious comfort of Mrs. Cowper Temple's séances, and though the psychic experiences he enjoyed at Broadlands were never very definite, he derived a vicarious satisfaction from the beliefs he heard expressed there. Himself he saw nothing; but an apparition of Rose was asserted by the medium to have hovered near him in the darkened room; and henceforward he began to regain his hopes of immortality.[1] He liked to imagine that Rose was his guardian angel; and gradually his recollection of the young girl who during her life had involved him in so much human anguish, for whom his adoration had had so strong an earthly colouring, joined those imaginary princesses, Dante's Beatrice and Carpaccio's St. Ursula. It was as if all three were manifestations of the same celestial Aphrodite. In his mind, Beatrice and Rose had always been associated: Rose, like Beatrice, passing him in the street, had "denied her salutation"; and now St. Ursula, her cheek on her hand, absorbed some of the passion he had once poured out to Rose. She was wrapped in the slumbers of an inviolable innocence; yet, as he copied Carpaccio's painting, when the room was very quiet he almost feared to wake her.

Hints of a similar conflict emerged in Ruskin's general attitude, both in his treatment of his friends and acquaintances, and in his demeanour as a public man; for just as the sensuous and the ascetic sides of his temperament, hitherto uneasily reconciled, now threatened to wage open war, so the aspect of his character which was submissive and affectionate became dissociated from the tyrannical and aggressive self, which demanded complete obedience and flamed into instant wrath at the smallest hint of

[1]To Holman Hunt, at a later period, Ruskin spoke of "the unanswerable evidence of spiritualism," which, though it included "much vulgar fraud," convinced him that "there is personal life independent of the body."

opposition. His manner grew more effusive, till the endearments that he dispensed were somewhat overwhelming. Kisses he bestowed with a remarkable exuberance, not only on attractive women and children but on a mendicant Roman friar or a Venetian archæologist; while "Darling" was a favourite form of address, whether it was applied to Downs, his elderly gardener, Miss Kate Greenaway, the spinster protégée whom he advised and teased and scolded, or some seven-year-old girl whom he had encountered in a drawing-room. His worship of youth was vehement as ever; but it remained always strangely innocent. There was nothing about him of the lickerish middle-aged man; for his masculine ardour was counterbalanced by a touch of feminine delicacy, and his femininity had increased with age as his masculine passions were denied their proper outlet. Many admirers noted this ambiguous charm; with his "small bird-like head and hands," his celebrated blue cravat, "and the collars and the frock-coat, which made him look something between an old-fashioned nobleman of the Forties, and an angel that had lost its way," he moved one (wrote Canon Scott Holland) as one might have expected to be moved by some frail and charming woman. But "the bushy eyebrows gave a strength to the upper part of the face which was a little unexpected"; and under those cavernous brows were fiercely attentive eyes, ready to blaze forth in an explosion of rage or sparkle with resentment.

The poet was still a wrathful prophet—but a prophet whose motives were confused and whose comminations often ill-directed. Righteous indignation and petulant exasperation frequently became mixed in the same prophetic utterance; and unfortunate friends suffered the chastisement that he had once reserved for adversaries. His staunchest supporters did not escape. Among the victims was Miss Octavia Hill, the gifted and high-minded reformer, who had been associated in a scheme—far more successful than most of his projects—to provide decent accommodation for the London working classes. Having ventured to express a private doubt of Ruskin's "ability to conduct any practical enterprise successfully" (which, no doubt, was injudicious, but natural enough considering the fate of the Master's recent enterprises) she received in *Fors Clavigera* a stinging public reprimand. At Oxford he was equally a law to himself, inconsequent as it suited him, extravagant as it pleased his mood. The results "verged on the grotesque"; extraordinary improvisations were accompanied by fantastic gestures; a passage from the Psalms of David reminded him of a Mendelssohn anthem that he had heard and much disliked in a certain college chapel; and, chanting derisively "*Oh! for the wings of a dove*," he flapped the skirts of his gown, as he danced an antic minuet. There was "the oddest look on his excited face." Friends with an insight into his personal life, who knew the conditions in which he worked and the accumulation of plans, some half-completed, some scarcely begun, that overflowed his writing-table, were greatly concerned for his health and mental balance. Ruskin's own view of his future was by no means optimistic. He saw the dangers that he ran, and more and more distinctly felt intimations of some approaching breakdown. That his mind was "tottery" he had at times admitted; and, whereas in 1870 he had remarked to Norton that, so far as he knew, he had been "entirely insane . . . only about Turner and Rose," by 1874 he was obliged to agree that madness was a real danger. ". . . I am so alone now in my thoughts and ways" (he told the workmen of Great Britain) "that if I am not mad, I should become so, from mere solitude," but for the manual work—the wood-hewing and stone-laying—in which he found refreshment. What hope was there that he could persuade his brain to pause? The intricate rapidity of his mental processes was by this time uncontrollable.

He had "too many irons in the fire," too many demands on his last reserves of intellectual energy. "There is no use" (he had written in 1872) "saying tired or ill; always now." He knew that his "eddies of thought" were constantly sweeping him "into apparently irrelevant, and certainly unprogressive inlets." There were a thousand things in his head pushing each other like shoals of minnows; and elsewhere he likened himself to an exhausted juggler, concerned, "with a touch first to one, then another," to keep innumerable globes revolving. In 1876, having obtained leave of absence from the University, he retired to Venice, where he remained from the end of August until the following June, and enjoyed such spiritual solace as St. Ursula could give him. Nor was her angelic influence unavailing: she sent him heavenly tokens—by the hands of an Irish friend a pot of the self-same pinks that Carpaccio had painted upon her bedroom window-sill, and from England a dried sprig of the second flower framed within her casement, "the sacred vervain," a symbol of domestic purity. St. Ursula also "sent her love." Both tributes made a profound impression; and Lady Castletown's pretty gift (which she had playfully accompanied by a message from his patron saint) acquired a mystical significance that might have surprised and disconcerted her. For she could not have guessed that, according to Ruskin's fancy, "the Greek Proserpina, and the Gothic St. Ursula" were legendary phases of a single "living spirit," personifications of Heavenly Love, opposed to the reptilian goddess he castigated in *St. Mark's Rest.* Yet the cult of his divinity was not completely unshadowed. Rival divinities continued to demand attention; and once again, in analysing Ruskin's character, we are suddenly taken aback by a hint of downright worldliness. There were times when the prophet was flippant—occasions when he was apt to disclose a shade of underlying cynicism. Now and then, he succumbed to self-indulgence; and after dining at three o'clock (he wrote to Charles Norton from Venice on October 5th, 1876) he would lie upon his sofa and "read any vicious book I can find to amuse me—to prevent St. Ursula having it all her own way. Am greatly amused with the life of Casanova at present."

Neither Casanova nor St. Ursula could relieve the gathering tension. During the summer of 1877 he returned at length to England; but, almost as soon as he had started work, he was oppressed by sensations of giddiness and

John Ruskin with Joan Severn

dizziness. He felt " overworked . . . in head and eyes," while the " sense of blood going to head " caused him some anxiety. His thoughts were flitting beyond his control. " Dim-eyed and confused " (he recorded in August) " with mixture of music, Yewdale streams, and St. Mark's mosaics, buzzing in my head with free trade and Venice fruit law all the morning." Lacking the ability to assemble his ideas, he grew morose and captious; and it was in such a mood that, having walked into the Grosvenor Gallery where the " *Nocturne in Black and Gold* " was then on exhibition, he delivered himself in *Fors* of a petulant and spiteful reference to the art of James McNeill Whistler, whose paintings Swinburne in the past had often recommended. Here was a picture that the admirer of Turner's shimmering sun-scapes might have been expected to examine, if not with admiration, at least with sympathetic interest. But something in the " Nocturne " touched off his rage: he was infuriated perhaps by the presence of a talent he could not wholly understand, and retaliated with a burst of invective as coarse as it was ill-conceived. He was astonished, he announced to the readers of *Fors*, that a coxcomb should ask two hundred guineas for flinging a paint-pot in the British public's face.[1]

Sometimes he saw more clearly; but clarity of vision rarely brought him comfort. Thus, on his way to visit land which St. George's Guild had purchased in the neighbourhood of Bewdley, he had a further brief terrifying glimpse of the industrial machine at work. He passed through a district where nails were manufactured, entered a cottage and beheld two women, ominous *Clavigerae*, labouring at the hot iron " with ancient Vulcanian skill. Foot and hand in perfect time: no dance of Muses on Parnassian mead in truer measure. . . . Four strokes with the hammer in the hand: one ponderous and momentary

[1]The famous libel action that resulted belongs to Whistler's rather than to Ruskin's story ; for, although Ruskin looked forward eagerly to defending his opinions in court, when the case was tried in November 1878 he was too ill to attend. Burne-Jones, somewhat reluctantly, gave evidence on his behalf ; and Whistler, having scored a brilliant tactical victory, received a farthing damages.

blow of the balanced mass by the touch of the foot; and the forged nail fell aside finished on its proper heap; . . . level-headed, wedge-pointed, a thousand lives soon to depend daily on its driven grip of the iron way. So wrought they—the English Matron and Maid . . . from morning to evening—seven to seven. . . . The wages of the Matron Fors, I found, were eight shillings a week—her husband, otherwise and variously employed, could make sixteen. Three shillings a week for rent and taxes, left, as I count, for the guerdon of their united labour . . . fifty-five pounds a year, on which they had to feed and clothe themselves and their six children; eight souls in their little Worcestershire ark. . . ." The letter containing this impression was the eightieth of the *Fors* series; and, though they include occasional flashes of eloquence, the letters that follow it are for the most part wildly disconnected. 1878 began, cheerfully enough, with "thoughts of Immortality, as taught to us by every happy work and true soul of man"; he visited Mr. Gladstone at Hawarden, and Prince Leopold at Windsor, both of them refreshing and flattering experiences; but at Oxford he was distracted by the apparent impossibility of getting through his daily work; and, among "things that shriek out to be done," he was crushed to the earth by an increasing sense of powerlessness. Then, on the penultimate night of January, after he had withdrawn to Brantwood, he found himself wandering in the labyrinth of an extraordinary and vivid nightmare. Seven years earlier, during his serious illness at Matlock, his dreams had been remarkable. At that period, however, they were exciting and inspiring; for he had imagined that he was a brother of St. Francis, that an Italian woman had sung to him in a voice more divine than he had ever heard with waking ears, and that he had watched the golden horses of St. Mark's putting on their harness. Very different were the dream landscapes in which he was now condemned to grope his way—"some ornamental Tuileries-like gardens" where he had overturned a great sarcophagus and rolled it down a hill. Fearing detection, he had tried to escape. The gardens were deserted, and he entered an ugly town, only to discover that he could not talk coherently. Still he dreaded the arrival of the police who, he felt, could not be far off. But, when he endeavoured to board an express train, he had been left behind on the platform because he could not summon up resolution to climb into a carriage—"every one going faster and faster past me." The hurtling procession, he said, reminded him of "those days of January." His thoughts whirled, and time was rushing by. He sank deeper and deeper into "dreamy scatterment and bewilderment."

Where did his dreams end, and where did life begin? "I *must* get to work" (he noted midway through February) "or I shall get utterly into dreamland." But as he wrote, his pen seemed to become entangled in a mesh of thickest cobwebs; and the eighty-seventh letter of *Fors*, entitled "The Snow Manger," proved almost unintelligible. His present undertaking was to catalogue his Turners and compose a preface to the catalogue—a task he would have vastly enjoyed, had it not been for the too-acute emotions with which Turner's drawings filled him. The preface was finished on February 12th, while day was slowly breaking across the fells of Coniston, and "level mists, motionless, and grey beneath the rose of the moorlands," veiled the lower woods, and the roofs of the village, "and the long lawns by the lake-shore. Oh, that someone" (he lamented) "had but told me in my youth, when all my heart seemed to be set on these colours and clouds . . . how little my love of them would serve me, when the silence of lawn and wood in the dews of morning should be completed; and all my thoughts should be of those whom, by neither, I was to meet more!" It was a final effort; and from that point he descended rapidly into the shadows of his dream-life. Visions surrounded him: spirit-voices spoke to him. Rose and St. Ursula, and men and women from the pictures he most admired, came crowding out the real world. Among the last sentences he committed to paper were Tintoretto's "*Sempre si fa il mare maggiore*" and a line from the *Te Deum*: and "his mind was overthrown" (observes the pious biographer) "with the praise of God in his heart."

That comfortable suggestion, alas, is unsupported by Ruskin's own recollections of the development of his mental crisis. Mixed with fantasies about feminine saints, there was an appalling conviction of sin, translated by his imagination into many lurid symbols. Up and down the terraced gardens of Brantwood strayed an ancient peacock which, like every bird of its kind, uttered discordant cries at the approach of bad weather. The season was dim and rainy; and as the bird shrieked from the garden below, Ruskin imagined that he was in a farm-yard, the plaything of a tyrannical demon who willed that he should commit some hideous act of wickedness. He could never resist the temptation, and his inevitable fall was saluted by a girding shriek of glee. This yell of triumph, he remembered, was more terrible than he could express in words. One night he expected the Devil himself and, stripping off all his clothes, prepared to meet him boldly. The night air was bitterly cold; but he strode naked to and fro in his room, "to which I had retired about eleven o'clock," suffering intense agitation, yet "entirely resolute as to the approaching struggle. Thus I marched about my little room, growing at every moment into greater and greater exaltation. And so it went on till dawn began to break. . . ." A blue light filtered through the window; but, as Ruskin approached the panes, from its hiding-place behind the looking-glass sprang a huge black household cat. "I darted at it (he remembered) . . . and grappled with it with both hands, and gathering all the strength that was in me, I flung it with all my might and main against the floor . . . Nothing happened—I had triumphed! Then, worn out with bodily fatigue, with walking and waiting and watching, my mind racked with ecstasy and anguish, my body benumbed with the bitter cold of a freezing night," he cast himself on his bed and lapsed into unconsciousness. From that dark lake he slowly struggled ashore, to find his room occupied by demons in corporeal shape, "almost too horrible to think of." His mahogany bed-knob was the face of a witch; but as if to suggest the inward conflict which since his lonely youth had haunted and tormented him, fear and horror brought in their train a heightened sense of beauty. The Turner drawings that had lined his walls had never looked more radiant. Even the curtains and wallpaper seemed for a while transfigured.[1]

[1]This account of Ruskin's delusions is derived from an article, entitled "The late Mr. John Ruskin : Mr. Ruskin's Illness Described by Himself", signed "H" and published in the "British Medical Journal" of January 27th 1900.

Epilogue

"BRAIN-FEVER" was the verdict of the nineteenth-century experts—a disturbance brought on by over-work, by having "too many irons in the fire" and exploit-ing his mental resources too continuously and recklessly. It was an affliction often described in the stories of Victorian novelists, whose heroes and heroines were inclined to undergo a sharp attack of brain-fever if destiny had visited them with some severe emotional mishap. He might recover; and, indeed, he seemed to recover. After so deep and desperate a plunge, few men of Ruskin's tempera-ment have arisen with such buoyancy. By April 7th he was once more in his study, capable of reading Plato and deter-mined to settle down to a course of soothing, quiet labour. When he appeared among his friends, they felt that he was almost unscarred. Without false shame he spoke and wrote of his recent awkward misadventure. To a woman friend he remarked that he had "tumbled down the stairs of his wits," and that he was positively embarrassed by the display of good-will his clumsiness had brought him; and to Prince Leopold he confided that although he had been "very thoroughly out of my wits for a while," he hoped that they had "been only what the Scots call 'wool-gather-ing,' and I may even make a web some day of what I have gathered." The beauty of existence was still undimmed: he had still his plants and illuminated manuscripts: the rocks were still as absorbing, cloud-formations still as fascinating. Under the Severns' care he quickly improved, and promised that never again would he allow himself to overwork. For the moment there was no reason to suppose that the last decades of his existence, given sensible precautions, might not be safe and happy: that he had not emerged from the inferno unscathed, and that " The Long Dream," as he called his delirium, had not been dreamed through to its end in the dreadful weeks at Brantwood. Certainly the awakened dreamer talked of his experiences with reassuring frankness.

A modern student has painful advantages. He knows that Ruskin did not recover: he sees that for the injury done to the spirit no degree of kindness or attention could provide any genuine remedy, and that the remaining years of his life can only be regarded as a lengthy, tedious epilogue. During that epilogue the main themes of the drama were repeated and enlarged on. New books were written and new lectures were delivered; but with a single dazzling exception, they did not measurably enrich our view of Ruskin's genius. More and more he preferred to live among his memories of past times, until in his own person he resembled a ghost—now the eccentric apparition who wandered back to Oxford, now the pathetic and dignified *revenant*, whose eloquence had the charm of another world or century. It was in this guise that, less than two years after his breakdown, he confronted an Eton literary society who had invited him to speak to them. Ruskin, wrote A. C. Benson,[1] was " one of the most singular figures " that he had yet encountered: his clothes had an antique oddity: his " tight-waisted dress coat " displayed a velvet collar: " the sleeves were long, and the delicate hands that emerged were enveloped in long, somewhat crumpled cuffs; and he showed a soft and many-pleated shirt-front over a double-breasted waistcoat. . . . His hair was thick and grew very full especially over the forehead; he had large side-whiskers and bushy eye-brows; his face was extraordinaily lined, and the big mouth, with a full underlip, gave him, I thought, a rather formidable air." As for the discourse he delivered, that struck the young man as " very impressive, though not natural; it had something ghostly, remote, magical about it," which chilled and yet attracted. While he spoke, " quick glances, half-friendly, half-

[1] Memories and Friends by A. C. Benson.

mournful," swept from the blue eyes beneath the shaggy brows across his wondering audience. But "there was never a sign of placid or easy mastery, no appearance of enjoyment, even of interest: it was a duty he had to perform, a service he might do; and at the end he looked old and weary."

Oxford, whither he returned during 1883,[1] saw him in a rather different mood. Outside the lecture-room he might produce an impression of overwhelming melancholy; but once he had reached his desk, he entertained the undergraduates with all his old extravagance. At some lectures he exceeded their expectations; and his lecture on Protestantism, which was attended and wildly applauded by many fervent Catholics, established a new record in hilarious originality. First St. Ursula was exhibited as "a type of Catholic witness": then the Professor, warming to his subject, inquired by what types and emblems the spirit of Protestantism might be fitly represented. Well, here, he said, was his answer; and to an audience that gaped with excitement he unveiled two complementary pictures—Mr. Stiggins, the hypocritical Protestant, with his umbrella and his concertina, and, as representative of "earnest Protestantism," an engraving of a pig by Bewick—"a good little pig, which is alert and knows its own limited business. It had a clever snout, eminently adapted to dig up and worry things, and it stands erect and keen, with a knowing curl in its tail, on its own native dunghill." Such explosions evoked embarrassing echoes: London newspapers began to stigmatise Ruskin's professorship as an "academic farce": and his friends commented with disapprobation on the habit he had developed of playing to the gallery. At any cost he seemed anxious to raise a laugh; but what his well-meaning critics perhaps did not appreciate was that although the "perversity of spirit" they deplored might to some extent be held responsible, his "wish to arouse hilarity" was also bred of loneliness,

[1]After Ruskin's collapse, the Slade Professorship was taken over by his friend Sir William Richmond, who resigned on hearing that Ruskin was anxious to re-assume it.

and that since he thirsted for the smallest hint of response, he was resigned to eliciting in the rôle of comedian the enthusiasm he had ceased to expect in the capacity of tragic seer. But the excitement his lectures induced was plainly growing dangerous. His friends did all that they could to keep him calm and rational; and Jowett, who had forgotten his former suspicions, entertained him at the Master's Lodge "with a watchful and almost tender courtesy." But they were too late; ideas gathered like an Alpine avalanche; and once the avalanche had started to descend, no human power could check its motion. Theories and fancies and speculations, inextricably involved, rushed down upon his listeners; and the effect, which should have been tremendous, was sometimes merely ludicrous. His last lecture had a tragic conclusion; for though he began to speak in clear, but excited tones, his periods soon degenerated into incoherent violence. There was an outburst of profane, and even obscene, expressions, accompanied, it is said, by corresponding gestures, before his startled attendants could coax him from the lecture-room.

At this moment of his own accord he resigned the Slade Professorship—not, however, because he admitted that his mental powers were failing him, but because a "vote endowing vivisection" had been passed by the University, and, as a secondary reason, because he had been refused a financial grant to enlarge the Ruskin drawing-school. "Double motives are very useful things": he confessed to his disciple and future biographer, E. T. Cook, "you can do a thing for two that you couldn't for one." Oxford as a whole was undoubtedly relieved; and Ruskin, who from that moment would never again agree to cross the city's limits, withdrew to the seclusion of Brantwood, dispirited and out of patience. He felt very old; and age, he observed to Norton, was "threatening to be a weary time for me. I'll never mew about it like Carlyle, nor make Joanie miserable if I know it, but it looks to me very like as if I should take to my bed and make everybody wait on me." It seemed to him that he was peculiarly alone: for Norton was in America, and Carlyle, whose companionship, notwithstanding the uncharitable reference to his old friend's gift of self-pity, he always sought in times of crisis, had shuffled off his remaining burdens in February 1881. Since his first collapse Ruskin's appearance had changed: he was now a bearded patriarch; and Edward Burne-Jones—his " darling Ned "—who saw him after a long interval in 1883, noted that, " the hair he has grown over his mouth hides that often angry feature, and his eyes look gentle and invite the unwary, who would never guess the dragon that lurks in the bush below." Burne-Jones was also glad to be able to record that he " looks well—really looks stronger." But Norton who, on a brief visit to England, stayed with him at Brantwood, was shocked to see the results of ten years' gradual transformation. He had left him in 1873 a vigorous middle-aged man: it was an old man, bent and long-bearded, with an " habitual expression of weariness, with the general air and gait of age " whom he met in 1883. Ruskin had become " more positive, more absolute in manner, more irritable "; but his " essential sweetness " frequently prevailed; he had many returns of gaiety and his smile was still disarming. In the long winter of his discontent there were numerous days of placid Indian summer, when nature and humanity both contrived to please him: the small cherry tree outside his window suggested " twenty coral necklaces with their strings broken, falling into a shower "; he was happy studying a wild snapdragon—" blossom with upper two petals thrown up like the sharpest little fox's ears . . . more like some bat's—veined purple on white, the swollen lip below pure white touched with yellow in the throat "; or walked among purple cyclamens, " thick as violets in spring—vividest pale red-purple, like light of evening." As early as 1880 he had been strong enough to go abroad; and the habit of foreign travel continued with some regularity till 1888, when he was joined at Abbeville by two devoted young enthusiasts, Sydney Cockerell and Detmar Blow, in whose pleasant company he admired the ancient town and explored the neighbouring countryside. Much had vanished that he had been used to love—here old houses demolished, there a streamlet bricked over; but many buildings had preserved their former majesty; and hour after hour throughout the night a watchman still sounded his horn from one of the towers of St. Wulfran.

For young men he had an irresistible charm; and with girls and women of any age it pleased him to develop close and sentimental friendships. These associations were akin to love. Even Miss Susan Beever, an elderly invalid, and Miss Kate Greenaway, the illustrator, who had neither youth nor elegance, received their share of romantic endearments and were addressed in tender "little language." Miss Greenaway was his "Sweetest Kate." He was inspired to make preposterous claims for the merits of her child-drawings, which had re-established, he said, the manners and customs of fairyland "throughout gentle Europe"; and in long and affectionate letters he urged her, as he had once urged Rossetti, to improve upon her natural gifts, to remember that girls had not only frocks but also limbs beneath them, to draw "flowers that won't look as if the leaves had been in curl-papers all night" and children's shoes not "*quite* so like mussel-shells." He signed himself her "loving Dinie"—otherwise her "Demonie," or her aesthetic familiar-sprite. For each correspondent he had a separate nick-name signature. To Miss Beever he was "Phoca," the seal; to Joan Severn, "Di Pa," an abbreviation of "Dear Papa," while Mrs. Severn was his "Di Ma," his dear or dearest mother. A young girl with whom he corresponded between 1884 and 1887, was saluted as his "Darlingest Pitcher"; and, since he was known as "The Professor" at Brantwood, he eventually became her "Ever loving Fessie." To the schoolchildren of the neighbouring village he devoted the same paternal care as he had formerly lavished upon his class of girls at Winnington. He welcomed them to his study, where, since his parlourmaid objected to the scattering of crumbs, he would help to lay and clear the tea-table, taught them geography, botany and music, and coached them to sing the nursery chants he wrote for them. Joan Severn did not wholly approve—perhaps she feared that

"Di Pa's" eccentric warmth of manner might, at times, be misinterpreted: his pupils, on the other hand, though generally puzzled, were by no means unappreciative. "*He's a foony man is Meester Rooskin*," concluded one little girl, "*boot he likes oos to tek a good tea*."

While friendship and affection were kept awake, an ancient enmity was laid to rest. He had forgotten his hatred of Lacerta, forgotten the intense bitterness with which her treatment of his love had years before inspired him; and Mr. and Mrs. La Touche presently called on him at Brantwood. Such was his declining existence in calm and lucid intervals. But those intervals were constantly overshadowed. "The Storm Cloud of the Nineteenth Century" still scourged the English landscape; and, under that title, in 1884, he delivered two lectures at the London Institution, describing the malignant manifestations of the "plague-cloud" and the "plague-wind," and linking their appearance with the growth of moral evil. The storms, which he did his best to externalise, had their real existence elsewhere. It was as if demoniac forces, long and painfully subdued, now burst from the nether regions of consciousness, sweeping all before them, defying every attempt at control and overthrowing every sanction. Then the personality that needed love was replaced by a personality that expressed itself in violence. Normally the most courteous of men, with a particular distaste for the English trick of swearing, in periods of distraction Ruskin, like Swift, very often fell into a strain of repetitive profanity. His *damns* were incessant and monotonous—wrung from him, no doubt, not so much by physical exasperation as by a psychological compulsion to damage and offend himself. In his happier moods sympathetic and considerate even to extravagance, when the plague-cloud descended he became intensely quarrelsome: Joan and Arthur Severn were not always spared; and during the spring of 1887, Joan having ventured to suggest that his music classes for the village maidens might well be discontinued, he left Brantwood in a "white hot" passion and took temporary lodgings nearby. As the attack passed, he would revert to all his former gentleness: till once more a gathering gloom spread darkly through his waking hours, and at night, visions, "grotesque, terrific, inevitable," heralded the approach of yet another "Long Dream" which for agonising weeks or months would cut him off from rational life.

Ruskin suffered his second onset of delirium in February, 1881: his third, in March, 1882: his fourth, soon after he had, not a day too early, resigned the Slade Professorship in 1885: and his fifth in 1886. Convalescent during 1887, he was emboldened to go abroad in 1888, visiting Abbeville and Beauvais. There, as has already been related, he had two engaging young companions—"Detmar," he wrote, "is as good as gold," and Sydney Cockerell carried his umbrella for him "as if he were attending the Emperor of Japan." Sydney Cockerell was recalled to England; but Detmar Blow accompanied him southwards on the sacred pilgrim's road that led, through Burgundian France, to Switzerland and Venice, guarding the box that enshrined his precious "rose-leaves." At Venice Ruskin remarked to the Presbyterian chaplain what a blessed thing it was "to be able to do anything for the cause of Christ" and, when the chaplain spoke reassuringly of his spiritual achievement, replied that he was astonished: "I feel as if I had only led a selfish, useless life." He appeared vague and distraught; and, in Paris, at the end of his homeward journey, a further brainstorm struck him down. Joan Severn, who had hurried across the Channel, brought him back to Brantwood. He seemed to rally, but at length collapsed. He could no longer assemble his ideas: it was difficult to write: the gift of drawing left him. All his faculties threatened to crumble and dissolve. His friends understood that he could never face the world again.

Yet, during the previous decade, in spite of "terrific" attacks of mania, the periods of gloom by which they were preceded and the spell of langour and weakness by which each attack was followed, he had been able to resume *Fors*,[1] publish works on botany, English prosody and the in-

[1]The last letter in the *Fors Clavigera* series, entitled "Rosy Vale," is dated Christmas, 1884.

iquities of money-lending, collect his letters to the press,[1] and, in *The Bible of Amiens*, originally intended to form part of a general history of Christendom, produce one of the most popular of his architectural studies. Himself, he refused to believe that his recurrent lapses from sanity, though disturbing as long as they lasted, were necessarily weakening. His bouts of "delirious imagination," he declared, were "simply states of prolonged dream—sometimes of actual trance, unconscious of surrounding objects; sometimes of waking fantasy, disguising or associating itself with the immediate realities of substance and sound; but whatever its character, recognised afterwards as a dream or vision. . . . There is no physical suffering in the state . . . and so far as I can trace the effects of illness on my mental powers, it leaves them only weaker in the patience of application, but neither distorts nor blunts them, so long as they can be used." Ruskin's optimistic conclusions were not entirely justified. Each mouthful that he was obliged to digest of "Nebuchadnezzar's bitter grass" left him a little older, a little feebler, a little further removed from realms of light and reason. But some of the early attacks had a stimulating, as well as a weakening and demoralising, tendency. They turned his imagination back into the past; "both these illnesses," he wrote, after his second collapse in 1881, "have been part of one and the same constant thought, far out of sight to the people about me . . . as *they* go on in the ways of the modern world, and *I* go *back* to live with my Father and my Mother and my Nurse, and one more—all waiting for me in the Land of the Leal." Past years re-emerged with an extraordinary vividness and distinctness: the past seemed as brightly warm as the present was cold and clouded. *A la recherche du temps perdu* he embarked upon *Praeterita*.

His autobiography, begun in 1885, was not finally laid aside until 1889. The last passages were written with effort, and are plainly the work of an aged and exhausted man. But the earlier chapters have an incomparable distinction, for Ruskin at length was prepared to please himself,

[1]Under the title *Arrows of the Chace*.

and no moral design, no ulterior didactic motive, stood between the writer and the subject he was contemplating. That subject was his own beloved youth. As through a sudden break in the clouds, he surveyed the distant landscape from which he had ascended, and traced the wandering line of the path he had travelled spread out far beneath him. A lost landscape: yet every detail and every colour retained its virgin freshness. Nor was the prospect filmed by sentimentality: a deep devotion to the memory of his mother and father was combined with a clear appreciation of their intellectual shortcomings. But the resentment he had once expressed—so forcefully, on occasions so harshly—had altogether disappeared: and the portraits of James and Margaret Ruskin are at the same time frank and tender. His point of view was now almost completely detached; the cumbersome prophetic mantle was slipping from his shoulders; and it was with the imaginative passion of the artist, rather than with the interpretative zeal of the teacher or the moralist, that he reviewed the preliminary stages of his long and devious life's journey, reliving the pleasures of his childhood, suffering again the exquisite frustration of his love for Adèle Domecq. Like Proust he sought to recapture the past—not merely an historical skeleton, but the spiritual essence that gave the past reality. Ruskin's memory was extraordinarily retentive—perhaps even more retentive than he had at first suspected; and as he wrote, scene after scene returned in undimmed splendour: Herne Hill, a flowery suburban Eden, dominated by the presence of two majestic guardian-spirits: wonderful jaunts across country in Mr. Telford's carriage: the Tay, eddying over its pebbly bed, "an infinite thing for a child to look down into": his parents at the tea-table beneath the white-heart cherry tree: their original journey abroad, and the evening walk round Schaffhausen, with a range of far-away Alpine snow-peaks glimmering on the skyline.

His opening chapters are a record, if not of unmixed happiness, at least of an existence in which faith and hope predominated. But the tenth chapter of *Praeterita* introduces Adèle Domecq; with the appearance of love, doubt and anxiety had begun to do their fatal work; a conviction of guilt had impaired his natural candour; and we read of the collapse which had overtaken him at Oxford, and of the sense of haunting inward dissatisfaction which accompanied him through Italy. His second volume, Ruskin feared, would be "less pleasing to the general reader"; for he must now write more of himself; and, "as I look deeper into the mirror, I find myself a more curious person than I had thought." In fact, he did not pursue the study; and his narrative, which had seemed to promise a year-by-year account of the education of his heart and mind, gradually abandoned any attempt at chronological exactitude. Long periods remain undescribed; many important events receive not the smallest mention; and though Effie appears as an unnamed little girl for whom he had once written *The King of the Golden River*, there is no reference to the fact that he had ever married. But Rose, still a persistent phantom, could not, of course, be shut out; and in the third volume, written on the verge of a catastrophic breakdown, he revisits the memorable year 1858, and describes the first brilliant apparition of his grave-eyed youthful mistress, as she had stepped towards him across the drawing-room carpet and extended her hand "as a good dog gives its paw." From that point the interest of the work declines. The last chapter, "Joanna's Care," composed after his attack in Paris, while he was recovering at the seaside, is a heartfelt but somewhat incoherent tribute to Mrs. Severn's virtues. Such a tribute he was determined to pay; but hour upon hour, as he sat in his bedroom, with an unwritten page beneath his eyes, the words and ideas he was struggling to assemble faded into nothingness, and the completed text, though it includes many decorative passages, is fragmentary and disappointing. His last sentences were a reference to the fireflies at Siena: "*How* they shone! moving like fine-broken starlight through the purple leaves. How they shone! through the sunset that faded into thunderous night as I entered Siena three days before, the white edges of the mountainous clouds still lighted from the west, and the openly golden sky calm behind the Gate of Siena's heart . . . the fireflies everywhere in sky and cloud rising and falling, mixed with the lightning, and more intense than the stars."

Praeterita was Ruskin's final essay in imaginative composition; yet, despite his age and weariness, it contains some of his most memorable additions to modern English prose-literature. His descriptive style is seen at its best, and also at its simplest, rippling smoothly as the surface of the Tay, with a suggestion here and there of mysterious depths and whirlpools. In these pages he united the strain of colloquial eloquence already displayed in parts of *Fors Clavigera* to the more elaborate and sonorous style which he had once assumed in *Modern Painters* and in *The Stones of Venice*. His pictures of life with his parents are quiet and clear and low-toned; but when he was describing the Rhone at Geneva he gave his virtuosity free play:

" Fifteen feet thick, of not flowing, but flying water. . . . Waves of clear sea are, indeed, lovely to watch, but they are always coming or gone . . . Here was one mighty wave that was always itself, and every fluted swirl of it, constant as the wreathing of a shell. No wasting away of the fallen foam, no pause for gathering of power, no helpless ebb of discouraged recoil; but alike through bright day and lulling night, the never-pausing plunge, and never-fading flash, and never-hushing whisper, and, while the sun was up, the ever-answering glow of unearthly aqua-marine, ultra-marine, violet-blue, gentian-blue, peacock-blue, river-of-paradise-blue, glass of a painted window melted in the sun, and the witch of the Alps flinging the spun tresses of it for ever from her snow."

" Joanna's Care," is dated from Brantwood, June 19th, 1889. That summer he was at the seaside; but during August he returned to his country house, where violent delirium descended, keeping him a prisoner in his room till the summer months of 1890. He was not again to leave home, and, buried at Brantwood, he became a living legend, honoured in decrepitude by his soft-hearted countrymen with unanimity unknown in the days of his youth and vigour. Behind him lay a gigantic life's labour, many hundreds of delicate drawings, and printed works of which the collected Library edition, when it eventually appeared, ran to no less than thirty-seven extremely massive volumes. What had he accomplished? In his own considered opinion, little—almost nothing. Often his effect had been positively harmful; and he admitted that through his encouragement of Venitian-Gothic mannerisms, he was responsible for the production of some of England's ugliest edifices.[1] Public houses and banks and town halls had a smear of Gothic affectation, without Gothic grace and dignity. He passed from life believing that his mission had failed; but although many of the crusades he undertook ended in catastrophe, and his crusading-spirit had repeatedly misled him, we must not underestimate the practical influence that the prophet's writings exercised. Both at home and abroad, the doctrines he proclaimed had spread through widening circles: thanks to Ruskin, ignorant restoration and ruthless demolition of Europe's ancient buildings no longer went unnoticed: efforts were made to drain and level the vast industrial quagmire: the self-satisfaction of the *laissez-faire* economist was measurably shaken, if not completely pulverised. But more important than Ruskin's practical influence was the modification of sensibility we owe to his æsthetic criticism. True, his attitude was frequently perverse: the relationship of art and ethics involved him in questions to which he could find no satisfactory answer: yet, by breaking down the artificial restrictions with which art had been surrounded, by suggesting that it was a "universal language," the highest expression of the aspiring human spirit, impossible to dissociate from all the other manifestations of the heart and the intelligence, he opened new and impressive vistas,

[1] ". . . I would rather, for my own part, that no architects had ever condescended to adopt one of the views suggested in this book, than that any should have made the partial use of it which has mottled our manufactory chimneys with black and red brick, dignified our banks and drapers' shops with Venetian tracery, and pinched our parish churches into dark and slippery arrangements for the advertisement of cheap coloured glass and pantiles." *Preface to the Third Edition of the* "*The Stones of Venice*", *1874*.

not only to the art critic and the poet but also to the novelist. The genius of Marcel Proust, we are told by a French admirer,[1] cannot be fully appreciated unless we acknowledge his indebtedness to Ruskin, who became for him just such an " *esprit intercesseur* " as Poe had been for Baudelaire, a type of the artist-saint, devoted to the pursuit of an unattainable perfection. " *Cette Beauté* " (Proust wrote of his master) " *à laquelle il se trouva ainsi consacrer sa vie, ne fut pas conçue par lui comme un objet de jouissance fait pour la charmer, mais comme une réalité infiniment plus importante que la vie, pour laquelle il aurait donné la sienne. De là vous allez voir découler toute l'esthétique de Ruskin.*" Proust's view of Ruskin's æsthetic beliefs was no doubt unduly simplified: there were complications he did not suspect, limitations that he passed over. But Ruskin's shadow falls recognisably across innumerable Proustian paragraphs: he flits into the church at Balbec: we are aware of him beneath the flowering hawthorns in the sunlit lanes round Combray.

Proust's was an exceptional cult; and during the last twenty or thirty years Ruskin's fame has slowly dwindled. His qualities and his defects alike are ill calculated to appeal to twentieth-century prepossessions; for the strain of wilful extravagance that moved Matthew Arnold (who distrusted Ruskin personally) to call him a " provincial " writer offends those critics and readers who set their minds on classicism; while his romantic flow was constantly impeded by a desire to preach and moralise. Nor can his career be readily explained in terms of any current dogma. If we suggest that he was the victim of an " Œdipus complex," we merely skirt the problem: John, James and Margaret Ruskin must also be considered as characteristic products of their social class and period; and yet the sociological explanation proves, in the last resort, as unconvincing as the Freudian. We remain face to face with the mystery of an individual character, separate, lonely, passionately self-absorbed, perpetually at war with a world that did not welcome it. At no time would Ruskin's fate

[1]*Proust et Ruskin* par André Maurois. Essays and Studies by members of the English Association, 1932.

have been easy; but many earlier periods might have treated him less harshly, or offered some tolerable refuge from the difficulties of private life. During the age to which he was born, however, a romantic revival coincided with an industrial revolution; and artists whom the romantic poets had taught to dream and suffer must make their peace (should they aspire to peace) with a society that, besides its gigantic material achievements, had built the pestiferous slums of London, Leeds and Liverpool. Spiritual offspring of Byron and Shelley confronted the growing wealth and rapidly-deepening squalor of mid-Victorian England. To their forebears it had still appeared that "perfectibility" was no idle vision, and that some sudden explosion of benevolence—such as, to men of good will, had seemed very close in 1789—might yet introduce the reign of freedom, equality and universal happiness. Gradually romantic optimism gave way to economic fatalism. While the industrial machine required its toll of victims, according to the inexorable laws of supply and demand they would always be provided.

For the resultant conflict there were alternative remedies: one might subscribe to the belief in "progress," a concept which Ruskin with all the indignation at his command had repeatedly rejected, but which Alfred Tennyson, resolutely thinking the best of his age, had rather vaguely sponsored: or one might seize hold upon religious faith, which promised supernatural rewards crowning mundane toil and misery. In England, revivalism and industrialism were contemporaries, even allies. Steam-power and the Gospel had made almost simultaneous inroads; and the rise of Evangelical faith had coincided with the emergence of the triumphant middle-classes. During Ruskin's early manhood, "the religious movement of the last century" (as Arthur Hugh Clough recorded in his *Epilogue to Dipsychus*) "beginning with Wesleyanism, and culminating . . . in Puseyism," had provoked that "over-excitation of the religious sense," which induced an "irrational, almost animal irritability of consciences. . . ." Dangerously alarmed by the possession of an immortal soul, continuously disturbed by the recurrent crises in which it might be lost or saved—so that a suitor, before he dared to propose, would carefully examine his beloved on her religious tenets—thoughtful Victorians lived through hells of doubt but, if they were fortunate, climbed to heavens of certainty. Ruskin was not fortunate. He could neither accept the stern Evangelical creed of Denmark Hill and Harristown, nor succumb to the diplomatic solicitations that sometimes came from Brompton Oratory. Manning, his "darling Cardinal," who flattered him and entertained him, giving him "lovely soup, roast beef, hare and currant jelly," together with exquisite puff pastry, delicate (he said) as Papal pretensions, was wonderfully persuasive, subtly unobtrusive; but Ruskin's restless intelligence could never quite be brought to bay. He was still an Anglican who mocked at Protestantism, a Catholic sympathiser who declined to take his final vows.

He had needed a faith—few men more acutely—and no faith that accorded with his spiritual wants had ever been presented to him. But in 1889, all that he needed was rest; and, so far as his distracted brain would permit, he began to float away into a state of deep quiescence. At moments his calm was broken. Then every step upon the stairs would be punctuated by a furious *damn*; and the same expletive was sometimes interpolated into every sentence of his conversation. He had loved children; and it is sad to learn that in the twilight of his old age some children came to dread him. There he sat on the lawn at Brantwood, an ancient long-bearded figure, stared at them with eagle eyes and beckoned them incessantly; but if they approached, their reception was very often startling; and the words "*Bow-wow—Damn!*" pronounced with dreadful emphasis, might send them scurrying homewards. As before, there were storms and hideous unbecoming outbursts. Acland, his old friend, hearing that the Professor declined to eat, ventured to take him up a fried sole, was struck with the sole across the face and obliged to give ground hastily. But the general tenor of his life was monotonous and placid. With his dog and his trusty valet, he would roam in a pensive trance around the Brantwood gardens; or, seated in his study, he would receive a favoured visitor. He had little to say: sometimes he would nod, and sometimes smile: a fragmentary remark occasionally passed his lips: as a rule, however, he preserved a brooding silence. Usually his expression was benign, and as long as he lived he was always very carefully dressed, with blue cravat, old-fashioned gold watch-chain and double-breasted waistcoat. To work he could no longer pretend. In 1893, when he learned that Susan Beever was lying on her death-bed, he wrote her one of his last letters—a message of eight brief quavering lines, signed "in all sympathy ever your grateful and loving Phoca," accomplished at the expense of three hours' strenuous effort. His few subsequent letters were generally dictated; but on the death of Gladstone in 1898 it occurred to him to condole personally with the elder statesman's daughter, and yet once more, against overwhelming obstacles, he struggled to express himself. In an hour he had formed eleven words; and then his concentration broke down.

If mental derangement is an escape from life, Ruskin had now escaped beyond all fear of apprehension. With folded hands, he gazed out over the lake, only to return if some familiar voice, some exceptionally stirring memory, had roused him from his stupor. "That's my dear brother Ned," he observed one night on his way to his room, nodding affectionately at Edward Burne-Jones's portrait; or he recollected that he had been a writer of books and, extending his finger and thumb, remarked "half-regretfully" that they would never hold a pen again, adding that it was probably just as well, such was the trouble they had brought him. The rooms he inhabited were lined with Turner drawings; but towards the end he noted that they appeared to have lost "something of their radiance," concluding resignedly that "the best in this sort are but shadows." One day a pair of young men, both enthusiastic Ruskinians, were admitted to his study, and found the Professor, attended by Mrs. Severn, seated beside a table on which were many flowering potted plants. He was livelier than usual, and talked with some broken flashes of the old angelic eloquence; but after a while, indicating his Turners, he complained that they had faded. *There* was a picture that would never fade, declared Mrs. Severn, it may be a little too brightly, pointing through his study window. " For *me* it has faded," said the author of *Modern Painters*; and his young disciples felt that the time had come to bid him good-bye. John Ruskin lived on into January 1900—into an epoch that saw the materialisation of a few of his hopes, but also the confirmation of some of his most distressful prophecies. He died, after a short attack of influenza, on January 20th. Mrs. Severn refused the offer of a grave in the Abbey, close to Tennyson in the Poets' Corner. She decided that, as he had once desired, he should be interred at Coniston.

SELECTED BIBLIOGRAPHY

Life of Turner *by William Thornbury*. Hurst & Blackett. 1862

Letters & Memorials of Jane Welsh Carlyle *ed. by J. A. Froude*. Longmans. 1883

The Gentle Art of Making Enemies *by J. M. Whistler*. Heinemann. 1890

The Life of John Ruskin *by W. G. Collingwood*. Methuen. 1893

John Ruskin *by Alice Meynell*. Blackwood & Son. 1900

John Ruskin *by Frederic Harrison*. Macmillan. 1902

Rossetti Papers: *compiled by W. M. Rossetti*. Sands. 1903

Memorials of Edward Burne-Jones *by Lady Burne-Jones*. Macmillan. 1904

Pre-Raphaelitism & the Pre-Raphaelite Brotherhood *by Holman Hunt*. Macmillan. 1905

William Allingham, A Diary. Macmillan. 1907

Life of John Ruskin *by E. T. Cook*. George Allen. 1911

Ruskin: A Study in Personality *by A. C. Benson*. E. Smith. 1911

Memories and Friends *by A. C. Benson*. E. Smith

The Tragedy of Ruskin *by Amabel Williams Ellis*. Jonathan Cape. 1928

John Ruskin: an introduction to the further study of his work *by R. H. Wilenski*. Faber & Faber. 1932

Reminiscences of a Specialist *by Greville MacDonald.* Allen & Unwin. 1932

Ruskin, the Painter, and his works at Bembridge *by J. Howard Whitehouse.* O.U.P. 1938

Friends of a Lifetime. Letters to S. C. Cockerell *ed. Viola Meynell.* Jonathan Cape. 1940

Octavial Hill *by E. Moberly Bell.* Constable. 1942

Against Oblivion *by Sheila Birkenhead.* Cassell. 1943

The Order of Release *by Admiral Sir Wm. James.* John Murray. 1947

For the Time is at Hand *by R. S. Lambert.* Melrose. 1947

Ruskin at Oxford: An Inaugural Lecture *by Sir Kenneth Clark.* O.U.P. 1948

Dreamers of Dreams *by Holbrook Jackson.* Faber & Faber. 1948

The Life and Times of Coventry Patmore *by Derek Patmore.* Constable. 1949

Ruskin, The Great Victorian *by Derrick Leon.* Routledge & Kegan Paul. 1949

INDEX